MANAGING

WITH A CONSCIENCE

How to Improve Performance Through
Integrity, Trust, and Commitment

SECOND EDITION

FRANK K. SONNENBERG

ISBN-13: 978-1466461024 (pbk.)
ISBN-10: 1466461020 (pbk.)

Library of Congress Control Number: 93030795
CreateSpace, North Charleston, SC

Cover and interior design by Carrie Ralston, Simple Girl Design LLC.

TO MY WIFE, CARON,
AND MY DAUGHTERS, CATHY AND KRISTY,
WHO MAKE EVERYTHING WORTHWHILE

CONTENTS

PREFACE   XI
ACKNOWLEDGMENTS   XIII

1 IF A TREE FALLS IN THE FOREST . . .   **1**
   COMPETING IN THE NEW AGE OF INTANGIBLES

   Are We Using Yesterday's Weapons to Fight Today's Wars?   1
   The New Age of Intangibles   2
   Deciding What's Important   5
   What Goes Around Comes Around   6

2 FROM OBEDIENCE TO COMMITMENT   **9**
   BUILDING AN ORGANIZATION WITH PASSION

   Why Love a Company That Doesn't Love You Back?   13
   Employee Satisfaction Continuum   16
   A New View: Employees as Assets   18
   A New Management Paradigm   20
   Management by Principles   22

3 IT'S A GOOD IDEA, BUT . . .   **29**
   BUILDING AN INNOVATIVE ORGANIZATION THAT
   REINVENTS ITSELF EVERY DAY

   Unlocking the Creative Mystique   31
   Running the Creative Gauntlet   33
   Management Style   33
   Operational Style   40
   The Organizational Culture   47
   Reaching the Winner's Circle   52

4 INTERNAL COMMUNICATION . . . MORE THAN LIP SERVICE   **53**
   BUILDING AN ORGANIZATION WITH TOTAL CONCENTRATION
   AND FOCUS

   Stress to Success   55
   Communicating in the Information Age   57
   The Role of Leadership   58
   The Role of First-Line Management   66
   The Flow of Information   72
   Honest, Open Communication   77
   The New Way to Communicate   78

5   IF I HAD ONLY ONE CLIENT   **81**
BUILDING AN ORGANIZATION DEVOTED TO SERVICE EXCELLENCE

The Q Word   84
The Long-Term Consequences of Your Actions   85
Taking a Holistic View   86
The Road to Quality   87
Conclusion   105

6   CHANGE . . . WINNING IN THE FAST LANE   **107**
BUILDING AN ORGANIZATION THAT ADAPTS WELL
TO CHANGE

We Must Change the Way We View Change   108
Fallacies About Change   111
Change . . . Why Bother?   115
The Only Thing We Have to Fear Is Fear Itself   116
Learning . . . K Through Life   120
Learning to Learn   123
Organizational Learning   128
Conclusion   132

7   WHEN FAST ISN'T FAST ENOUGH   **133**
BUILDING AN ORGANIZATION THAT RESPONDS WITH SPEED

Picking Up the Pace   136
Organizational Effectiveness   138
Management Style—Getting the Most Out of Others   147
Personal Time Management   153
Conclusion   158

8   PARTNERING . . . ENTERING THE AGE OF COOPERATION **159**
BUILDING A FLEXIBLE ORGANIZATION

What Causes Relationships to Fail?   162
The Anatomy of Relationships   169
When Does the Relationship Begin?   170
Creating the Right Environment for Growth   171
Maintaining the Relationship   173
Making It Happen   176

9 NETWORKING 179
A WORLD OF UNLIMITED RESOURCES

The Underlying Structure 181
Building Relationships 182
Turning Talk into Action 183
Why Doesn't Everyone Network? 184
How to Make Networking Work 185
Networking Protocol 188

10 TRUST ME . . . TRUST ME NOT 191
BUILDING A TRUSTING ORGANIZATION

Trust—The Miracle Ingredient 194
The Four Stages of Trust 197
Conclusion 212

11 FOLLOWING YOUR CONSCIENCE 213
A RECIPE FOR PEAK PERFORMANCE

NOTES 237
INDEX 253

PREFACE

In the turbulent, frenetic, dog-eat-dog times that marked the end of the 20th century, many believed that the only way to achieve success was to be unscrupulous. Acting like slumlords, corporations let their assets deteriorate by exploiting customers, mistreating employees, and squeezing suppliers. What they overlooked, however, was that their obsession with short-term results significantly damaged their company's long-term performance as well as its competitiveness.

Today, it is more critical than ever to put an end to these shortsighted tactics. The 21st century is a time of unprecedented change as the world continues its transition from the Industrial Age to the Information Age. This new age is characterized not by tangible products but by the intangible resources that involve the intellect and the ability to gather, analyze, transmit, and synthesize information. The result has been the birth of new companies and entire industries, everything from information services to software and biotechnology companies.

This new edition of *Managing with a Conscience* sets forth and clearly defines nine factors critical to success in the new Age of Intangibles. To succeed today, companies must encourage employees to be passionate about what they do, to remain laser focused on their organization's mission and goals, and to be obsessed with customer service excellence. Furthermore, organizations must reinvent themselves every day through creativity and innovation, increase their ability to move quickly by cutting red tape, and adapt well to the changing landscape. Organizations that remain flexible by creating win-win partnerships, that tap unlimited resources through old-fashioned networking enhanced by modern technologies, and that value trust and integrity will be best positioned for success in the 21st century.

Managing with a Conscience spells out a better option for improving long-term success, restoring traditional values, and injecting trust and integrity into all business practices and relationships. *Managing with a Conscience* is about replacing the old "us versus them" mentality with a new "us" approach that encourages the growth of win-win relationships with employees, customers/clients, suppliers, and alliance partners. When this kind of culture takes hold, people work at a higher level, are proud of what they do, and achieve goals once thought to be unattainable. Remember, although the Golden Rule may be considered cliché, it still represents remarkable value. When you do right by people, most people will reciprocate. It's that simple. And, when you operate with the highest levels of trust and integrity, it makes you feel good about yourself, the people you work with, and the organization that you represent. It impacts how you view yourself and the way other people view you.

Managing with a Conscience was written to help reanimate the values that count and to demonstrate how to improve performance through integrity, trust, and commitment. We seem to have forgotten the amazing rewards of living up to a higher ideal of what is right and good. This book is my attempt to say that managing with a conscience will enable us to achieve the personal and business success that we seriously desire.

Frank K. Sonnenberg

ACKNOWLEDGMENTS

This book represents the contributions of many people to whom I am most grateful.

Kathy Dix served as editor and proofreader of this book. I cannot say enough about Kathy. She is an incredibly intelligent, experienced, and conscientious person whose attention to detail is second to none. Her ideas and suggestions have been invaluable. It is clear to me that Kathy puts her heart into her work. Words cannot express my appreciation.

Carrie Ralston designed the cover and the interior of this book. I've worked with Carrie for over six years. All I can say is WOW! Carrie is an exceptionally talented and thoughtful person who possesses a work ethic rarely found these days. Carrie gives every undertaking her level best, and then a little more. Whenever I compliment Carrie for going above and beyond, she says, "It's just my job." It's an absolute pleasure to work with Carrie.

My wife, Caron, performed valuable research for this book. With the abundance of information that's available these days, this is a heroic effort akin to drinking water from a fire hose. Caron also reviewed early manuscripts and served as a continual sounding board for ideas. Thank you, Caron, for your encouragement, patience, understanding, and insightful feedback.

There are several other individuals I particularly want to recognize for the impact they've had on my life and who provided teachable moments, the lessons of which are reflected in this book.

When I think of positive role models, I think of my good friend Mark Sandberg, PhD, Dean Emeritus, College of Business, Rider University. In my wildest dreams I never could have imagined the impact that one individual could have on my life. Mark is an incredible individual. Tom Brokaw once said, "It's easy to make a buck. It's a lot tougher to make a difference." That being said, if a person's life can be measured by the number of lives that he or she has touched, then Mark is the most successful person I know. I've come to learn some of the most important lessons of my life through countless hours spent with Mark and being a member of DAARSTOC, a leadership development program he founded. First, life is one big learning process. It is possible to learn from every experience and from everyone with whom you come into contact. While some open their eyes and grow to their full potential, others put on their blinders and stagnate. Second, it's a strength, not a weakness, to admit fault and recognize personal deficiencies. While some people are too proud to learn this way, others grow through this process and turn weaknesses into strengths. Third, you must find peace within yourself before you can be truly comfortable with others.

When I think about leadership, David Tierno, former Senior Partner, Management Consulting Group, Ernst & Young, comes to mind. Dave is one of the finest individuals I know and was a wonderful mentor to me. Dave taught me the importance of having a vision. His emphasis on trust and teamwork in business, his strength of conviction to do what is "right" rather than what is politically expedient, and his ability to create a working environment conducive to excellence, all make him the very special person that he is. I thank Dave for his years of leadership, his personal and professional counsel, and for his friendship. I am honored and privileged to have worked for Dave for over a decade.

When I think about a strong work ethic, Larry Frankel comes to mind. Larry and I have been friends for over 30 years. It doesn't take much effort to see why he's so successful. Larry is proof positive that "If you love what you do, you'll never work a day in your life." Even though he's become one of the most accomplished professionals in his field, he continues to have an insatiable desire to learn and to serve as a mentor to others. Larry is living proof that integrity leads to happiness and success.

My friend and editor, Beverly Goldberg, helped me write the first edition of this book. I couldn't have completed it without her assistance. I want to thank her for her patience, her energy, and her brilliant and thoughtful insight. When I think about philanthropy and personal service, Beverly clearly comes to mind. Beverly has taught me that real success is measured, in part, by giving of oneself to help others in need. Beverly is an exceptional individual; if more people were like her, we'd have a better world in which to raise our children.

My mother and father were wonderful role models who instilled the strong set of values in me that are so much a part of this book. My two bothers and I grew up in a home where honesty and integrity presided over all else, where people's worth was measured by their character rather than their personal wealth, and where people got more joy out of giving than by asking for more. They instilled in us the confidence that we could be anything or do anything, as long as we put our minds to it and worked hard to achieve it.

Being a parent to the two best daughters in the world, Catherine and Kristine, has taught me that parents can learn as much from their children as children learn from their parents. Catherine and Kristine have taught me the importance of having the proper balance in life: it's the moments in life, not the days, that we remember; to recognize the beauty in the simple things that we often take for granted; and to accept the importance of living in the moment while planning for the future.

Caron is my wife, best friend, and business partner. We've been married for 31 years and literally spend 24 hours, 7 days a week together. Caron has taught me that if two people are five steps apart, the best way to meet in the middle is for each person to take three steps forward; that life is filled with "ups and downs," so make the most of the "in-betweens"; and that life is so much more rewarding when you can share every moment with someone you love.

Thank you all.

BE PRACTICAL AS WELL AS
GENEROUS IN YOUR IDEALS;
KEEP YOUR EYES ON THE
STARS AND KEEP YOUR FEET
ON THE GROUND.
COURAGE, HARD WORK,
SELF-MASTERY AND
INTELLIGENT EFFORT
ARE ALL ESSENTIAL
TO A SUCCESSFUL LIFE.
CHARACTER IN THE
LONG RUN IS THE
DECISIVE FACTOR IN
THE LIFE OF AN INDIVIDUAL
AND OF NATIONS ALIKE.

—THEODORE ROOSEVELT

1

IF A TREE FALLS
IN THE FOREST . . .

COMPETING IN THE NEW AGE OF INTANGIBLES

The 21st century is a time of unprecedented change. The world continues its transition from the Industrial Age to the Information Age, a new age characterized by intangibles that have far-reaching implications for everything we do. And clearly, our ability to successfully weather this transition will determine our competitive position in the world market, which will, in turn, affect generations to come.

If we are to succeed as a nation and as individuals, nothing is more important than our ability to identify our priorities and allocate our precious resources. Nothing would be worse than discovering, too late, that the processes we used to make decisions for our future were flawed. When it comes to business, this means that, first, we must decide what investments to make. Then, we must determine the most effective management styles for making those investments pay off, which means we must choose the optimal organizational structures and reward systems for motivating our employees.

ARE WE USING YESTERDAY'S WEAPONS TO FIGHT TODAY'S WARS?

Many people will tell you that such things as empowering your workforce, creating an environment that encourages risk and discourages fear, eliminating waste and improving business processes, encouraging continuous education and training of employees, communicating in an open and honest manner, building trust among employees, nurturing long-term relationships with suppliers and clients, working hard to develop an impeccable reputation, living according to sound business ethics, and unifying your organization around a mission and shared values are likely to be among the key determinants of success in this new age. Others will tell you that these are "soft" issues.

What do people mean when they say these issues are soft? Are they saying that they are not effective management practices and that they do not enhance results? Or are they saying that because these things are difficult to quantify and measure, they make management uncomfortable and uneasy? Do they mean that because these practices cannot be isolated from other management practices, as in a scientific experiment, they are not worth doing?

There is a tendency in this country to believe that if something cannot be quantified, it does not exist. It brings to mind the question associated with Bishop George Berkeley, an early 18th-century British philosopher: If a tree falls in the forest and no one is there to hear it, did it make a sound? To apply this to management practices: If someone enhances performance in an organization using an approach that cannot be quantified, did the improvement take place?

This philosophy—that something must be quantifiable to exist— permeates American life. For example, even after there was a considerable body of evidence that smoking was hazardous to one's health, it was only after the Report of the Surgeon General of the United States revealed a direct statistical link between smoking and certain medical problems that people began to heed earlier warnings. Another example was our failure to recognize that the Japanese focus on quality would capture market share in electronics and automobiles; only when we saw the hard evidence of increasing sales of Japanese products did it become clear that quality, a "soft" issue, made a difference to customers.

THE NEW AGE OF INTANGIBLES

The Industrial Age brought us products such as cars, heavy farm equipment, refrigerators, washing machines, and computers—equipment that could be seen, touched, and demonstrated. In contrast, the Information Age is characterized by intangibles—those resources that involve the intellect and the ability to gather, analyze, transmit, and synthesize information. The result is the birth of new companies and entire industries, everything from information services to software and biotechnology companies.

Companies in the Industrial Age thrived because of their access to and exploitation of raw materials, standardization of goods and services, and ability to maximize volume. Today, however, the speed with which products are becoming commodities has increased dramatically, and companies are experiencing greater and greater cost pressure from competitors. Now, as soon as new products are introduced into the marketplace, clones marked by similar features appear in months or even in weeks. Unless consumers can see the value in premium brands, many will buy products solely on the basis of price. That is why the only companies that will be able to charge a premium in the future will be those that use intangibles—such as product innovation and design, reputation, and the customer experience—as a way to clearly differentiate themselves from their competitors.

THINKING ACROSS THE AGES

The differences in the thought processes between the two periods are evident in the terminology in the following table.

INDUSTRIAL AGE	INFORMATION AGE
Capital intensive	Knowledge intensive
Capital expenditures	Education/training
Natural resources	Educated workforce
Inventory	Data (information)
Production enhancements	Process enhancements
Hierarchical management	Employee empowerment
Tangible rewards	Psychic rewards
Issuing orders	Communicating
Top-down planning	Employee commitment (buy-in)
Inspection	Quality built in
Equipment failure	Employee turnover
Equipment uptime	Morale building
Purchasing	Recruiting
Sales	Customer satisfaction
Laborer	Knowledge worker
Defending turf	Innovation
Company push marketing	Consumer pull marketing
Company relationships	Networking

Clearly, the critical success factors of the Information Age are intangibles. And just as you cannot measure liquids in pounds or nuclear fusion in quarts, you cannot use yesterday's measurements of physical inventory to gauge the results of empowerment, brand awareness, creativity, or commitment. Moreover, the unmeasurables include the results of numerous instinctive judgments that are made by executives after years of experience. A senior lending officer for one of the nation's largest banks said to me, "Today's MBAs just don't understand. Sure, they know the formulas, the financial ratios. They've read all the case studies. They learned all that in business school. But sometimes, it is the gut feel that is the most important indicator. Some say it comes with experience, and others say it's a sixth sense. But I'm convinced that many problems today are the result of not following these instincts because we cannot logically explain them."

To take another example, Americans are enamored with technology. But they tend to forget that technology in and of itself does not deliver results; the way it is implemented does. Unfortunately, some organizations focus only on purchasing the latest equipment. They do not understand that the way technology is introduced—the efforts made to overcome resistance to change, to provide training for those who will use the equipment, and to put methodologies in place to support the technology—is what brings results. As a consequence, new technologies are acquired and then underutilized.

This kind of behavior is not limited to technology; it affects entire companies. A good example of the value of unmeasurable behavior is the case of Johnson & Johnson's Tylenol. Years ago, a deranged person inserted poison into some Tylenol capsules with fatal results. As soon as the first incident was discovered, Johnson & Johnson pulled all Tylenol off the shelves nationwide without any hesitation and started a massive warning and recall campaign. This decision was far easier for Johnson & Johnson to make because of their commitment to their credo: "We believe our first responsibility is to the doctors, nurses, and patients, to mothers and all others who use our products and services. In meeting their needs, everything that we do must be of high quality."

The speed and certainty of Johnson & Johnson's response enabled Tylenol to make a strong comeback. The existence of their credo and their firm belief in it, something many would call a "soft" component of their business, made a critical difference to the decision-making process. But the value of a credo isn't usually measurable.

Creativity is another intangible that cannot be measured. The 3M Company puts a great deal of effort into creating a climate that stimulates innovation. How does that climate translate into business? Or, how do you measure the value of brand recognition and customer loyalty? According to research conducted by Interbrand, "Coca-Cola, IBM, Microsoft, Google, GE, McDonald's, Intel, Nokia, Disney, and Hewlett-Packard" rank highest in perceived value or brand equity.[1] How do you measure the value of employee empowerment to GE or Google? Or the value of reducing a workforce with compassion and sensitivity? And how do these things translate into a stronger competitive position? How do you measure the manager who builds camaraderie, trust, and lasting relationships with his team? Or the manager who exhibits strong ethical values, commands loyalty, and has a reputation for keeping his word?

DECIDING WHAT'S IMPORTANT

In this new edition of *Managing with a Conscience*, I examine nine critical success factors for competing in the 21st century. You won't find these attributes in an annual report because they are intangible and difficult to quantify. But that doesn't make them any less important to an organization. These critical success factors require that companies:

- Seek to develop employees who will be deeply committed to the organization's mission and values and, most important, who will be passionate about reaching its goals (see Chapter 2)
- Create an environment that stimulates creativity and innovation and reinvents itself every day (see Chapter 3)
- Set priorities that focus the company's efforts and people on the resources that provide the greatest potential return (see Chapter 4)
- Believe that the main reason for the company's existence is to provide service excellence to its clients and customers (see Chapter 5)
- Be able to continually adapt to a changing marketplace (see Chapter 6)
- Recognize that time is both a valuable resource and a fixed commodity and, therefore, that speed provides a competitive advantage (see Chapter 7)

- Build a flexible organization by collaborating with other organizations (see Chapter 8)
- Emphasize that personal networking provides a highly efficient and effective way to solicit ideas, access new sources of information, increase business development, and attract new hires (see Chapter 9)
- Understand that a foundation of trust between an organization and its employees, suppliers, and clients is what brings and keeps people together (see Chapter 10)

WHAT GOES AROUND COMES AROUND

The common thread throughout this book is "What goes around comes around." If you hire the best people and treat them with dignity and respect, invest in them and display confidence in their abilities, motivate them and help them grow personally and professionally, and create an environment conducive to excellence, they will reward you by striving for peak performance. Further, if you treat suppliers as part of your own organization, create an environment where everybody wins, and build relationships based on trust, honesty, and integrity, your colleagues and suppliers will reward you with their commitment and with a long, fruitful relationship. Last, but not least, if you view clients (or customers—these two words are used interchangeably throughout) as long-term assets rather than immediate sales transactions, develop policies and procedures based on the overall impact they have on client service (not for the benefit of your own employees), and migrate from mass marketing to niche marketing to personal marketing (carefully listening to and then satisfying the specific needs of your clients), they will reward you with increased market share and profits. Treating employees with integrity increases productivity, encourages loyalty, and promotes passionate performance. Developing relationships with suppliers through a flexible, borderless organization results in quality improvement and the ability to rapidly adapt to changing customer needs. And a long-term focus on service excellence creates a strong customer base, which is especially critical as the production process becomes less of a differentiating factor and everything leading up to, during, and after the sale becomes key.

When companies manage with a conscience, their investment pays tremendous dividends. The winners of the 21st century will be those who treat clients, employees, and suppliers according to the Golden Rule. Reverend Robert Fulghum, author of *All I Really Need to Know I Learned in Kindergarten*, put some basic rules into language that everyone can understand. His rules included the following: "Share everything. Play fair. Don't hit people. Put things back where you found them. Clean up your own mess. Say you're sorry when you hurt somebody. When you go out in the world, watch out for traffic, hold hands, and stick together."[2] Soft issues are all very like the tree that falls in a forest. In the Information Age, if we don't believe that there was a sound, maybe it's time to get our hearing checked. In the Information Age, if we don't change our view of employees as a necessary evil—if one leaves the company, he or she can be replaced by another—we will fail. If we measure employees solely by their ability to increase the quantity of their output, we will lose the best of them. We must learn to encourage employees to create new product innovations and design improvements, to be on the cutting edge of technology, and to enhance the company's reputation for service excellence. In today's world, in manufacturing companies as in service companies, it will be hard to separate the actual product from those who deliver and produce it. Not only will today's employees produce products, but their knowledge, experience, and skill sets will be a part of the products themselves. Thus, as discussed in Chapter 2, the organization's working environment and its ability to attract, develop, and retain the best and brightest employees will determine its success.

2

FROM OBEDIENCE
TO COMMITMENT

BUILDING AN ORGANIZATION WITH PASSION

For the first 100 years of American history, plantations were one of the primary forms of corporations, mostly located in the southern states and commonly associated with slavery. The Civil War and the Emancipation Proclamation ended slavery and virtually ended the plantation era, although for many Americans, plantation management has continued uninterrupted. . . .

Plantation managers tend to see local workers as indentured servants who are born to pick their cotton. [They] . . .have no name, no identity, because they are not real people. You can abuse them, not pay them fairly, and claim all of the monetary returns on their work.

Modern plantation management involves the subjugation of people through more subtle means than slavery, but the end result is about the same. People feel like slaves—they feel trapped, owned, enslaved.

—Ken Shelton, *Executive Excellence*[1]

Plantation managers—now as in the days of the Old South—view people as disposable objects. They treat people according to their positions and degree of power: Superiors are treated with respect and dignity, subordinates as worthless beings. Focusing on the bottom line, they have forgotten that everyone has certain inalienable rights.

You can find evidence of plantation management everywhere. Stephen Covey, consultant and best-selling author, tells the story of a manager who bragged to him about his tough management style. He explained that when confronted with problem employees, "he told them to either shape up or ship out." Covey says he then asked the manager "why he didn't tell his customers that if they weren't prepared to buy the goods and services at the prices requested, they should either shape up or ship out. [The manager explained that] he didn't have the same right to do this with customers as he had with his employees."[2]

The problem is that all too many managers really believe that employees are little more than slaves who obey orders and follow the rules. In return for their good behavior, and if they're lucky, employees may keep their jobs—and be paid just enough to keep body and soul together. Back in 1995 when I was writing the first edition of this book, I quoted a *Training* magazine article that said, "Chiefs who make 100 times the average Indian's pay are no longer rare."[3] How quaint that notion seems now. According to the 2010 Institute for Policy study, "In 2009 CEOs of major U. S. corporations averaged 263 times the pay of the average American worker."[4]

This kind of arrogance has been accompanied by an unhappy trend to quick-and-easy divorce. Many organizations no longer remain faithful in sickness and in health; instead, their relationships with employees are beginning to look more like one-night stands. In fact, according to Linda Barrington, managing director of human capital, The Conference Board, commenting on a job satisfaction report issued in January 2010: "The newest federal statistics show that baby boomers will compose a quarter of the U.S. workforce in eight years, and since 1987 we've watched them increasingly losing faith in the workplace."[5] According to The Conference Board report, 20 years ago, some 61 percent of that generation was satisfied with their jobs, compared to 45 percent at the time of the report.

Additionally, the drop in job satisfaction between 1987 and 2009 covered all categories in The Conference Board's survey, from interest in work (down 18.9 percentage points) to job security (down 17.5 percentage points) and crossed all four of the key drivers of employee engagement: job design, organizational health, managerial quality, and extrinsic rewards.[6]

When you work in a place that doesn't care about you, it's hard to be enthusiastic about what you are doing. It's hard to go the extra mile if you believe that nobody cares. It's hard to see where caring, loyalty, and team-work fit in if the value of your work is measured only in dollars and "what have you done for me today." Not only is plantation management damaging to the morale of workers and the soul of management, it is a direct cause of low productivity rates, disaffected workers, and a dreadful bottom line.

To the plantation manager, there is nothing wrong with stealing talented people from well-managed companies rather than investing, nurturing, and training the company's own employees. It is not unlike "being a corporate slum landlord. Keep raising the rent while letting the assets deteriorate."[7]

Why then are managers puzzled by employees who are highly motivated outside of work but show little initiative on the job; people who put in time but no energy; people who spend more time working on their résumés than on the activities at hand. A management style that produces these results obviously won't be enough to compete in today's global economy, especially given changes taking place in the attitudes of workers today. In fact, the result of this plantation-style management is already causing a disastrous collision between the needs of businesses and the demands of today's workforce.

According to *U.S. News and World Report*, "fast-trackers who floored it to the finish line, hyper achievers who slept, ate, and breathed work, now. . . are taking weekends off and muttering about personal fulfillment and quality of life."[8] *Fortune* magazine calls it the "boomer backlash. The busters look around the office and observe the 40ish crowd who neglect their families and avocations for. . .What? By the time the boomers have made it, they've had it. This scares the younger folk to no end." *Fortune* goes on to characterize the new baby-bust generation as people who "want to be happy and fulfilled—socially and culturally—and to progress in the work world to the point where [they're] happy with [themselves]."[9]

"Challenging and meaningful work is vitally important to engaging American workers," says John Gibbons, program director of employee engagement research and services at The Conference Board. "Widespread job dissatisfaction negatively affects employee behavior and retention, which can impact enterprise-level success." In fact, according to The Conference Board's research, 22 percent of respondents said they don't expect to be in their current job in a year. "This data throws up a big, red flag because the increasing dissatisfaction is not just a 'survivor syndrome' artifact of having co-workers and neighbors laid off in the recession," adds Gibbons.[10]

This new breed of employees wants to work for an organization that they can feel proud of: an organization that has values and viewpoints compatible with their own; an organization that is oriented toward the long haul, working toward the prevention of ills, not just curing the symptoms; an organization that cares about morals and ethics, doing what is in the best interests of its clients; and an organization that cares about the impact it has on the environment. Employees want this because they recognize that such an organization will also care about them. The fact is, according to research, being a good corporate citizen is also good for your company.

> There is now an extensive body of research that demonstrates that corporate citizenship has positive effects on employees' motivation and morale as well as on their commitment and loyalty to the organization. . . . A survey of almost 25,000 people across 25 countries found that 80 per cent of people who worked for large companies stated that they felt greater motivation and loyalty towards their jobs and companies the more socially responsible their employers became. . . . Similarly, a survey of European employees found that almost 90 per cent expressed greater loyalty to employers who were socially responsible. Another study of employees in U.S. companies found that a company's corporate citizenship activities had a positive effect on the average employees' satisfaction and loyalty. In particular, employees involved in employer-sponsored community events were 30 per cent more likely to want to continue working for their employer and help it succeed.[11]

This new breed of employees knows that the kind of organization just described conducts a never-ending search for the best and brightest people; that it encourages managers to develop their people both personally and professionally; that it recognizes and rewards employees for their unique contributions; that it delegates responsibility not just accountability. They want to work for a company where they are encouraged to make a meaningful contribution; where procedures, policies, and paperwork are never more important than results; and where building bonds between people is considered as important as the bottom line. The question is, "Is it possible to create this kind of environment and strive for market leadership?" The answer is, "You don't have much of a choice."

WHY LOVE A COMPANY THAT DOESN'T LOVE YOU BACK?

A TNS/Conference Board report on "Employee Engagement and Commitment," issued in September 2005, found that "the greatest challenge facing business is an increasingly disengaged workforce. Forty percent of respondents reported feeling disconnected from their employers and a quarter said that they only show up to collect a paycheck. What's more, this trend appears to be hitting all levels of the workforce. A mere 26 percent of higher-paid respondents reported feeling motivated at work. Thirty-four percent reported feeling 'detached.' The numbers were 20 percent motivated and 48 percent detached for lower-paid workers."[12]

We must keep in mind all the costs of mistreating employees. Employees can express their dissatisfaction in a number of ways—all of them damaging: They can resign, taking important skills and customer knowledge with them; they can voice their discontent, thereby hurting morale; they can use every "sick day" available or continually show up late; or they can become apathetic, producing only enough to avoid being fired.

"I QUIT"

Employees leave an organization for a number of reasons. Among the most common are that they:

- Don't get along with their colleagues or supervisors
- Believe they could make a stronger contribution if given the freedom to do so
- Believe they are not being paid enough or receiving enough recognition for their contributions
- Feel they are stagnating and not being challenged
- Feel they don't have control over their destiny
- Disagree with the direction the organization is taking
- Believe the organization lacks direction
  (They're asked to do one thing today, the exact opposite tomorrow.)
- Are frustrated by the red tape
- Feel they're working in the dark and lack the resources to do their jobs

- Think they're not working in a fun environment

  And last, but not least:

- They simply cannot turn down that better offer.

It does not matter why employees leave; the costs and consequences of turnover are the same. The bonds between customers and your organization are severed. Employee industry knowledge and ability to network within the organization are lost. Replacements have to be attracted, hired, trained; then they have to learn to navigate their way through the organization. Moreover, if someone leaves the organization dissatisfied, and mentions it even discreetly to others, recruiting will suffer and your reputation may become tarnished.

In addition, the former employee may be a potential client in the future but may pass up your organization in favor of another because of unhappy memories. Thus, even if it's too late to persuade someone to stay, don't burn bridges.

"THIS IS A TERRIBLE PLACE TO WORK"

Plantation management also results in unhappy employees who decide, for any number of reasons, not to leave. Instead, they express their dissatisfaction by voicing their discontent. These employees quickly get the ear of new hires as well as veterans, telling them tales of woe.

Furthermore, dissatisfied employees who spend much of the workday complaining create an air of dissension, hindering concentration and lowering everyone's morale.

"I WON'T BE IN TODAY"

Unhappiness in the workplace also manifests itself in physical and psychological ailments that cause workers to be less productive. Unhappy people tend to notice minor physical ailments more. They escape their job frustration by focusing on their aching back or cold. Other employees, so distressed by their work, can become seriously ill.

According to a *Wall Street Journal* article, "An advertising salesman treated by Bruce Yaffe, a New York internist, screamed so loudly when he argued with his boss that he punctured a lung. Another patient, an office receptionist, had such stress-induced vomiting that she eventually had to quit her job. And a third, a Wall Street broker treated by physician Larry Lerner for hypertension, was so certain his death was imminent that he refused to take his children to the park for fear they would be abandoned when he died. Human resource managers, as well as doctors, psychologists, and pollsters agree that workplace stress is way up. Layoffs—and the pervasive fear of dismissal—are jangling nerves."[13]

Employees can also become so disaffected that they take time off because they cannot face another day at the office. *The Worklife Report* notes that "the more interesting and challenging the work, the less likely people are to be off work. If you like what you are doing, if you feel you are indispensable, you are not as likely to take off without a good reason."[14]

The obvious costs of absenteeism are easy to delineate: loss of productivity, increased costs of temporary workers, medical benefits and disability payments, and even possible lawsuits. The less obvious costs of absenteeism can also be identified: loss of morale among other members of the organization, loss of productivity as other employees pick up the slack for a "wounded" colleague, and loss of expertise if a "generalist" picks up the slack.

Moreover, an organization can face a contagion if this behavior continues unabated. A healthy body and a healthy mind may be a cliché, but clichés contain truths; it's in every organization's interest to consider the analogue: a healthy employee, a healthy organization.

"I DID AS MUCH AS I HAD TO . . ."

Another way that individuals express dissatisfaction—and maybe the most deadly of them all—is apathy. This silent killer strikes without warning or telltale signs that a problem exists. Apathy is a problem that raises its ugly head in different ways. According to the January 2010 Conference Board report on U.S. job satisfaction press release, "Americans of all ages and income brackets continue to grow increasingly unhappy at work—a long-term trend that should be a red flag to employers, according to a report released by The Conference Board. The report, based on a survey of 5,000 U.S. households conducted for The Conference Board by TNS, finds only 45 percent of those surveyed say they are satisfied with their jobs, down from 61.1 percent in 1987, the first year in which the survey was conducted."[15]

This loss of commitment is rampant in American business today. When researchers Yankelovich and Ammerwahr examined the situation, they found that the number of American workers who said they were working at their full potential was shockingly small—23 percent. They also discovered in their random sampling of American workers that "nearly half (44%) say they do not put any more effort into their jobs than is required to hold onto them. The overwhelming majority, 75%, say that they could be significantly more effective on their jobs than they are now."[16] Furthermore, according to a Watson Wyatt survey of nearly 13,000 workers in all job levels and industries, "fewer than two out of five employees today have trust or confidence in their senior leaders."[17] The implications for productivity are startling.

Apathy is difficult to remedy because it's intangible. However, employee satisfaction can be identified more easily if you view it on a continuum starting from a high of employee commitment to a low of apathy. By measuring employees on this scale, apathy may be more apparent—and therefore something you can rectify.

EMPLOYEE SATISFACTION CONTINUUM

The stages of employee satisfaction, ranging from commitment to apathy, are as follows:

- *Committed.* Every organization wants to strive for committed employees. These individuals have moved beyond loyalty. They are so deeply moved by the organization's values and purpose that they continually look for creative and innovative new ways for the organization to grow and develop. Their excitement, with its passion and sense of ownership, spills over onto others.

- *Loyal.* These are employees who enjoy coming to work, believe that they are making meaningful contributions, acknowledge that they are fairly recognized and rewarded, but most of all care deeply about the organization. Loyalty, however, does not always encourage creative and independent thinking, stimulate initiative, or instill a sense of ownership.

- *Motivated.* Management is doing a good job of keeping these employees happy. They are content with their present situation, but that feeling may be temporary. The things that motivate them today may be taken for granted tomorrow. At this stage, an individual may also care more about personal than organizational success. The result is that a better offer may be tempting.

- *Obedient.* These employees do enough to get by. Whether they are acting out of fear or trying to avoid personal conflict, they are unwilling to do anything that would set them apart. They are good soldiers who follow orders, but they have little interest in doing anything to make the organization more successful.

- *Disgruntled.* These individuals' hopes, desires, and expectations are not being met. However, they still care enough to try to change the situation by voicing their discontent. They demonstrate their displeasure by telling you that they'll do something "as soon as they can get to it." If you're listening carefully, you will know something is bothering them. If you don't catch the signals they're sending, they will either reach their limit and leave the organization or become apathetic.

- *Apathetic.* These employees are commonly known as deadwood. Their behavior can be characterized as having a lack of interest and/or caring. They sit at their desks shuffling papers and watching the clock; they take every sick and personal day allowed. They never make a suggestion or volunteer for anything. They accept assignments and deadlines with little visible reaction and respond with a shrug when asked if there is a problem. This general air of lassitude and disaffection is as contagious as enthusiasm in an organization.

The obvious question is, "How do you inspire commitment?"

A NEW VIEW: EMPLOYEES AS ASSETS

It's time for a new style of leadership. Workers don't like to be micromanaged or treated like cogs in a wheel. In a search to increase productivity, management has been taught various theories, techniques, and approaches believed to motivate employees. But they are all based on the fundamental premise that it's management's role to motivate—that is, management's job is to corral employees by changing or controlling their behavior. Great managers, however, know that it's much more desirable to win employee commitment through the organization's beliefs and values.

Successful leaders know that motivational techniques work for the moment—enough to achieve short-term goals. If you supplement short-term motivational techniques with a belief in and emphasis on your organization's mission and the vital contribution that employees are making, you instill commitment to an organization that your employees can feel proud of—one that contributes back to society. For today's employee, being a part of something that "makes a difference" is much more important than the rewards sought by yesterday's "me" generation.

Doing this, however, requires a very different organizational structure than the traditional hierarchical organization. According to Robert Haas, former chairman and CEO of Levi Strauss, [hierarchies] limit people to "strait jackets of narrow job definitions, rigid functional distinctions, and the mark of not sharing the information that people need to be successful." He added that "the first challenge for all of us is to cut through the ways that we, as managers, inhibit the intelligence, energy, commitment and excitement that already exists in our organizations." He said that in order to succeed, organizations must abandon "the myriad policies and procedures that shackle people today, the archaic command-and-control mentality of many managers, the unwillingness to listen and engage in two-way dialog, to value the opinions of people in the workforce [that] is cutting the organization's IQ in half."[18]

In a later interview with *Harvard Business Review*, Haas acknowledged that it is very "difficult to unlearn behaviors that made us successful in the past. Speaking rather than listening. Valuing people like yourself over people of different genders or from different cultures or parts of the organization. Doing things on your own rather than collaborating. Making the decision yourself instead of asking different people for their perspectives. There's a whole range of behaviors that were highly functional in the old hierarchical organization that are dead wrong in the flatter, more responsive, empowered organizations that we are seeking to become."[19]

Only those organizations that can provide employees with the responsibility, authority, and information to get the job done will thrive in today's competitive environment. But new structures and policies are only a start; to achieve true success, a new way of thinking must also become the norm. In these organizations, the "soft" side of business—the intangible beliefs, values, and philosophies espoused by management—must become of peak importance.

What we are discussing here is social motivation: the controls we impose on ourselves when we work with people with similar expectations and goals. An article in *California Management Review* stated, "With formal systems [of control] people often have a sense of external constraint which is binding and unsatisfying. With social controls, we often feel as though we have great autonomy, even though paradoxically we are conforming much more."[20]

The kind of self-motivation that results from a belief structure is in sharp contrast to leadership by command and control. Think of the terms associated with command-and-control "leadership." In *The Renewal Factor*, Robert Waterman says that it is interesting to "look up the word boss in a book of synonyms. At the start of the list you find manage and direct. Not bad. Then the list continues with control, order, command, take charge, preside over, oversee, supervise, superintend, domineer, dominate, push around, ride herd on, ride roughshod over, trample under foot, and shove around."[21] Obviously, managers who would wear the word "boss" proudly, knowing it carries all of those connotations, do not have the "right stuff" to be leaders in today's organizations, to inspire people to be the best that they can be.

A NEW MANAGEMENT PARADIGM

Stephen Covey says that commitment building is a four-phase process:

Covey calls the first phase the scientific management phase. In it, employees are seen primarily as stomachs (economic beings). In these organizations, management motivates employees primarily through use of the carrot and the stick. This is the stage at which managers are likely to say that their responsibility "is to motivate through the great jackass method . . . the carrot in front to entice and intrigue them, lead them to their benefits, and the stick behind." It says that I, the manager "am in control, I am the authority, I am the elite one, I know what is best, I will direct you where to go, of course the rewards will be fair."[22]

Covey calls the second phase the human relations phase. This is the stage at which management accepts that people also have hearts. They see "that people have feelings. . . . [and thus treat them] not only with fairness, but with kindness, with courtesy, with civility, with decency. . . . [In this] shift from authoritarian to benevolent authoritarian—we still know best. The power still lies with us, but we are not only fair to people but are kind."[23]

The third phase emphasizes human resource principles, recognizing that people have, in addition to stomachs and hearts, minds. Such recognition means that as managers, "we make better use of their creativity, imagination. . . . We begin to delegate more realizing that people are more committed to a goal when they're involved. . . . We begin to explore ways to create an optimal environment, a culture which taps their talents and releases their energy. . . . People want to make meaningful contributions. They want their talents identified, developed, utilized, and recognized."[24]

A recent article in *The Wall Street Journal* confirms the robust effect of Covey's first three phases of commitment building. The article stated, "A study of 60 business teams in the journal *American Behavioral Scientist* found teams with buoyant moods who encouraged each other earned higher profit and better customer-satisfaction ratings. A 2001 study at the University of Michigan says people who are experiencing joy or contentment are able to think more broadly and creatively, accepting a wider variety of possible actions, than people with negative emotions. And a 2005 research survey in the *Psychological Bulletin* shows happier people miss work less often and receive more positive evaluations from bosses."[25]

Covey calls the fourth and final phase the whole person paradigm. This is the best of all worlds. When an organization enters this phase, it provides its employees with "meaning, a sense of doing something that matters. People do not want to work for a cause with little meaning, even though it taps their mental capacities to their fullest." In this phase, leaders manage by tapping into "values, ideals, norms, and teachings that uplift, enable, fulfill, empower, and inspire people."[26]

According to Covey, "the scientific management (stomach) paradigm says, 'Pay me well.' The human relations (heart) paradigm says, 'Treat me well.' The human resource (mind) paradigm suggests, 'Use me well.' The principle-centered leadership (whole person) paradigm says, 'Let's talk values and goals.' "[27]

The time has come for business to enter the fourth phase. To do that, leaders must exercise their power by creating a vision and instilling a sense of purpose and mission in those they lead.

In *Leadership Is an Art*, Max De Pree, former chairman and CEO of Herman Miller, Inc., points out that "in a day when so much energy seems to be spent on maintenance and manuals, on bureaucracy and meaningless qualification, to be a leader is to enjoy the special privileges of complexity, of ambiguity, of diversity. But to be a leader means, especially, having the opportunity to make a meaningful difference in the lives of those who permit leaders to lead. . . . The measure of leadership is not the quality of the head, but the tone of the body. The signs of outstanding leadership appear primarily among the followers. Are the followers reaching their potential? Are they learning? Serving? Do they achieve the required results? Do they change with grace?"[28]

An article in *Fortune* exploring the exercise of power discussed the view of John Kotter, a professor at the Harvard Business School, who said that there are five kinds of power: "The first is the power to reward—to give someone a promotion, a raise, or a pat on the back. Its twin is the power to punish, to fire someone; . . . third is the power that experts call authority. Authority can be specific, and specifically granted—the right to sign $100,000 contracts. . . . The fourth kind of power derives from expertise. Finally, psychologists speak of referent power, which attaches to a leader because people admire him, want to be like him, or are wowed by his integrity, charisma or charm."[29]

The article went on to discuss other views of this theory. It stated that Jane Halpert, a professor of industrial and organizational psychology at Chicago's DePaul University, points out that "the first three—reward, punishment, and authority come with the office. The higher your rank, the more you usually have. But expertise and referent power inhere in the person. The better the leader . . . the more likely he [or she] is to rely on the personal sources of power. . . . Really effective leaders almost never have to put the screws on someone."[30]

Additionally, the article said that Ralph Stayer, former CEO of Johnsonville Foods, agreed that "real power is getting people committed. Real power comes from giving it up to others who are in a better position to do things than you are. Control is an illusion. The only control you can possibly have comes when people are controlling themselves."[31]

MANAGEMENT BY PRINCIPLES

More than 200 years ago, our forefathers brought forth a Bill of Rights for America. Remarkably, the words they wrote, reinterpreted as times changed, have withstood the test of time. The principles embodied in that document, which have always stood us in good stead as a nation, can be applied to business. Its values can help us migrate to that fourth phase of the paradigm—the stage at which leaders grant all employees those inalienable rights that inspire them to be the best they can be.

Before presenting the following Employee Bill of Rights, it is worth reminding today's leaders that embarking on a never-ending search for the right people is a prerequisite. It sends a message: You believe that your employees are your most important assets; they must be treated with dignity and respect. Furthermore, the more time you spend searching for the right people, the more effort you will make to develop them. This ultimately translates into higher expectations and greater trust. It also demonstrates your commitment to creating an exceptional working environment that will attract and retain valued employees. But most of all, this sends a strong message to all employees that they are special, thus creating a sense of pride and camaraderie within the organization. All of this will happen if you keep the following guidelines in mind.

AN EMPLOYEE BILL OF RIGHTS

Employees have the right to decide how best to achieve their goals. People work best when they have the responsibility and the authority to get the job done. Even though they may not determine the overall direction of the organization, they should have input into the process and choose the right path to effect results.

Employees have the right to be treated as part of the engine, rather than as interchangeable parts. People want to be part of something special and to know that they are making a valuable contribution. They want their work to be meaningful, and they want to be given a clear picture of how their daily activities impact the overall success of the organization.

Employees have the right to be viewed as unique individuals. Every person brings unique talents to the organization. Employees want to spend most of their time making the best use of those skills.

Employees have the right to be challenged. Employees should be given challenging responsibilities that utilize their strengths and stretch their potential. Their input should be solicited, their continuous improvement welcomed; and their contributions valued.

Employees have the right to be treated with dignity and respect. People should be treated with dignity at all times. Harsh criticism and temper tantrums must be replaced by civilized behavior and mutual respect. Everyone's contribution should be recognized and valued, and people should be made to feel part of the same team.

Furthermore, it is important to recognize the personal and professional needs of every employee. Many organizations believe that employee treatment affects only that individual, but that is not the case. It is rare for transfers, promotions, or reprimands to affect only the individual involved. For example, when three people are laid off in a department, those remaining, and those in other departments, may spend a great deal of time speculating about "who will be next" or even job hunting in preparation for the "next round."

Employees have the right to try and to fail. When people don't make mistakes, they aren't trying anything new. Mistakes, discussed in the next chapter, are an important stage in the learning process. Employees need to have confidence that failing in their attempts to try something new won't have repercussions.

Employees have the right to know that their employers have confidence in them and in their abilities. People do not like being second-guessed or micromanaged. They want to know that management trusts and respects them to do a responsible job. This leads to superior employee performance. In fact, "formal psychological research, as well as a large amount of casual empiricism by others, leaves no doubt that the power of expectation alone can influence the behavior of others. This total phenomenon is called the Pygmalion effect."[32] Studies have shown that the IQ scores of children, especially on verbal and information subjects, can be raised "merely by expecting them to do well. . . . A study showed that worker performance increased markedly when the supervisor of these workers was told that his group showed a special potential for their particular job."[33]

When employees feel like helpless drones, they tend to perform that way. If they believe that they are vital to the operation's success, they will take ownership, accept greater responsibility, and ultimately increase productivity.

Employees have the right to be treated in a fair and honest fashion. An article in *Industry Week* reported that "while 87% of the workers polled in a survey think it is very important that management is honest, upright, and ethical, only 39% believe that it is." It's not surprising that employees don't trust management that condones poor treatment or dishonest dealings with customers and suppliers. Furthermore, "three-quarters of those polled also indicated that it was very important to them that management truly cares about employees as individuals, but just 27% believe that anything like a caring attitude truly exists."[34] This belief that there is a lack of caring is a direct result of policies that fail to extend to employees the same level of loyalty and relationship building used with suppliers.

Employees have the right to have their professional standing recognized. For many individuals, performing well in their jobs isn't completely fulfilling. They want to continue to learn on the job and remain current in their field through professional affiliations, networking, or formal education. An organization's willingness to support these efforts helps develop employees both personally and professionally and increases productivity, loyalty, and commitment.

Many organizations feel that the costs associated with these activities are prohibitive. They fail to consider that these activities ultimately help the organization adapt to change and reduce employee turnover. Money spent recruiting new employees can be redirected to programs aimed at building commitment through training and employee development. (This subject is discussed in greater detail in Chapter 6.)

Employees have the right to freedom of expression. Employees should feel confident that they could make suggestions and provide input, as well as receive constructive feedback, without fear of recrimination or retaliation.

Employees have the right to be informed. Employees should have access to all information needed to do their jobs. This includes knowing the rationale behind why decisions are made, rather than being expected to just follow orders. Furthermore, they should be made aware of *major* events affecting the organization through formal channels rather than through the grapevine or by hearing about them through the media.

Employees have the right to approach management. Management should announce an open-door policy. But announcing it is not enough. Employees should feel comfortable approaching management. Ask yourself if you're in your office long enough to be approached. Are you available at convenient times or only at 7:00 a.m.? Has your administrative assistant done everything to screen you from "outsiders" except put barbed wire outside your office? When a concern was brought to your attention, in confidence, did you divulge any part of the information? Do you just go through the motions of listening? It is up to you to take the initiative and get out of your office to meet with employees. Be seen on a regular basis so people don't think you're avoiding them.

Employees have the right to know that their efforts are appreciated. In an article in *Industry Week*, David Kearns, former chairman and CEO of Xerox Corporation, said, "If you have a pot of gold, it's easy to manage. Just keep giving out cash, holding those carrots out. But when that pot of gold isn't there, it's a lot more difficult to manage. That's when the true managers emerge."[35]

Clearly, everyone wants to get paid for a day's work. But all things considered, pay is far from the greatest motivating factor. Numerous studies point out that recognition for a job well done is as important as salary differentials.

For example, a survey conducted by the Houston-based American Productivity Center reported that "90–95 percent of the responding members said that recognition when I've done a job well is important or very important as a motivational factor. In fact, it ranked above competitive salary and pay clearly tied to performance."[36]

Personnel Journal reports that "recognition and praise on the job are so important that one in four workers surveyed by Motivational Systems of West Orange, New Jersey, said they would leave their current jobs—to work at the same salary and benefits—for another company with a reputation for giving special notice and appreciation."[37]

EMPLOYEE RECOGNITION PROGRAMS

As a general rule of thumb, recognition programs should meet the following criteria:

- *Be simple enough that everyone understands how, why, and when people will be rewarded.* I'm always amused to hear that an organization launched an Incentive Program that no one can figure out.
- *Communicate continuously.* I know an individual who won an award from a program she didn't even know existed.
- *Stage ceremonies.* People should be praised in public so that others will then emulate their behavior. A note of thanks on someone's desk, while nice, is a limited management tool.
- *Mandate senior management involvement.* Senior management's involvement in award giving adds emphasis and significance to any award.

- *Display consistency with major goals.* Recognition should reinforce the areas most important to the organization. If the program is not consistent with or does not reinforce the strategic direction of the organization, it will be ineffective. For example, rewarding people for tenure rather than performance encourages longevity rather than success.

- *Provide ongoing recognition.* The best programs offer constant and timely feedback; they do not depend on a formal review process.

- *Ensure informal and formal rewards.* While formal recognition programs are vitally important, sometimes the most effective programs are spontaneous. Examples include such programs as Lightning Strikes and ABC (Above the call of duty). In these programs, awards can be given out any time at the discretion of management. Recognition can also take the form of creating a sense of ownership. For example, when some organizations announce a new development or product, rather than have a public relations professional or a senior executive make the announcement, they let the creator and development team present and discuss the innovation.

- *Have goals that are perceived as realistic and achievable.* If the requirements for winning an award are unrealistic, the program is useless. The opposite—setting goals so low that everyone wins—is just as meaningless.

- *Make rewards meaningful.* Every reward need not be materially significant; it may be just a token. Of course, there must be balance. But I have seen the Dale Carnegie organization give out an inexpensive pen for the best speaker at a meeting, and watched the proud expressions of the recipient too often to believe that small rewards are unimportant. The critical element is that a reward be given in a sincere—and timely—manner.

CARING

There is a story told by Fran Tarkenton that sums up so much of what is being said here—and does it so well—that it is worth repeating in its entirety:

A month after my election to the Hall of Fame, I stood in the kitchen of our house in Atlanta with suitcases stacked all around me. The day had arrived for my son to leave home for Princeton University. He left the kitchen for a moment, and when he came back, he had an envelope for each of us.

That's when the realization hit me: My son is saying goodbye to everything he's known. The security of his family, his home . . . he knows it will never be the same. He's going off to start all over again. And then it happened. He came around the kitchen table to me and I saw the tears. As I put my arms around him, I felt the tears. His tears wet the shoulder of my shirt, my tears spilled freely for the first time in my life. For long moments, we just held each other, saying nothing.

Later, thinking about that moment, I realized that a great change had occurred in my relationship with my son. We really, truly, unequivocally cared. We cared more than macho would let us admit. And when we saw and felt how much good it did, we both knew there was no weakness in letting our feelings be known.

It took strength. Only real men can cry.

The more I think about the mood of business, the problems of management, the more I am convinced that what is missing is tears! Maybe not literally, of course, but certainly what tears represent in terms of personal caring and commitment.[38]

3

IT'S A GOOD IDEA, BUT . . .

BUILDING AN INNOVATIVE ORGANIZATION
THAT REINVENTS ITSELF EVERY DAY

Constant reinvention is the central necessity at GE. . . . We're all just a moment away from commodity hell.

—Jeffrey Immelt, Chairman and CEO, General Electric[1]

When was the last time that someone in your organization came up with a good idea? Do your new ideas come from a select few or is it everyone's responsibility to contribute? Do you reward innovation or stifle it with politics, protocol, and procrastination? Do you welcome ideas with outstretched arms or listen because you have to? Do you have a formal plan for stimulating ideas or just allow them to happen? Do senior managers break down old barriers or construct new ones? Do you actively encourage the exploration of new ideas as a corporate philosophy or do so only when forced to?

In this new age of competitive intensity, an organization's ability to create and then act on new ideas can make the difference between a winner and an also-ran. Warren Bennis, a recognized pioneer in the field of leadership studies, told a management conference in the year 2002 that in the current age, the main asset of any organization—whether private, public, or nonprofit—is human imagination, and that if an organization does not understand this and act accordingly, "they won't be in the phone book come 2005."[2] But just as capital equipment must be properly maintained and repaired to protect its value, creativity—an organization's greatest natural resource—must be nurtured if it is to provide the greatest benefits.

Creativity makes a difference at every level and in every type of organization—whether in creating new products and services, managing business relationships, or finding ways to solve long-standing problems by using imagination to throw an old ball with a new twist.

In some organizations, creativity is encouraged by the corporate culture, by the organization's operational style, and by individual management practices; in others, it is stymied at every turn. According to a 2010 Boston Consulting Group (BCG)/*BusinessWeek* study of 1,590 executives worldwide, "A large majority of companies consider innovation a top strategic priority for 2010. Seventy-two percent of respondents said that their company considers it a top-three priority, versus 64 percent in 2009." According to the study, executives identify a risk-averse corporate culture as one of the top two factors holding down the return on their innovation spending.[3]

Organizational barriers to creativity are numerous, and the difficulty of bypassing them depends to a large extent on the level at which they are found. The most difficult roadblocks to creativity are found in organizations where the cultural mind-set encourages politics, where there is a caste system, where the organization resists change of any kind, and where failures represent a death knell to an individual's career. This is the first, or most basic, level where roadblocks occur.

Operational style, the second level, is a less formidable roadblock because at this level, it is easier to identify the problems and pinpoint the remedies. The procedures and protocol that dominate, the bureaucratic morass that hinders action, the delayed and inadequate hearings given to new ideas, and the lack of incentives for rewarding people can all be changed to nurture creativity.

Last, the easiest obstacle to remove is an individual's management style that quells creativity. Removing that barrier requires an understanding on the part of all managers that keeping people in the dark, managing with a dictatorial style, making requests with unrealistic time frames, and procrastination are not in management's best interests.

UNLOCKING THE CREATIVE MYSTIQUE

Many people have little understanding of or have difficulty assessing the creative process. They try to issue orders to stimulate, put time limits on, or insist that the creative process conform to preconceived notions. The fact is, the better you understand the creative process, the easier it is to encourage creativity.

In his intensive studies of creativity, best-selling author Roger von Oech notes that "there are two main phases in the development of new ideas: a germinal phase and a practical one. In the germinal phase, ideas are generated and manipulated; in the practical phase, they are evaluated and executed. To use a biological metaphor, the germinal phase sprouts the new ideas and the practical phase harvests them."[4]

Von Oech warns against concentrating in only one area. Instead, he says, the best thinking comes from playing four different roles—explorer, artist, judge, and warrior—at appropriate times. To start, you

> need the raw materials from which new ideas are made: facts, concepts, experiences, knowledge, feelings, and whatever else you can find . . . so, you become an *explorer* and look for the materials you'll use to build your idea. . . . They may form a pattern, but if you want something new and different, you have to give them a twist or two. That's when you shift roles and let the *artist* in you come out. . . . Now you ask yourself, "Is this idea any good? Is it worth pursuing? Will it give me the return I want? Do I have the resources to make this happen?" To help you make your decision, you adopt the mindset of a *judge*. . . . Finally it's time to implement your idea. You realize, however, that the world isn't set up to accommodate every new idea that comes along. . . . So you become a *warrior* and take your idea into battle . . . you may have to overcome excuses, idea killers, temporary setbacks, and other obstacles.[5]

Von Oech's interpretation is particularly interesting in light of the common notion that we use different sides of the brain for different kinds of thinking. The left side of the brain is logical, concrete, and judgmental, very specific and consistent. The right side of the brain, in contrast, is capable of abstract thought, of putting various pieces together and creating something new; it is the place where intuition flourishes. Thus, the roles of explorer and artist may work best using right-side thinking; judge and warrior, left-side thinking. The difficulty arises when a person who is primarily a right-brain or left-brain thinker is responsible for playing all four roles and has a problem switching gears. An additional difficulty occurs when the role of management requires being a judge while at the same time, being on the creative team calls on the artist role; in forcing their different ways of thinking onto each other, the two sides come into conflict.

Some companies excel at creativity. According to senior executives surveyed by The Boston Consulting Group, the 10 most innovative companies in 2010 were Apple, Google, Microsoft, IBM, Toyota Motor, Amazon.com, LG Electronics, BYD, General Electric, and Sony.[6] Of course, there are pockets of creativity within companies and among managers, but organization-wide creative thinking is more difficult to find.

One organization known for innovation is Apple. "Over the past decade, the pride of Cupertino has produced a mind-boggling parade of accomplishments:

- "Having been dismissed as a footnote in the personal computer industry, Apple is now the market leader in computers costing more than $1,000. In one recent month, its market share in this segment exceeded 90%.

- "Though it was a late entrant into the mobile phone business, Apple currently makes more money from roughly 3% of the global handset market than Nokia makes from more than 30%.

- "Within six years of launching its online music store in 2003, Apple had become the world's largest music retailer.

- "Apple's first physical store opened in 2001. Five years later, Apple's sparse, elegant shops were generating four times more revenue per square foot than its big box competitors, and its Fifth Avenue store in New York is thought to be the most profitable retail outlet in the world.

- "At $180 billion, Apple's market value is currently three and [a] half times that of Nokia, and more than 60% higher than Hewlett-Packard's—a company with three times Apple's revenue."[7]

Another organization best known for innovation is 3M, the company responsible for such products as Post-it Notes and Scotch tape—a company that strives to get 25 percent of each year's sales from products that are less than five years old. Extolled as "masters of innovation" and "new product champions," 3M has, over the years, been a perfect example of how to promote the creative spirit among employees.

One reporter, examining what makes 3M different, said that " 'Thou shall not kill an idea' is 3M's 'eleventh commandment.' " This commandment is carried out through establishment of a climate that puts a premium on "patience in the nurturing of developing projects; respect for the ideas of others; a constructive attitude toward failure as a necessary by-product of innovation; and an atmosphere of open communication."[8]

RUNNING THE CREATIVE GAUNTLET

According to an IBM survey of more than 1,500 chief executive officers from 60 countries and 33 industries worldwide, "chief executives believe that—more than rigor, management discipline, integrity or even vision—successfully navigating an increasing complex world will require creativity."[9] The first step in encouraging creativity is recognizing roadblocks and the reasons for them—some of which are unconscious. A good place to start is with the roadblocks that are easiest to tear down: those created by management because they lack the skills required to manage the creative process or because they believe they must maintain tight control at all times or because of their own inadequacies as managers.

After discussing management style, we'll tackle the roadblocks that exist in operational style and then finally, the most challenging roadblocks of all—those that exist in the corporate culture, in the very mind-set of an organization.

MANAGEMENT STYLE

According to Eric Schmidt, executive chairman of Google, "More than ever, innovation is disruptive and messy. It can't be controlled or predicted. The only way to ensure it can flourish is to create the best possible environment—and then get out of the way. It's a question of learning to live with a mess."[10]

In the most creative environments, the line between working and having fun is blurred. People come to work not because they have to but because they want to. Creating that kind of environment is the responsibility of management. Jack Welch, Jr., former chairman of the board and CEO of General Electric (one of the greatest business leaders of our times), describes this environment well in GE's 1989 *Annual Report*:

> We want GE to become a company where people come to work every day in a rush to try something they woke up thinking about the night before. We want them to go home from work wanting to talk about what they did that day, rather than trying to forget about it. We want factories where the whistle blows and everyone wonders where the time went, and someone suddenly wonders aloud why we need a whistle. We want a company where people find a better way, every day, of doing things; and where by shaping their own work experience, they make their lives better and your company best.
>
> Farfetched? Fuzzy? Soft? Naive? Not a bit. This is the type of liberated, involved, excited, boundary-less culture that is present in successful start-up enterprises. It is unheard of in an institution our size; but we want it, and we are determined we will have it.

In this kind of organization, employees are given excellent direction by senior management, colleagues work together rather than at cross-purposes with one another, and most important, everyone from the top of the organization to the lowest-level employee is committed to and has a personal stake in achieving the organization's goals.

In such organizations, management transfers authority and responsibility for getting the job done to employees, leaving the process for reaching goals to their discretion. Management's responsibility then is to ensure that employees have the resources they need to do their job and that barriers inhibiting their progress—such as keeping people in the dark, dictating creativity, setting unrealistic time frames, and procrastination—are torn down.

KEEPING PEOPLE IN THE DARK

> *"Why do you have to know what we are doing? All I want are a few ideas."* How can someone come up with ideas in a vacuum? The time you invest providing background information often helps ensure that the ideas developed are consistent with your organization's overall strategy. Moreover, such information often becomes a catalyst for new ideas.

"It's just not right. I can't tell you why, but I just don't like it." Managers who don't take the time to evaluate an idea and provide constructive feedback (rather than criticism) will be disappointed when employees make the same errors again.

"I know exactly what I want, but can't explain it. When I see it, though, I'll tell you." The inability to provide direction or to verbalize your expectations sets your employees up for failure. Perhaps you need to spend more time figuring out what you want before requesting assistance.

"Discuss the project with Harry, Tom, and Bill. Their input is important." Don't ask someone to get direction from others unless you're sure that consistent input will be received or that the group will be able to resolve inconsistencies together. Otherwise, the person may end up playing the role of mediator rather than creator. The old adage "too many cooks spoil the broth" applies here. *The Wall Street Journal* told the sad tale of a speechwriter requested to circulate a draft of the CEO's speech to some of the company's executives. The writer said that "he received copies of his draft from 24 executives—'with 24 sets of comments.' And the chief executive hadn't even seen the draft. 'Twenty-four people rewrote it from their point of view,'" he lamented, adding that the result was he quit his job.[11]

"Your job isn't to meet with the client. It is to deliver results." The "creative team" should have direct access both to their clients and to those on "the front line," that is, those closest to the customer, such as salespeople and dealers. After all, the closer one gets to the customer, the less chance there is that something will get lost through translation or modified by individual bias.

To ensure that people are not kept in the dark, even unwittingly, management must promote free and open communication throughout the organization, both vertically and across disciplines. That openness is part of the nurturing environment that spurs creativity, dampens distrust, and fosters a climate in which everyone pulls together to achieve a common end. In this environment, new ideas are encouraged and constructive feedback is offered. Internal communication is not hoarded by a few people because what seems important to one person may be insignificant to another. Instead, management works hard to break down barriers to communication and create forums encouraging people to exchange ideas and network both within and outside their organization. (A new model for internal communication is introduced in Chapter 4.) In companies known for innovation, communication flows freely and experimentation and smart risk taking are encouraged. In an article in the *MIT Sloan Management Review*, the author notes that Google Inc. runs 50 to 200 search experiments at any given time and comments:

> In one case, Google asked selected users how many search results they would like to see on a single screen. More, said the users, many more. So Google ran an experiment that tripled the number of search results per screen to 30. The company found that traffic declined.
>
> What happened? On average it took about a third of a second longer for search results to appear—a seemingly insignificant delay that nonetheless upset many of the users. The greater number of results also made it more likely that a user would click on a page that did not have the information he or she was seeking.
>
> In an environment where experimentation is this quick and efficient, many traditional practices make less economic sense. For instance, current research-and-development efforts are often driven by considerations that the company's technicians think are important but customers really don't care about.[12]

Despite the negative results in this case, the significant takeaway is that the practical application of an idea is key. Furthermore, in this successful corporate culture, questions are continually being asked and experiments pursued. After all, who knows who will spark the next great idea!

DICTATORSHIPS

> *"Here's my idea and how to execute it!"* When you tell people not only what you want but dictate the process as well, people shift into automatic pilot, stop thinking about a better way to attack a problem, and execute the action as directed. Because your orders indicate a resistance to—and perhaps punishment for—finding new and perhaps better ways to do something, you negate any possibility of developing a new approach that might result in greater efficiency.

"Here's my idea, what's yours?" When managers present their ideas before allowing employees to present theirs, employees may hold back suggestions rather than insinuate that their bosses' ideas are inferior. This places boundaries and parameters on employee thinking, discouraging independent thought.

"Find me the optimal idea." When you're looking for only one answer—The Best One—it's too easy to stop the creative process after just one idea is presented. Remember, the first good answer may not always be the best. Encourage employees to brainstorm ideas until all possibilities have been exhausted.

"Why are you wasting your time doing background research?" Don't let your personal bias toward the creative process influence how others proceed. Remember that right-brain thinkers like to explore ideas on the road to new developments; don't let your manager's bias toward left-brain thinking prevent that exploration. Those doing the research know what works for them. In many ways, "managing talent is like raising children. Talents are children who never completely grow up; managers are people who do grow up, but many of them forget they were ever children. They lose that child-like wonder. They don't know how to relate to children—or to talent. Managers who eliminate the child in their personality can never manage talent well."[13]

"Don't waste your time brainstorming, just come up with a great idea." As Klaus Kleinfeld, the former CEO of Siemens AG, once said, "You can only win the 'war' with ideas, not with spending cuts."[14] Remember that many of the best ideas result from using one thought as a springboard to another. Furthermore, many innovations result from applying an idea from one industry or company to a completely different situation.

"Stop playing around and get back to work." The authors of *The Creativity Infusion* say that "another barrier to creativity often cited is the lack of discretionary time. When you work for an organization, you're generally deemed to be fully employed. Fully employed means that if you're not visibly doing something during all of your hours of employment—and usually beyond—then obviously you don't have enough to do. . . . From another perspective, however,

truly dedicated managers will sometimes make sure you can't be creative. They'll pile onto you things that are really unnecessary, again with the theory that if you have your feet up on the desk, you're obviously not fully employed."[15]

"What you came up with is okay, but let's do it somewhat differently." Don't alter ideas by introducing subtle, meaningless changes in order to justify the time you spent reviewing them. Furthermore, it is important to provide recognition for creative new ideas. When employees know that their suggestions are appreciated and adopted, they work harder to implement them.

"Here's $300,000 to try out your idea." Being too generous can often kill an idea. The size of an investment can raise expectations before an idea has had time to move out of its infancy. It is often better to test an idea in incremental steps, learning from mistakes, than to increase its visibility and smother it with money.

Managers often turn to a dictatorial style of management out of fear that they will lose control by providing too much latitude. Such managers maintain tight control to avoid having anyone "mess up." They have lost sight of the conviction that if you believe in your people, they will believe in themselves. Organizations should adopt the philosophy of executives such as Dick Madden, former CEO of Potlatch Corporation, who said that it is far better to "think of the boundaries within which your staff operates as you would the walls of a room. Make sure that the walls are far enough apart to give people maximum space, but never so far apart that management can't support people if they stumble. The walls are there to strengthen and guide; they aren't there to neglect or confine. As skills develop, the boundaries can be enlarged."[16]

UNREALISTIC TIME FRAMES

"It's only one page. It shouldn't take more than an hour to complete." You can't put a timetable on creativity. Doing so will result in ideas that are not fully developed and in frustrated employees who hand in their work but have second thoughts about their efforts the next day.

"I know there's no reason to have it tomorrow, but I want it then anyway." Some managers believe they must exert pressure to force

creativity, that people respond to pressure with inspired break-throughs. Although people often do rise to an occasion, pressure or fear is a short-term approach that doesn't always yield results. Furthermore, if you cry wolf too often, when you really need something extra from your employees, they won't have it to give to you.

"I gave you two days to do this; I can't believe there's a typo in it." By first setting unrealistic time frames and then ridiculing an individual's best effort, not only do you destroy employee morale, you also reduce confidence, which will negatively affect future work.

Management must resist the pressure to accept projects that have unrealistic deadlines and then force them onto their employees. According to a survey of senior managers by the Wharton School, "problems arise when senior people's approach to new products does not recognize the learning process. . . . Another problem is impatience. Once management (finally, in the eyes of some) makes the go decision, they want the product out immediately."[17]

PROCRASTINATION

"We really do want suggestions. It's not our fault if we're too busy to act on them." In many organizations, employees are asked for suggestions and told that management will get back to them upon review—but no one ever does. Employees begin to assume no one cares, so they stop trying. This problem is compounded when managers are so overextended that they view a new idea as an annoyance, an attitude that is "communicated" to employees.

"I think we've got it now. I only have minor corrections to the thirteenth draft." Some managers change things just for the sake of changing them. Others make changes because proper attention was never given to an earlier draft. A creativity survey reported in *Marketing News* said, "over-evaluation and competitiveness among group members were mentioned by 41 percent of the participants as a cause of failure."[18]

"Thanks for the information. Our committee meets in a few weeks. We'll decide whether to go ahead with it then." Delays cause a loss of momentum. A frequent complaint is that "senior people are willing to entertain new ideas, but tend to drag out investment decisions too

long. . . . The hamper to innovation is the analysis process we get into. Rather than use judgment, they'd much rather gather lots more data."[19]

"With all the problems I have on my plate, you can't expect me to think about that now." Maybe if you had listened to someone else's idea six months ago, you wouldn't be faced with all these problems now. It takes just as much effort to find excuses as it does to listen.

Today's competitive environment places a premium on speed—which is discussed in great detail in Chapter 7. That is why procrastination—waiting until problems are critical before addressing them—creates problems at every turn. You end up spending all your time putting out fires rather than lighting them. Moreover, setting unrealistic deadlines creates cynicism and dulls enthusiasm among employees.

OPERATIONAL STYLE

Every organization is unique in the way it conducts its day-to-day business. This is evident in its structure, its policies and procedures, and its reward system. It is important to remember that rules can be changed to encourage creativity. This is less challenging than trying to change the corporate culture, which permeates the mind-set of the entire organization.

FORMALITIES AND PROTOCOL

"Put it in writing." This action stifles creativity in two ways. First, individuals may feel more comfortable expressing their ideas verbally. And second, many individuals may lose interest before having the time or inclination to put their ideas in writing.

"Make sure your ideas conform to our format." This is the case of putting boundaries on an idea—style over substance. First, evaluate an idea on its own merit before considering how to package it.

"Come up with something really creative, but be sure it doesn't run more than eight pages, has limited text, and uses line art." Injecting personal preferences or limiting creative freedom may hinder the creative process. Or, it may end up changing the basic idea enough that it is no longer valid.

"Don't ask questions, just follow the rules." Every organization needs procedures that organize basic activities; the danger is in establishing rules that stifle creativity and innovation. As Roger von Oech says, "There is a lot of pressure in our culture to follow the rules. This value is one of the first things we learn as children. We are told, 'Don't color outside the lines,' and 'No orange elephants.' Our educational system encourages further rule-following. Students are usually better rewarded for regurgitating information than for playing with ideas and thinking of original uses for things. As a consequence, people feel more comfortable following the rules than challenging them. . . . If, however, you are trying to generate new ideas, then the value 'follow the rules' can be a mental lock because it means 'think of things only as they are.' "[20] In an article in *Business Week* discussing the creative climate at 3M, traditionally known for its innovation, the author points out that "the scarcity of corporate rules at 3M leaves room for plenty of experimentation— and failure [which is not considered a death knell of any kind]."[21]

Organizations develop procedures such as standard design formats to increase consistency and make the organization function more smoothly— in fact, the absence of any rules would lead to chaos. Many times, however, either the rationale for developing a rule disappears as circumstances change, or the procedures themselves take on greater importance than achieving the ultimate goal. Employees must be empowered to bend the rules when it serves the best interest of the organization. In the article mentioned previously, Eric Schmidt, executive chairman of Google, said, "Addressing the innovation deficit requires rethinking our innovation model. We can no longer rely on the top-down approach of the 20th century, when big investments in the military and NASA spun off to the wider economy. Now that the Internet has put abundant information and powerful tools in everyone's hands, innovation is often driven from the bottom up. The ideas that power our next generation of growth are just as likely to originate in a coffee shop as in the laboratory of a big corporation."[22] Therefore, company procedures should serve as strict guidelines, but never be so set in stone that they can't be modified. They should be revisited and tested over time to ensure that they still serve their intended purposes.

BUREAUCRACY

"It's a great idea. Now just get the 10 required signoffs and we're ready to roll." There are two ends to the bureaucratic continuum. One is centralization, where a few people approve everything, leading to excessive queues. The other end, consensus, ensures that quick decisions are close to impossible. The speechwriter quoted earlier, who had his draft reviewed by 24 executives, noted that the result of taking everyone's suggestions into account was "minestrone." He recalled that "a marketing manager . . . wanted the speech to tell the audience how certain financial products could be adapted to fit its specific needs. A lawyer wanted to talk about the legislative battle the company was prepared to wage. An economist wanted to focus on trends."[23]

"Run the idea up the flagpole. You need the approval of the five unit heads." This scenario is all too common: Some of the changes being requested are inconsistent with one another, one person is on vacation for two weeks, and two other reviewers are out of the country for five days—but you have three days to complete the work. If approvals are important, those involved must be available to mediate differences among themselves and provide direction in a timely fashion.

"I personally thought it was a good idea, but when I presented it to my boss . . . ." Those who generate an idea are usually the best people to sell it. They have the enthusiasm and are best equipped to answer questions to gain approval. Therefore, when running an idea "up the flagpole," try to bring the idea's champion or champions with you to the presentation meeting. After all, one of the greatest benefits of generating a good idea is getting the opportunity to present it to upper management.

"You can't have him for your new design group . . . he's in sales." The authors of *The Creativity Infusion* point out that "it seems fairly reasonable and logical that if a company's managers are investing in the organization's future survival and growth, they should staff creative projects with their best and brightest. Yet they often do this reluctantly because these folks are so valuable and essential in other important or critical areas. The boss then may be reluctant to volunteer them for a high-risk assignment that takes them away from their already invaluable contribution."[24] The Wharton study mentioned

earlier reported that "one product manager said that the biggest problem was that it took 3 months to pull the people out of their existing organization and get them working temporarily on his project. He has continuing problems making sure that these people's bosses recognize the value of their work on the new project so that the people will not suffer in their performance reviews."[25]

The ability to respond promptly to a client's request, to get a new product to market quickly, to be the first to introduce a new idea is key in today's competitive environment. As the General Electric *Annual Report* mentioned earlier states:

> Being on top of things, controlling them, must give way to sharing, trusting. Most of the bureaucracy that infects business institutions— the reviews, layers, routines and reports—stem largely from a lack of trust . . . controlling people doesn't motivate them. It stifles them. We've found that people perform better, even heroically, when they see that what they do every day makes a difference. When they see that—when they are allowed to make real contributions to win—they quickly develop increased self-confidence. That self-confidence in turn promotes simplicity—of action, of design, of process, of communication—because there is no longer a psychic need to wrap oneself in the complexity, trappings and jargon that, in a bureaucracy, signify sophistication and status.

When a highly promising or time-sensitive idea is not screened as a priority but rather receives the same plodding attention as a rudimentary idea, it may die as a result. Furthermore, management will be unable to respond to the volume of ideas on a timely basis. As a result, employees will stop sending ideas to management, knowing they will never hear back from them anyway. In both cases, the organization loses.

Why do organizations insist on developing elaborate bureaucracies? In some cases, people are merely protecting their fiefdoms. Other times, managers impose a rigid style because they fear the loss of power and control.

In yet other organizations, the bureaucratic style develops as managers, afraid of making decisions, pass anything requiring a decision along to the next level. Although several approvals are clearly required when decisions involve a lot of money, have major strategic consequences, or require a specialist's review (for example, by an attorney), in most cases, however, those best able to judge the likelihood of success are those closest to an idea.

DISCOURAGING NEW IDEAS

"I won't have time to meet with you, so why don't you drop it in the mail?" If you want to develop an innovative culture, being responsive to new ideas must become a priority. If you can't review an idea on a timely basis, provide an explanation and a promise to discuss it at a future date—and keep that promise!

"Sorry, I didn't review your idea yet. I already received 50 ideas like yours this week." Everyone thinks their idea is special. Don't turn them off by minimizing their effort.

"I personally wouldn't do it, but why don't you try anyway?" Watch how you phrase your direction. People work best when they feel they are making a valuable contribution to an organization. If you want someone to do something, hold back any qualifiers that plant seeds of doubt. Instead, indicate confidence in them and their ideas.

"Don't come up with ideas, just do your job." It's everyone's responsibility to come up with new ideas, not just a select few. The person you just discouraged might have had the next homerun idea.

"You've got a great idea . . . now all we have to do is figure out who to present it to." When people don't know where to go with ideas, the ideas unfortunately sit on the shelf. Innovative companies have a culture and a clear process for submitting new ideas.

"I know my idea is great; if only I could convince management." Many ideas fail, not because the ideas are flawed, but because they are not properly packaged. For example, when a great idea is presented to management but the PowerPoint presentation is amateurish, the idea is turned down. Management could break down this barrier by separating substance from fluff. If the idea lacks packaging, management could provide marketing support to aid the process.

"Why are you bothering me with that? Its impact would be minimal." Examining only big ideas is bad business. Hitting a lot of singles scores as many runs as hitting it out of the park. Besides, that small idea may turn out to be a first step on the road to something big.

The tone of an organization is set through good climate control. Organizations that understand this premise "regard new ideas as wild flowers.

They know you do not plant seeds for wild flowers; you find them by searching in many places. They concentrate on preparing the conditions for wild flowers to grow as they push for incremental change everywhere."[26]

This means that organizations should analyze their internal climate, norms, and personal biases that inhibit creativity and institute changes that will create a climate where new ideas are welcomed and allowed to flourish; where ideas are evaluated on their individual merit rather than on the status of the person introducing them; where people look for "the good" in every idea, trying to add value to it rather than trying to shoot it out of the sky.

THE EVALUATION PROCESS

"I ran it by the committee, and it didn't fly." Providing feedback on just the bottom line isn't enough. A summary of the factors and process used to evaluate an idea should be provided to the originator of the idea as well.

"Rather than take the time to give you my comments, it'll be easier if I take care of it myself." This reaction prevents people from learning from their mistakes, thus ensuring that the mistakes will be repeated. Moreover, by failing to let someone see a project through to the end, you steal the satisfaction most people get from completing an activity.

"I know I asked you to be creative, but this stuff is off the wall." When you rip apart a suggestion and demean the person who made it, you guarantee that you will receive "safe" solutions in the future. Explaining what was wrong without making disparaging remarks is far more productive.

"John, how do you expect me to approve this when you left out . . ." This is known as throwing the baby out with the bathwater. Be careful not to discard a great idea because of a detail.

Many times it is not negative feedback that stops the flow of ideas, but the way that the feedback is presented. Furthermore, reviewers must not be rushed or overextended; they must give new ideas the time and attention commensurate with the time and effort expended to come up with the ideas.

INCENTIVES

"Why say thank you? It's his job, isn't it?" People work for more than money. Most people want to be recognized for a job well done and experience an inner satisfaction.

"Why should we broadcast the fact that John had an idea?" By giving John the kudos he deserves, you create the incentive not just for John but for others to come up with more good ideas.

"Look at the great idea I just came up with." There's nothing more demoralizing to employees than having superiors take the credit for subordinates' work. When you have a breach of trust, people hesitate to present new ideas; furthermore, they are likely to look for a path other than innovative thinking by which they can be recognized for their contributions.

"Why provide incentives for ideas?" Concrete rewards evoke enthusiasm, dedication, and loyalty. They also inspire others to emulate the behavior of the person being recognized.

In an article in *Fortune*, Stratford Sherman explains that companies that encourage innovation and creativity "reinforce the fear of stagnation with rewards for success." He cites Jack Welch of GE who annually doled out $2 million in bonuses for extraordinary contributions. He notes, "Others rely less on money than on ego-boosters. 3M gives prizes—trophies and certificates—while Intel gives its design engineers the gratifying opportunity to present their new products to engineers at client companies."[27] Almost every innovative company has reward systems in place, but perhaps no company does it better than 3M, where the person "who champions a new product out the door then gets the chance to manage it as if it were his or her own business."[28]

Furthermore, at some organizations, dual career ladders have been set up to reward individuals who deserve promotions but are happy doing the creative work that resulted in their recognition in the first place. For example, at 3M, engineers who don't want to be managers are not punished. The company's dual-ladder approach, said Lester Krogh, the former vice president of research and development, "allows employees to go back and forth from management to research. As scientists, they can have the same benefits and monetary privileges as managers."[29]

Indeed, in organizations noted for their creativity, even failures that are the result of unusual effort receive special awards. Managers in such organizations recognize the nuances among their employees. They know that some people are less likely to be motivated by money or career advancement than by the inner satisfaction of hatching their own ideas. These managers make sure that they reward people who take chances by:

- Saying thank you in public
- Having a variety of methods for granting recognition, including internal newsletters, formal notes, and lunches with senior management as well as major gifts
- Making sure that rewards are given soon after the effort is made

THE ORGANIZATIONAL CULTURE

A participant in a study conducted by the Wharton School said, "First you have to learn how to bypass, obliterate or work through the culture to get the product to the marketplace. . . . A great deal of time is spent selling inside the organization. Then you go sell outside."[30] The most difficult roadblock to overcome is an organizational culture that militates against creativity and innovation, that fights change of any kind, that believes that the way things have been done in the past is the way they should be done in the future. The motivations for such behavior are fear of failure, playing politics, uneasiness with anything new or different (leaving the comfort zone), and a belief in a caste system.

FEAR OF FAILURE

"Even though you let me down last time, I'm going to give you another chance." Given this type of response, people will spend more time fearing reprisal than going all out to follow through on an idea. Furthermore, they will probably play it close to the vest, hesitating to reveal any part of the idea early on.

"Will you bet your job on it?" When managers demand assurances of success, employees gloss over problems and overestimate the potential for success, setting up false expectations. Organizations that foster innovation deter fear by treating mistakes as another step in

the learning process. They make it clear that if you're not making mistakes, you're not trying something new.

"I'm afraid that if it doesn't work, we'll all look foolish." Unless your organization accepts the premise that risks are worth taking, it will dampen the impulse toward creative thinking. Everyone should realize that "the need to be right all the time is the biggest barrier there is to new ideas. It is better to have enough ideas for some of them to be wrong than to be always right by having no ideas at all."[31]

A corporate culture that creates a fear of failure stifles creativity. A participant in the Wharton study said, "One must wonder how many potentially good ideas have not been brought forth because someone did the 'wise' thing career-wise. . . . It is easier to ride the wave than stick your neck out. If you do work on something new, it will be positive or negative—you will succeed or fail. If you fail, you're out. If you succeed, you're only a little bit ahead. It's not worth the risk."[32]

In corporate cultures that stimulate innovation, senior management understands how much you can learn from failure. Ronald Mitsch, former executive vice president of the industrial and consumer sector, corporate services, at the 3M Company, has said:

> If we gain a lot from each successful program at 3M, we also learn as much or more from every failure. For example, we tried to market a line of suntan lotions that adhered to the skin without being sticky; it protected the skin even after a 30-minute swim. There was nothing wrong with the product's performance; however, we were not successful in the marketplace. The suntan lotions were challenged by those of well-established competitors which offered broad lines of well-known skin care products.
>
> The experience reinforced our traditional wisdom that keeping one foot in a comfort zone enables us to compete more successfully. So we try to leverage our existing marketing strengths as often as we can when we embark on new products. But we also learned never to give up too easily. Some astute laboratory people kept working on the suntan lotion technology and came up with a successful insect repellant.[33]

Moreover, according to Professor Jack Matson, quoted in a *U.S. News and World Report* article, "There are two ways to fail. . . . One approach, trying out things sequentially, [which he] calls slow, stupid failure, is the worst. The process is so drawn out that you get worn out and say the hell with it. The other way, intelligent, fast failure means launching several ideas at once and readying more for the next salvo. . . . Failure is a normal, natural way of mapping the unknown so you want to compress your trials into as small a time period as possible."[34]

A good approach to success, according to Thomas J. Watson, the founder of IBM, "is to double your failure rate."[35] And for that to happen, management must create a comfortable, stimulating, risk-free environment where individuals are free to offer speculative, imprecise, sometimes off-the-wall ideas. As Jeffrey Bezos, chairman, president, and CEO of Amazon, said, "You have to go down blind alleys. But every once in a while you go down an alley and it opens up into this huge, broad avenue. That makes all the blind alleys worthwhile."[36]

POLITICS

"What will the boss think?" People often look back to the last time they presented an idea. They remember if management was unreceptive. As a result, many ideas never get presented.

"Don't rock the boat . . . I don't know if it's good politics." Introducing change is never easy, but in nurturing environments, ideas are presented and built upon without fear of someone "getting even."

"I wonder if my idea will offend anyone." In a corporate environment marked by politics, there is good reason to believe that the originator will worry more about what people think than about the idea itself. People are afraid that snipers are behind the bushes waiting for them. As a result, ideas may be so compromised that by the time they are presented, they don't look anything like the original, having been tempered to raise the fewest possible objections.

"I wonder if someone at the meeting will shoot down my idea to get even with my boss." Where the good of the organization is subservient to the ambitions of its employees, the free expression of ideas takes a backseat to fears of backstabbing.

If everyone in an organization is pursuing their personal ends, the games that result will discourage creativity. Unless the culture can be modified so that everyone is pursuing common goals, stopping the gamesmanship and igniting creativity will be difficult.

RESISTANCE TO CHANGE

"If it's such a great idea, how come no one ever came up with it before?" Someone probably has, but the idea was shot down, either because of inertia, because the person was afraid to present it, or because no one wanted to take the initiative to follow through.

"We've never done it this way before." That may be so, but if it's right for the organization, why not start doing it that way now. Organizational cultures tend to perpetuate themselves by hiring people who "fit in." Second, organizations often have a tendency toward inward thinking as a result of either experiencing too much success or living in an ivory tower, out of touch with reality.

"We're doing great. If it ain't broke, don't fix it." New ideas are frequently rejected because they are unfairly compared with the great ideas of yesterday. This is particularly true in organizations that have a long and successful history. Unfortunately, this is a one-way ticket to mediocrity because what made the company a winner yesterday may not hold true tomorrow.

"How can you say you have a better idea? Don't you realize how long it took us to come up with the present system?" If you fall in love with the present way of doing things, you will become stale and complacent. A mentality that focuses on the past, that likes the reassurance of "We've always done it this way," is bad for business. Instead, learn to question why things are done in a particular way, and ask yourself whether an alternative might be better. Remember that many ideas are discounted because there isn't enough information available to make the decision. And most of all, remember that everybody fears the unknown.

THE CASTE SYSTEM

"Why should I listen to you? It's not your area of expertise." It is often possible to be too close to the forest to see the trees. Someone

with a different perspective can often find a better way of approaching a problem. In the article evaluating the success of 3M, Thomas Osborn said, "Many of 3M's most successful innovations came from personnel in sales and other departments, not just technical lab people . . . for example, 3M's most famous consumer product, Scotch tape, was once manufactured strictly as an industrial product, until a salesman got the idea of packaging it in clear plastic dispensers for home and office use."[37]

"Why ask me about that? I'm only a salesman." It is important to keep employees from focusing solely on their area of expertise. According to von Oech, "Specialization can be dangerous because it can lead to the attitude, 'That's not my area.' When this happens, a person may not only delimit his problems to too small an area, he may also stop looking for ideas in other fields."[38]

"Why is everyone sitting around discussing this? That's what we have management for." Surely, the more people who try to come up with creative solutions, the better. In fact, in a creativity survey of 150 managers in 27 companies, participants said that they believed "groups surpass individuals for idea quality and quantity. Seventy-eight percent of the respondents said groups outperform individuals for idea quality, and 91 percent of the respondents said they feel groups outperform individuals on idea quantity." Furthermore, according to the survey, "Small groups are preferred for problem solving over working alone or in large groups. Seventy-one percent said they prefer to work in groups of six or less to solve problems."[39]

"Why ask Joe, Tom, or Harry for ideas? What do they know?" Some managers ignore employees because they are too low on the totem pole. They forget that "any part of the human body which is not exercised properly starts to atrophy. This is true, too, of the various parts of the human mind, and particularly true of imagination."[40] They have never escaped the ancient Roman belief that creative individuals were "endowed by the gods with transcendental intellectual and/or artistic powers . . . geniuses were born, not made."[41] Managers forget that deciding who is creative may prove a self-fulfilling prophecy; it may also mean that if the "creative type" doesn't come up with ideas, nothing can happen.

Organizations with cultures based on an "old-fashioned snobbery of the kind that took for granted that the common man was incapable of creating anything . . . [that] the universe functioned according to a cosmic pattern in which everything and everybody had a place," are organizations that will not survive in today's competitive, rapidly changing, technology-driven world.[42] This condescending culture must be changed if an organization is to meet the demands of modern competition.

REACHING THE WINNER'S CIRCLE

It is not enough, however, to simply remove the roadblocks to creativity and innovation. Internal communication, the subject of Chapter 4, must be viewed as an avenue to release the creative genius in an organization. Furthermore, you must also encourage everyone in your organization to look at things through new lenses. Remember that most people have been educated in the American school system, which emphasizes—and rewards—rote learning. Try to encourage your employees to be broad thinkers and not to have tunnel vision. Let your employees know that their jobs are not just a series of tasks but that they are responsible for finding new and better ways of doing things. Let them know that coming up with a new idea that fails is not regarded as a personal failure, and perhaps most of all, let them know you value creativity. Tearing down the roadblocks to creativity is the only way to achieve victory.

4

Internal Communication . . . More Than Lip Service

BUILDING AN ORGANIZATION WITH TOTAL CONCENTRATION AND FOCUS

Companies with highly effective communication had 47 percent higher total returns to shareholders over the five-year period (mid-2004 to mid-2009) compared with companies with less effective communication practices.

—2010 Towers Watson Communication ROI Study Report[1]

O
ver the past 10 years, the world has changed dramatically." When I first wrote those words in the mid-nineties, no one ever could have contemplated that we were only at the *beginning* of spectacular change that would transform the world forever! The enormous increases in globalization and in technology, the power of "social media" to upend everything from buying behavior to political campaigns, the explosion of information resulting in increased consumer knowledge and expectations are just some of the significant developments that forever changed the way we conduct business. Time is now so compressed that where it was once a victory to launch a product in two years, the competitive environment today dictates that it be done in months. To keep up with these changes and expectations, employees need information readily available to them. They can't wait until tomorrow. To make matters even more difficult, people are constantly bombarded with information. The burden and the challenge of

this information overload are growing steadily every day. The concepts discussed in Richard Wurman's groundbreaking book, *Information Anxiety*, still give us pause, even though they were written several years ago. According to Wurman, "The weekday edition of *The New York Times* contains more information than the average person was likely to come across in a lifetime in 17th century England."[2]

Add to these changes the avalanche of takeovers, outsourcings, restructurings, downsizings, divestitures, and leveraged buyouts, and you have the makings of a confused and anxiety-ridden workforce. The challenge facing us all today—more urgently than ever before—is finding ways to increase employee loyalty, build bonds between people, and improve productivity during a time of unprecedented change, global competition, and information overload, coupled with the necessity to move quickly.

Human resource studies over the years have confirmed that effective organizational communication has a significant effect in reducing employee stress and improving performance and productivity. In an article for *Training and Development Journal* a number of years ago, behavioral scientists reported that "individuals prefer to exert control over their environments . . . particularly . . . in stressful situations such as an organizational acquisition. Because information increases an individual's sense of control, open and honest managerial communication can help employees gain a feeling of personal control."[3] This is totally consistent with the findings of a study conducted by the Columbia University School of Business and Dunhill Personnel System Inc.: "When 225 middle managers were asked the top on-the-job stress points, 43 percent of the respondents pointed to a lack of information while 31 percent of the respondents cited conflicting information."[4] The need for information can be seen everywhere. For example, there's the case of a large multinational corporation that installed an 800 number to provide a daily, recorded update of company news to the media. Much to their surprise, most of the calls they received were from their own managers throughout the world who wanted to know what was going on in their company.

Along these same lines, according to the Towers Watson study quoted at the beginning of this chapter, there is a direct correlation between corporate communication to keep employees engaged in supporting the company's vision and productivity.

The results of our 2008/2009 WorkUSA survey further support the value of helping managers keep employees engaged during times of change. That study found that keeping employees engaged correlates to an average 26 percent higher productivity rate, and that highly engaged employees miss fewer days of work and are three times as likely as their less-engaged peers to exceed performance expectations.[5]

Employees are saying they need information today because it's obsolete tomorrow; they are saying it must be relevant, customized to meet their specific needs, or they're just not interested. What brought about this fierce desire to know more and know it now? It's driven by the belief that in an age of abundant information and rapid change, you can't be productive by waiting until the end of the month to receive a generically written, watered-down newsletter that doesn't provide relevant information. While that may have been satisfactory yesterday, in today's fierce global economy, it isn't enough.

STRESS TO SUCCESS

Think about your organization's communication effectiveness. If you randomly selected 50 employees and asked them basic questions about the heart of your organization, would their answers be similar? For example, ask them: What is our organization's mission? What are our core values? What factors are most important to our future success? What are our core competencies? How does someone get ahead in our organization? How do we differentiate ourselves from the competition? What are our key initiatives this year? How will our industry change over the next few years? How will we respond to this change? What's the impact of this phenomenon? According to a 2005 Conference Board survey, two–thirds of workers do not identify with or feel motivated to drive their employer's business goals; 40 percent of workers feel disconnected from their employers; and another 25 percent of employees are just "showing up to collect a paycheck."[6] Unless your employees give similar answers to these most basic questions, waste, redundancies, inefficiencies, confusion, and anxiety are likely; the result—employees working at cross-purposes.

In *Innovative Employee Communication*, Alvie Smith, former director of corporate communications at General Motors, compares communication to the cardiovascular system of the human body: "The management organization is the prime top-to-bottom link with employees. It represents the network of arteries that hold the corporate body together. And communication is the lifeblood which draws its informational strength from various sources, recasts it into digestible forms, and transmits the revitalized materials to every part of the corporate body."[7]

"The Gallup organization estimates that disengaged employees cost U.S. employers a significant amount of money, between $250 and $350 billion a year."[8] In 2002, Mercer conducted a study of over 2,500 U.S. workers to gauge why better communication by management is related to employee engagement and company financial success. It found that "When senior management communicated a clear vision for the future direction of the organization, fewer employees were dissatisfied with the organization compared to when senior management did not communicate its vision effectively (7% vs. 39%, respectively); fewer employees said that they did not feel a strong sense of commitment to the organization (6% vs. 32%); and fewer employees said that they were seriously thinking about leaving the organization (16% vs. 40%). Thus, better communication from company executives was associated with better engagement from employees."[9]

To succeed in today's competitive marketplace, organizations must give internal communication the priority that it deserves. They must view it as an avenue to release the creative genius of an organization, not as a bothersome chore. After all, communication acts as a powerful agent of change, a source of continuous improvement, and a catalyst for moving the organization forward. Finally, organizations must address internal and external audiences with a single voice to avoid sending mixed messages to the marketplace.

Unfortunately, internal communication programs must compete with external communication programs for an organization's limited resources. External communication includes time and money spent communicating to customers, suppliers, shareholders, and the local communities in which the organization resides. Furthermore, internal communication is usually one of the first items to be cut in tough times; it is treated as a stepchild compared to external communication, and overall, organizations consider it a chore rather than something that they want to do.

Today and in the years to come, organizations will have to focus on winning employees back; building trust, respect, and teamwork between people; being receptive to and then acting on the best ideas; and once again instilling employees with pride in and commitment to the organization. Internal communication will be a major force in achieving those ends.

COMMUNICATING IN THE INFORMATION AGE

Internal communication has to keep up with the changes taking place in the world. Where the bimonthly newsletter was considered a preferred source of information for 45 percent of employees in 1980, today, according to an IABC (International Association of Business Communicators) study, it is frequently used by only 31 percent and rarely used as a communication method by 41 percent of respondents.[10] As a vehicle to keep employees informed, the employee newsletter is as out of place in today's new organization as the adding machine. Just as external communication migrated from two-day mail, to the fax, to the Internet, internal communication is following the same path. It is interesting to note that, according to research, "Email (83%) and intranet (75%) are reported as the most frequently used communication vehicles for engaging employees. Face-to face meetings are used 54% of the time."[11] However, according to other research conducted by IABC and Buck Consultants, findings show that "While social media is perhaps the hot topic among communicators, it is not the solution to effective employee engagement."[12] One explanation for its ineffectiveness may be explained by JoAnne Yates, a professor at MIT's Sloan School of Management, who studies e-mail usage in the workplace. "[She] advises people to use electronic communication only to transmit and confirm simple information, and have actual conversations for anything that could possibly be sensitive."[13]

Where employee communication was once created by a group of professionals, it is now created on the fly by laypeople. Where it was once broadcast from the ivory tower, it is now transmitted through the grapevine. Where communication was once formal, social networking and chat rooms make communication very familiar. Where communication was once highly controlled, it is now haphazard. Where executives had the first and last word, everyone now has an equal voice. Where the purpose of internal communication was to report on the completion of an event, it now plants seeds that will grow into new ideas. Where communication was once infrequent, it is now constant. Where there was once lag time in reporting an event, communication is now instantaneous. Where formal mass communication was once commonplace, customization and personalization are now the norm.

Everyone in the organization must face the fact that internal communication is a philosophy, not an activity. There is no longer room for statements such as "We should communicate more with our employees, so let's put up bulletin boards" or "Morale seems a little weak this month; let's hold some meetings." There is no room for believing in the efficacy of a magic communication wand that will make problems go away. Instead, organizations must commit to an ongoing process of communication that exists on four levels. The first is between the organization's leadership and its employees, the second is between first-line managers and those who report to them, and the third is between colleagues. Last, as we continue to break down walls between our organizations and the outside world, our external strategic and alliance partners deserve the same commitment to communication that our employees receive.

THE ROLE OF LEADERSHIP

An article in *Forbes* reports that "According to a survey conducted by Harvard's Kennedy School, 80% of Americans believe we have a leadership crisis. Only 45% of respondents say they have confidence in our business executives."[14]

In the past, leaders controlled the information employees needed to make day-to-day decisions. Leaders who continue along that path will become frustrated as they lose the confidence of employees whose desire for timely, customized, and truthful information is not satisfied. According to a Towers Perrin study, of the 1,000 U.S. workers polled, "just over half (51%) of the respondents believe their company generally tells employees the truth, while almost a fifth (19%) disagree. At the same time, 51% believe their companies try too hard to 'spin' the truth. The survey also shows that employees believe their companies communicate more honestly with shareholders (60%) and customers (58%) than with workers."[15]

Furthermore, employees will increasingly demand communication that is multidirectional, participatory, comprehensive, credible, open, relevant, and delivered in a timely fashion. They will use the Internet, social networking, texting, and evolving forms of technology in addition to networking to bypass formal communication vehicles.

Instead of trying to control information that will be obsolete before it is sent, today's leaders must provide employees with a different message. Jack Welch, the leadership guru, once said, "Leaders—and you take anyone from Roosevelt to Churchill to Reagan—inspire people with clear visions of how things can be done better. Some managers, on the other hand, muddle things with pointless complexity and detail. They equate it with sophistication, with sounding smarter than anyone else. They inspire no one."[16]

More urgently than ever before, today's leaders must communicate a clear and compelling vision that reinforces the beliefs and values on which the organization is based. They must provide consistent direction, clarify the rationale behind the policies that exist, and enroll everyone in a common cause. This can be aided by creating rituals and ceremonies that help establish heroes to emulate. And they must do this not only with words but also with consistent actions that provide validation.

CREATING THE VISION

In a study of 400 managers and professionals, Robert Kelley, business professor at the Carnegie Mellon University, discovered that almost two-thirds of those surveyed felt that their company's leadership failed to give them a "clear understanding of a corporate vision, mission and goals. . . . Only about one in five company executives were identified as having the skills to motivate employees and to implement a vision successfully enough to result in high performance. . . . Only one in three workers feels tied into the company's destiny and its performance goals."[17]

Leaders must create a shared vision that shapes the way employees feel about their organization. They must accept responsibility for making "the company," "our company"—a place where people work together instead of "doing their own thing." The vision may be precise or vague; it may highlight a specific goal or a dream of a better future. It is critical to present a clear and concise view of the organization that is compelling, realistic, believable, and attractive. Furthermore, it must promise a better future than prevailing conditions in visible and important ways.

It is important, however, that this vision not be so removed from the reality of the organization, or so difficult to achieve, that no one takes it seriously. The shared vision, statement of purpose, and operating values must be integrated so that they mesh with the day-to-day activities of the organization. Peter Senge explains this process in his book *The Fifth Discipline*: "Imagine a rubber band, stretched between your vision and current reality. When stretched, the rubber band creates tension, representing the tension between vision and current reality. . . . There are only two possible ways for the tension to resolve itself: pull reality toward the vision or pull the vision toward reality. Which occurs will depend on whether we hold steady to the vision."[18]

A shared vision must also make a connection with the personal values and desires of each and every individual. Here, a useful metaphor is a hologram, "the three-dimensional image created by interacting light sources. . . . If you cut a photograph in half, each part shows only part of the whole image. But if you divide a hologram, each part shows the whole image intact. Similarly, as you continue to divide up the hologram, no matter how small the divisions, each piece still shows the whole image. Likewise, when a group of people come to share a vision for an organization, each person sees his own picture of the organization at its best. Each shares responsibility for the whole, not just for his piece. But the component pieces of the hologram are not identical. Each represents the whole image from a different point of view. It's as if you were to look through holes poked in a window shade; each hole would offer a unique angle for viewing the whole image."[19]

Creating the vision, however, is not enough. It must be brought to life and then imbued in the corporate culture. The vision must be so omnipresent that employees old and new incorporate it into their personal and corporate belief structure, and then communicate it to customers and suppliers and the world at large. Moreover, it must be articulated clearly and frequently throughout the organization, so that it becomes ingrained in the organization's culture. Then the corporate structure and management style must be shaped to lend credence to the image created by the vision.

When the shared vision is embedded in the corporate culture, internal politics and game playing begin to diminish. As people begin to buy into the organization's vision and its future, they begin to work in unison, and discard their self-interest for the common good. Promoting beliefs and values is also good business. In research on 200 companies, John Kotter and James Heskett found that "companies that consistently valued and cared for employees, customers, and stockholders had much faster growth in revenues and jobs than other firms over an 11-year period. Values, or deeply held principles and beliefs, can be powerful motivators that, when shared, form a foundation for corporate culture."[20]

PROMOTING THE BELIEFS AND VALUES OF THE ORGANIZATION

Because beliefs and values form the heart of an organization's culture, great leaders never miss an opportunity to reinforce them. They know that once internalized, these beliefs and values affect the norms that influence day-to-day actions, determine what's important, reinforce appropriate behavior, and change attitudes.

If these norms are to be institutionalized, management must support them by clear and visible actions. Therefore, management must live these values in their heads and their hearts. Otherwise, they may be inconsistent in applying them, or worse, fail to promote them in times of stress. If commitment is perceived as rhetoric without substance, the effort will fail.

According to Terrence Dean and Allen Kennedy in *Corporate Cultures*, there are a number of clearly visible "signs of a culture in trouble; weak cultures have no clear values or beliefs about how to succeed in their business; or they have many such beliefs but cannot agree among themselves on which are most important; or different parts of the company have fundamentally different beliefs; the heroes of the culture are destructive or disruptive and don't build upon any common understanding about what is important; the rituals of day-to-day life are either disorganized—with everybody doing their own thing—or downright contradictory—with the left hand and the right hand working at cross purposes."[21]

Leaders make certain that everyone has "bought into" the organization's beliefs and values and that all are motivated to act on them. Leaders do this by walking their talk and by creating heroes, establishing rituals and ceremonies, and encouraging storytelling that sets the tone for the organization.

Heroes. Heroes are placed on a pedestal so that others can emulate their behavior. There are two kinds of heroes in an organization; the first serve as day-to-day role models for everyone to follow. They personify the values of the organization. Although they may not be at the helm of the organization, they frequently are placed in fast-track programs, hold visible positions, and are assigned to turnaround situations or to champion successful products. They are the employees who have gone the extra mile to serve the needs of a customer, to win back the business that was vulnerable to a competitor, or to lead the change effort within an organization.

The second kind of hero is the legend—the person (or persons) who built the organization and made it great, like Thomas Watson, Henry Ford, and Thomas Edison. These heroes are like the forefathers of this country— their stories should be captured and their words deeply embedded in the enterprise. They are the immutable source of inspiration. That is why they serve as role models.

Rituals and ceremonies. Rituals are day-to-day activities that demonstrate the cultural values of an organization, while ceremonies are the spectacles that are almost larger than life. Each serves an important function. If there are too many ceremonies, they soon become extravagant rituals with little meaning. Annual Veterans Day parades are rituals that allow us to remember and say thank-you. A spectacular ticker-tape parade welcoming returning heroes is a ceremony celebrating the nation and its accomplishments—in the course of which the contributions of veterans are honored. In business, ceremonies celebrate the heroes and myths of the organization. Rituals encompass everyday activities that are often taken for granted; there is no spotlight shining on them—they are a part of our subconscious.

As wonderful as ceremonies are, however, they do not continually emphasize or reinforce the importance that the organization places on key values. Rituals, the embodiment of the organization's culture, are the everyday events that reinforce the beliefs and values of the organization. Rituals run the gamut from the way meetings are conducted to the number held each year, from the way a promotion is announced to how a big sale is celebrated, from the way someone is introduced into the organization to the tone displayed when someone departs. Rituals set the climate of the organization and mold the actions of its employees.

Storytelling. In *Leadership Is an Art*, Max De Pree says, "Every company has tribal stories. Though there may be only a few tribal storytellers, it's everyone's job to see that things as unimportant as manuals and light bulbs don't replace them."[22]

Stories are nonthreatening; they expand perception, highlight new possibilities, and present different ways of working; they challenge the imagination and make difficult concepts engaging. Stories help us deal with complex feelings, open us to new relationships, and call us to action. But to be effective, stories must include aspirations achieved, dreams fulfilled, and goals reached.

There are several common story types. One kind helps employees know what will happen if they perform their jobs well. It addresses the questions people have about the organization they work for. Stories underscore a company's reaction to someone who breaks the rules or to the whistle-blower who reports the transgression. There is a pattern to these stories. According to an article in *Administrative Science Quarterly*, these stories send a message saying that "everyone should have to obey the rules; everyone is human; anyone should be able to rise to the top if he or she is sufficiently competent and hardworking. In the positive versions of these stories, these equalities do emerge. In negative versions, they could emerge and their failure to do so reinforces the inequality."[23]

The authors of the article tell two classic tales that demonstrate this point. The first, which took place at IBM, and the second, which happened at the Revlon Corporation, are good reflections of very different cultures:

> A twenty-two year old bride weighing ninety pounds whose husband had been sent overseas and who, in consequence, had been given a job until his return . . . was obliged to make certain that people entering security area wore the correct clearance identification. Surrounded by his usual entourage of white-shirted men, Watson [a former IBM chairman] approached the doorway to an area where she was on guard, wearing an orange badge acceptable elsewhere in the plant, but not a green badge, which alone permitted entrance at her door. I was "trembling in my uniform, which was far too big," she recalled. "It hid my shakes, but not my voice. 'I'm sorry,' I said to him, I knew who he was all right. 'You cannot enter. Your admittance is not recognized.' That's what we were supposed to say." The men accompanying Watson were stricken; the moment held unpredictable possibilities. "Don't you know who he is?" Someone hissed. Watson raised his hand for silence, while one of the party strode off and returned with the appropriate badge. . . . One possible message or moral of the IBM rule-breaking story for higher status employees is: "Even Watson obeys the rules, so you certainly should." For lower status people there is another moral: "Uphold the rules, no matter

who is disobeying. . . . Another type of organization is possible, one where bosses break rules with impunity and lower level employees do not dare challenge the infraction."[24]

The second story describes the behavior of Charles Revson, former head of the Revlon Corporation.

[Revson] was worried that employees were not coming to work on time, although Charles himself seldom arrived much before noon. Therefore, as late as 1971, . . . everyone was required to sign in in the morning. Everyone. Even Charles signed in. One day, when Revlon was in the process of moving from 666 Fifth Avenue up to the General Motors Building, in 1969, Charles sauntered in and began to look over the sign-in sheet. The receptionist, who was new, says, "I'm sorry, sir, you can't do that." Charles says, "Yes, I can." "No sir," she says. "I have strict orders that no one is to remove the list; you'll have to put it back." This goes back and forth for a while with the receptionist being very courteous, as all Revlon receptionists are, and finally, Charles says, "Do you know who I am?" And she says, "No sir, I don't." "Well, when you pick up your final paycheck this afternoon, ask 'em to tell ya."[25]

Storytelling can also be used to establish the boss as a "real" person. The story must first reinforce the boss's position within the organization—revealing status, usually through the title, say, CEO; then the story must afford the boss an opportunity to perform an act not expected of someone in a high position; and finally, it must be clear that the act does not cause the "boss" to lose status.

A few years ago, the director of a major nonprofit organization agreed to let two members of his staff who had plans to eventually open a catering service provide the meal at an important planning meeting. The night before the meeting, the city was hit by a major snowstorm. Many attendees who came from different cities were housed at a hotel across the street from the organization's headquarters. The meeting went on as scheduled, but one of the young women scheduled to cater the meal lived so far away from the city, she couldn't get in. The director, a noted gourmet and a fair cook himself, slipped out of the meeting from time to time to help the lone caterer.

When the lunch began, he announced that since he was helping in the kitchen for the day, he wouldn't be able to join them at the table till later. Because one of the waiters also failed to make it in, the director helped wait on the attendees. Once the main course was served, the director took his place at the head of the table and joined the conversation. His guests teased him about getting them refills, and asked about his availability if they needed assistance. It turned out to be a lunch they all remembered.

It is easy to see why senior people at that organization roll up their sleeves to get the job done; why the whole staff stays late when work has to get done in a hurry, with all hands pitching in to meet a deadline. Helping cook and serve a meal in no way diminished the director's status; instead, it showed the importance of pitching in.

Stories also help address questions and dispel rumors. In a downsizing situation, for example, employees are often concerned about who will be fired and what assistance the company will provide. If a precedent has already been established, and there are stories about people retrained for other jobs, assisted through an outplacement program, or receiving adequate severance packages, premature departures and gossip behind closed doors are less likely to occur.

Stories can be communicated through the grapevine, recounted before a meeting begins, incorporated into speeches, or disseminated through written internal communication when appropriate. There should be stories about people who perform above and beyond the call of duty, managers who motivate others to higher levels of productivity, and salespeople who achieve the impossible for a customer.

Stories should be perpetuated because they reveal critical information about the organization and influence employees by pulling them rather than pushing them toward their goals. Moreover, by linking actions with rewards and praise, stories give employees a sense of control. Questions that can be answered by stories include:

- Does the company value ethical behavior over short-term business? If it's the last day of the sales month, and the numbers look miserable, are people encouraged to do what's best for the client or close the sale— even if it may jeopardize the long-term relationship with the client?

- Are people rewarded only for the bottom-line performance or for the development of their people as well? Stories should show how individuals made it to the top of the organization while keeping the best interests of others in mind—rather than stepping on those in their way.

- Do people live up to their promises? Was a promise made and kept to a client even though circumstances changed after the promise was made? This sends a message to all employees, as well as clients, that the organization can be trusted.

- Are relationships lasting or made out of convenience? From a negative standpoint, are there stories about managers who disowned employees after they were promoted or transferred to another part of the organization?

- Are employees treated with understanding when taking care of a sick child or parent?

- What happens to someone who was once the star performer but who is now having a streak of bad breaks?

Remember, however, that stories that cast your organization in a bad light are as likely to find their way into the common currency as are those you choose to emphasize. Stories that communicate an uncaring organization that considers employees merely as insignificant cogs in a wheel are particularly damaging. No organization can long survive the barrage of stories such as the way a 16-year veteran was fired because of a downturn in business. Rather than thanking her for her contribution and treating her with dignity and respect, management had her escorted to her office to pack up, while someone stood guard and then escorted her to the door. That sends a message for everyone who stays—the inhumanity of the management team.

THE ROLE OF FIRST-LINE MANAGEMENT

While leadership enrolls everyone in a common cause, first-line management should serve as facilitators for removing communication barriers. To do this, communication must receive more than lip service. Employees should receive training not only in how to become better presenters of information, but also in how to become better receivers. They must develop a working environment that is conducive to open, trusting, caring relationships between people—an environment that welcomes new ideas and encourages constructive feedback; one in which management actively serves as a catalyst for nurturing and then disseminating new ideas.

One of the functions of a first-line manager is to recognize communication barriers so that the organization can avoid them. Discussed below are some of the most significant barriers to communication that should be avoided.

BARRIERS TO COMMUNICATION

Rigid adherence to organizational charts. It is important to recognize that organizational charts, while necessary, may inhibit communication. No organization should adhere to them so rigidly that they prevent the communication of ideas up the hierarchy, across departments and functional areas, and between units.

Therefore, it is important to recognize that "organization charts in a company neither define relationships as they actually exist nor direct the lines of communication. If the organization does not exist in the minds and hearts of the people, it does not exist. No chart can fix that. An organization's function is simple: to provide a framework, a format, a context in which people can effectively use resources to accomplish their goals."[26] The problem is that organizational charts imply that communication should only flow vertically. The fact is, communication must flow across organizational and functional units as well.

Management isolation. In an article in *Inc.* magazine, Alison Stein Wellner comments as follows:

> To be sure, e-mail is not inherently evil. But it can be the kiss of death when it's used to communicate anything sensitive, important, or complicated, says Ron McMillan, who is co-author of *Crucial Conversations: Tools for Talking When Stakes Are High* and who spent 10,000 hours observing how companies nationwide communicate. As text messages fly between desktops, laptops, and hand-helds, McMillan says, they arrive without the rich stew of nonverbal information, such as tone of voice, facial expressions, and eye gaze, that we typically rely on to figure out what someone really means. One study by UCLA psychology professor Albert Mehrabian found that 55% of meaning in an interaction comes from facial and body language and 38% comes from vocal inflection. Only 7% of an interaction's meaning is derived from the words themselves.

Since email is, by definition, just the words themselves, it's more easily misunderstood than an actual conversation. Yet managers and employees rely increasingly on text messages for nuanced conversations that really ought to be handled face-to-face or at least voice-to-voice, says McMillan.[27]

All too many managers isolate themselves from employees in various ways. Some CEOs do it by appearing in their offices infrequently because they spend much of their time serving on boards or making personal appearances. First-line managers do it by spending most of their time in meetings with other managers.

To rediscover the connection between productivity and communication, we should remind ourselves of the fantastic productivity of start-up companies, where a small group of people work closely with the founder— all giving enormously of themselves. On the other hand, saying the company has an open-door policy is meaningless if employees have to jump through hoops to make an appointment that's eventually canceled and rescheduled.

Managers should also keep in mind that creating lavish executive offices, having administrative assistants construct what amounts to barbed-wire enclosures around those executive offices, establishing perquisites— the corner office, executive parking spaces, separate executive floors, private washrooms and dining rooms, limos, private jets, even flying first class when others sit in coach—loudly proclaim who is boss. These "perks" increase personal distance, lead to suspicion, and ensure that people feel that their leaders are unapproachable.

The development of caste systems. The caste system is also a barrier to communication. Think of an employee "walking in from the back parking lot, through the snow, in zero-degree temperatures, who just before entering the building, sees one of the bosses pull his car into that sacred parking place. . . . The employee thinks why doesn't the son of a bitch have to find a parking place like the rest of us? When that happens, the executive parking lot has just moved the business backward."[28]

There are other artificial barriers that inhibit internal communication. For example, does your organization encourage clear language or is jargon the norm? Are there opportunities for people at different levels and in different functional groups to spend time with one another, or is there socializing only along status lines? Encouraging employees at all levels to participate in a softball league or to volunteer for a corporate social responsibility event is an effective way to break down barriers between people.

The existence of physical barriers. In my earlier book, *Marketing to Win*, I wrote that "distance poses another kind of problem in the workplace. Because people communicate most with those physically closest to them, those who work on special projects but spend most of their time in their assigned cubicles tend to communicate less. Thomas Allen of MIT notes that 'beyond a distance of 25 or 30 yards, personal interaction drops off markedly.' That is why it is important for management to try to bring together as much as possible those who work together."[29] This can be addressed by providing meeting rooms, by assigning people to different locations on a temporary basis, or by encouraging videoconference technology such as group chat rooms.

The ambiance surrounding meetings. The process of setting up a meeting as well as the nonverbal cues during a meeting often communicate as much as the content of the meeting itself. The answers to the following questions, for example, reveal an enormous amount about an organization's culture. How often are meetings held? Are people early or late for meetings? Is the boss late? Where are meetings held? What's the layout of the room? Who gets invited? What's on the agenda? How is the agenda prepared? What's the order of the agenda items? How long does the average meeting last? How much time is allotted to each subject? What time is the meeting held? Who sits next to the boss? Who introduces the speakers? Is the tone of the meeting formal or informal? What questions are asked at the meeting? How much dialogue is there? Is there give and take?

Consistency of words and actions. Are the actions of your organization consistent with its policies? Does management say that they care about innovation, but promote those who don't rock the boat? Do they say that they reward excellence, but give across-the-board raises? Do they say they reward creativity, but have a long-drawn-out approval process that frustrates anyone with a new idea?

A glaring example of the failure to match words and actions was reported by Timothy Schellhardt in *The Wall Street Journal*. Schellhardt referred to the Utilicorp United annual report, which said that "behind its growth 'have been the dedication and professionalism of our employees.'

Yet except for a picture of its chief executive, the report has only drawings of workers."[30]

Consistency of words and actions also means continuously reinforcing key messages at appropriate times; for example, at one company, when "management invited small groups of employees to 'no-holds-barred' discussions about company culture, goals, and the selling process [they discovered] . . . that employees hired within the past five years—more than 50% of the company's total population—believed their mission was to increase business, even if that meant neglecting existing accounts. In concentrating on expansion, management had not taken adequate steps to define and reinforce key cultural values for its new workforce. Rapid growth had weakened the company's culture at a critical time in its development."[31]

Political warfare. Some people hoard information for personal gain. They believe they increase their power when they know about a given subject and others are in the dark. Organizations must work to combat the idea that playing politics with information will bring personal gain. Organizations marked by politics, turf battles, and staff infighting lack adequate communication.

Listening. Everyone in the organization, from the top to the bottom, should strive to communicate more effectively. In *Marketing to Win*, I pointed out that according to research, we spend 7 out of every 10 minutes that we are awake communicating, and that communication time is devoted 9 percent to writing, 16 percent to reading, 30 percent to speaking, and 45 percent to listening. When report cards are given out for how well we listen, however, very few of us would receive passing grades. Barriers to listening include assuming a subject is uninteresting and tuning out, focusing on how something is said rather than on what is being said, reacting too quickly before the message is completed, picking up on emotional words and not hearing the rest of the message, listening only for facts rather than trying to absorb ideas, allowing yourself to be distracted, and avoiding listening to subjects that you don't understand. Everyone must learn to overcome these barriers.[32]

EFFECTIVE INTERNAL COMMUNICATION

Management should embrace new technologies and support the various forms of communication that are available. It must view information as a competitive weapon, not as a threat; it must support knowledge and learning at every level. First-line managers must keep in mind that effective internal communication must be:

- Multidirectional—upward, downward, lateral, diagonal
- Objective—expressing all sides of an issue
- Comprehensive—both in breadth of subject and depth of content
- Relevant—expressing issues that are meaningful; for example, providing the rationale behind policies
- Credible—expressed by those in the know
- Inviting—cutting through the information clutter
- Honest—truthful, factual, and error free
- Open—a fair and open exchange of ideas; bad as well as good news
- Thorough—containing more rather than less information
- Prioritized—filtered by importance so people aren't victims of information overload
- Timely—the most up-to-date information possible so that people don't have to go to other sources to get the information
- Consistent—actions consistent with words
- Appealing—easy to scan and understand
- Frequent—disseminated at regular intervals
- Reinforced—disseminated through multiple media
- Coordinated—in line with other communication elements
- Participatory—involving and relevant to the audience
- Measurable—evaluated regularly to determine effectiveness on the target audience

THE FLOW OF INFORMATION

Most people think communication only flows upward or downward in an organization, conforming to organization charts. Contrary to popular belief, it's everyone's job to encourage information to flow laterally and diagonally as well, breaking down the compartmentalization of knowledge. In this scenario, information sharing exists between different hierarchies, functional departments, and business units of an organization.

DOWNWARD COMMUNICATION

According to an A. Foster Higgins & Company survey, "more than one third (34%) of the CEOs indicated that they communicate with other CEOs daily or weekly. Forty-three percent said that they communicate with customers daily or weekly. Fifty-nine percent communicate daily or weekly with professional and technical staff; and fully 98% communicate daily or weekly with other top managers. Yet only 22% of the surveyed CEOs reported that they communicate daily or weekly with their company's rank-and-file employees."[33]

According to another study, while "top executives are a preferred information source for 62 percent of employees, only 15 percent of employees tell us that they are currently receiving information from their organizations' leaders."[34] And when they do receive information, its credibility is lacking. According to the survey *Enhancing Corporate Credibility: Is It Time to Take the Spin Out of Employee Communication?*, "employees view the information emanating from senior leadership as the least reliable, with almost half (48%) agreeing that they receive more credible information from their direct supervisor than from their company's CEO."[35] Downward communication is just not sufficient.

Leaders can dream up all kinds of excuses for failing to communicate: "I don't have the time." "Why ask them, anyway? I know how they feel." "I don't think they'll be able to handle negative information; it'll just demoralize them." "They won't understand the implications of the decision, so why bother explaining." "It's sensitive; I'm afraid someone may spill the beans." Furthermore, executives may not have the confidence to address the group—they're worried about being asked questions that they're unable to answer. And, of course, there's always the potential for disagreement.

Then there are executives who show up at offices with an entourage, fly through so quickly that no one sees them, except for the fact that in anticipation of the visit employees have been tidying up the office for weeks. Many executives fail to realize that they need to overcompensate for the fact that their position alone intimidates employees.

Even if employees have easy access to management, "too many bosses don't know how to talk to employees and too many employees are afraid to talk to their bosses. As a result, both groups are left stranded on the opposite banks of the same river, struggling toward a common goal but separated by a current of unshared information, stymied good intentions, misunderstandings, and fear."[36]

UPWARD COMMUNICATION

First-line supervisors should create an open environment where employees are willing to share their hopes, ideas, feelings, fears, criticisms; all it requires is sensitivity and empathy to the needs of employees. According to a study, of 5,000 workers nationwide surveyed by the Boston-based Wyatt Company, only 40 percent said that management seeks their input on important issues; about 25 percent said they had no freedom to express opinions.[37]

An example of the success that can be achieved by working together is described by Jack Shewmaker, former vice chairman and CFO of Wal-Mart. Shewmaker said that he

> remembers when in 1975, 14 out of the 100-plus stores were doing poorly, and management decided to confront the problem at the grass roots level. Sam Walton, chairman and founder and the rest of the management team visited all these stores. . . . On our visit to each store we simply said, you're doing lousy. We may have to close this store, though we've never done it before (or since for that matter) for lack of performance. We know you don't want us to do that, so tell us what we should do to be more successful.
>
> At first, the suggestions were seemingly minor, such as moving a clock from one wall to the next, or installing a new clock. In my own mind I wondered what difference does it make? So we'd either move the clock, or go out and buy a new one and mount it on the wall. We went through three or four suggestions of the same scope. Then all

of a sudden, they began to talk about what they could do to change the store. It wasn't a question of what management had to do, because management was receptive and attentive. It was what they had to do. Ten years later, management returned to those same 14 stores, which Wal-Mart had considered closing. All but one were among the top 10 percent as profit producers.[38]

There are many ways to encourage the kind of upward communication that made Wal-Mart such a success. For example, you might try management by walking around. Some organizations have breakfast meetings with their employees, where executives randomly invite a cross section of their organization to breakfast. In other organizations, advisory councils are established with employees from all areas of the organization. Other organizations have one-day meetings to address a timely problem or to spur new life into a project. Innovative programs designed to enhance communication are developed every day.

Suggestion systems and speak out programs are increasingly common. IBM uses a mail-in system, 'Speak up,' which allows employees to get individual responses to questions from high-level managers while maintaining their anonymity. Employees indicate their names and addresses, but these are removed by the 'Speak up' director and kept separately. When an appropriate executive has supplied an answer, it is mailed to the employee's home. Alternately, the employee may request a face-to-face or telephone response. Many large companies, including Anheuser-Busch and Eastman Kodak, now have similar programs.[39]

Other kinds of programs include telephone hotlines, focus group meetings, and skip-level meetings where managers meet with employees one level under their direct reports.

In order for these programs to work effectively, every question or idea must be taken seriously, and the results must be reported to management and to employees. These results should also include a plan for action. Many programs fall short because management only looks for big ideas rather than for ways to make big strides from incremental gains.[40]

LATERAL COMMUNICATION

It is important that employees understand how their actions affect others, and that they be held accountable for the impact their decisions have on other parts of the organization. Changes must be communicated among peer levels, within and between departments, and between shifts. Keep in mind the story of the CEO who "on one of the first days on the job . . . asked for a copy of every report used in management." He says that "the next day, 23 of them appeared on my desk. I didn't understand them. The manufacturing reports were written in manufacturing language, the finance reports in finance language, and the sales reports in sales language. . . . Each area's reports were Greek to the other areas, and all of them were Greek to me. Since we had to start cutting costs and products, we were going to have to do a lot of talking, but until we had a single market-driven language, we weren't going to have any common management information to talk about."[41]

The emphasis placed on vertical communication often overshadows the importance of lateral communication, which includes information sharing with others on the same level, but in different departments, or business units. But, "according to a survey, more than 60% of employees in a variety of organizations say that lateral communication is ineffective. More specifically about 45% say communication between peers within departments is inadequate, and 70% claim that communication between departments must improve."[42]

When employees fail to share information, efforts are duplicated, deadlines are missed, redundancies occur, rework increases, and interdepartmental relationships deteriorate. When coworkers stop communicating with one another, people often get tunnel vision, forgetting to consider other departments' needs. Problems also occur when people become so focused on departmental goals that they can't be bothered by problems that don't directly affect them. In these cases, work delegated laterally never gets done because everyone is looking to optimize their personal interests at the expense of the organization. Furthermore, inaction occurs when employees are not accountable to their peers.

Regular information exchanges between employees about key priorities, processes, and barriers that they are facing are important. In many organizations, however, employees communicate laterally only when a crisis or problem develops. As a result, they often don't understand the big picture: products being sold in other divisions, areas of overlap, the effect their work has on others, or who to contact for assistance.

There are many ways to foster communication within an organization. A good place to start is with the planning process. Plans are far easier to implement when employees take part in, and buy into, the planning process. Rather than retain a consulting firm or have an executive planning team that is far removed from the day-to-day action develop plans in isolation, management should involve employees in the strategic planning process. In addition, drawing groups from different areas of the organization fosters camaraderie and helps gain employee buy-in. The planning sessions that result offer a wonderful opportunity for the exchange of ideas among different areas of the organization and for employees to gain a better perspective about the problems and issues others face. Additional ways of stimulating communication across departments, functional areas, and units include establishing temporary task forces, job rotation programs, and organization-wide training programs.

DIAGONAL COMMUNICATION

In order for diagonal communication to flourish, employees must be encouraged to contact anyone who can help accomplish an activity, without regard to level, business unit, or other artificial boundary. This should include external networking. Management must actively develop forums encouraging employees to meet one another, build shared values, discuss emerging issues, and solve common problems.

When knowledge is divided, people fail to see the big picture. The only way to succeed is for communication to be downward, upward, lateral, and diagonal. Each plays an important role, and if all coexist, you end up with the kind of organization described by John Young, former CEO of Hewlett-Packard, who said that "communication is pretty fundamental. . . . We have the kind of company that is one team. There's no them-and-us managers or workers, and even though we have 40 companies around the world, 55 operating divisions, we think of the company as a single enterprise and everybody's a member. So good communication is a centerpiece of the way we approach employee relationships."[43]

HONEST, OPEN COMMUNICATION

Is your organization managed on the need-to-know principle because you are afraid to communicate with your employees out of fear that information may fall into the hands of a competitor? Donald E. Petersen, former chairman of the Ford Motor Company, says: "One of our fundamental objectives is to establish trust with our employees. One avenue is by communicating with them honestly on the facts about the company, its actions and its points of view. This must include our problems and controversies, as well as our attributes and achievements. . . . Good news and bad."[44]

Petersen's approach is very different from limiting information sharing to what employees "must have" to do their job. Organizations that subscribe to the need-to-know philosophy say they don't think that employees would understand more, that they can't be trusted with sensitive data, or that communication time is not productive time, so why bother. This is typical of many companies. In *Rude Awakening: The Rise, Fall, and Struggle for Recovery of General Motors*, Maryann Keller says that American companies "tend, fundamentally, to mistrust workers. There is a pervading attitude that if you give them an inch, they'll take a mile, because they don't really want to work. . . . More than anything else, GM's philosophy on people has contributed to its loss of the competitive edge. There is no trust. No respect."[45]

Information is so fundamental to our jobs that it can't be considered a privilege but a right. For example, innovation provides a key competitive edge. Information serves as the fundamental building block and catalyst to move innovation forward.

Communication is also vital to coordination. When in doubt, it is always better to err on the side of providing too much information rather than too little. Limiting information leads to second-guessing other people's intentions, to gamesmanship, politics, and maneuvering to secure information to do one's job. And the irony of it all is that the people who withhold information are usually the same people who say they can't understand why their organization isn't one happy family.

Wal-Mart sees open, honest communication as a key to success. Jack Shewmaker explains that

> the Company was not afraid to challenge a widespread assumption on the part of management that holds that it's risky to tell company employees too much about the business for fear that competition will find out. We decided that it was important that every single person associated with our company understands our mission, understands our direction, understands our progress or lack of it, and understands his or her role in making Wal-Mart a better company tomorrow than it is today.
>
> By withholding information from Wal-Mart's employees, we were penalizing the very people who needed some way of measuring their contribution to the company.[46]

THE NEW WAY TO COMMUNICATE

Internal communication has gone through several phases. The first phase was similar to the military model: Orders were given and obeyed. There was no opportunity to provide input. The second phase of communication involved the bilateral flow of information. Even though instructions were communicated down to employees, feedback was possible through formal means and selected channels. The third phase of communication encouraged two-way communication. Listening to employees was valued and mechanisms for doing so were created. The fourth phase of internal communication recognized the value of multi-channels. Just as some communication vehicles are more efficient and cost effective when communicating to the external environment, some media and processes are better for communicating internally; this knowledge was applied to employee communication. In the fifth phase, intimacy was introduced, but even with timely media like daily video and online broadcasts, employees' information needs still weren't being met.

It is the sixth phase—the one at which unilateral control of communication is abandoned—that organizations must strive to reach. In this phase, communication is continuous and multidirectional, the responsibility not of any single individual but of everyone within the organization. It is at this phase that good organizations stop dealing with the "tip of the iceberg." They no longer communicate by sending out a flurry of memos, letters, reports, and policy statements.

> We think that 90 percent of what goes on in an organization has nothing to do with formal events. . . . Even in the context of a highly controlled meeting, there is a lot of informal communication going on—bonding, rituals, glances, innuendos, and so forth. The real process of making decisions, of gathering support, of developing opinions, happens before the meeting—or after. In a strong culture, the network is powerful because it can reinforce the busy beliefs of the organization, enhance the symbolic value of heroes by passing on stories of their deeds and accomplishments, set a new climate for change, and provide a tight structure of influence for the CEO.[47]

Networking, or the "grapevine," is at the heart of the sixth phase. It is being enhanced and formalized today as a result of the changes that are taking place in technology and the comfort level of today's workers with those advances. Of course, networking is not likely to replace other forms of communication completely, but people are turning to it and to small group interaction more and more because these are highly personal. In networking, the message is usually delivered by someone you know and trust, as opposed to someone who is far removed from the issue giving you the "company line." In networking, the message is never discussed in generalities but is always customized. This gives you the chance to discuss the implications of what is said. Such personal communication is expressed with passion and received with great interest, but on the downside, the information is not always accurate.

Four elements are required to make communication thrive. First, every organization requires accessible, affordable, easy-to-use technology. Second, an open, honest work environment should be embraced. Third, people should be encouraged to break down the communication barriers that exist. Last, great leaders must communicate the guiding principles, beliefs, and values of the organization—this will rally everyone to a common cause. For just as the stars were used to navigate ships in the night, these guiding principles dictate what is important, how decisions are made, how people are rewarded, who gets promoted, what kind of person joins the organization, and how people communicate with one another. One value that should be communicated to employees is the company's main reason for existence: to provide service excellence to its clients and customers, as we shall see in Chapter 5.

5

IF I HAD ONLY ONE CLIENT

BUILDING AN ORGANIZATION DEVOTED TO SERVICE EXCELLENCE

If I had only one client, if my whole business and livelihood was solely dependent on that one client—boy, would I treat that client differently. They would really be special to me.

—Overheard in an Elevator

In August, a 76-year-old retired nurse named Mona Shaw smashed up a keyboard and a telephone in a Manassas (Va.) Comcast office after she says the cable operator failed to install her service properly. During her first visit to the branch outlet, the AARP secretary says she was left sitting on a bench in the hallway for two hours waiting for a manager. She returned, armed with a hammer, and let loose the rallying cry 'Have I got your attention now?' Afterward, she was arrested, fined $345, and became a media sensation, capturing the hearts of frustrated consumers everywhere."[1]

Even though your company may have hundreds or thousands of clients, some large and some small, each deserves to be treated as your sole client. In all too many companies, however, no client is treated as special. Why do companies make it so difficult to do business with them? Why do offices look drab and dirty? Why are e-mails filled with typos and promises broken with regularity? Why are customers ignored and treated as inconveniences? Why are employees indifferent, careless, and sometimes even rude? Why aren't employees well trained? Why don't they know their own products so they're able to answer the most basic customer questions? When problems surface, why are customers passed around the office like hot potatoes? And why do employees so often think: "I know it all and you know nothing," "It's not my job," or "I'm right; you're wrong."

This attitude has become all too pervasive in business. "They have taken away your pillows, your peanuts, and your dignity. You have been sitting on the runway for three hours. The stale, cold air is giving you a headache, but you can't ask for a blanket, or even a bottle of whiskey, because they've taken those away, too. You look desperately to the flight attendant, one of the nods to service that hasn't yet been removed from the airplane, but somebody apparently hauled off his work ethic. You're met simply with a blank, soul-crushing stare."[2]

The impact of these low levels of service is staggering. One reason this issue is often neglected is that today's metrics do not accurately reflect the true costs and benefits of customer relationships. For example, accounting practices ignore cash flows over the lifetime of a customer relationship. In fact, it is easier and five times cheaper to keep an existing client than to recruit a new one.[3] As a result of short-term thinking, many people view a sales transaction as an isolated event, rather than as a lifelong relationship with a customer; they believe that if a transaction is handled poorly, the cost is the loss of a single sale.

Unfortunately, the costs of short-term thinking go even deeper than the loss of unhappy customers: a Technical Assistance Research Programs study in the pre-Internet era said that the average person who has been burned by a company tells 9 to 10 colleagues about the experience, and 13 percent of dissatisfied customers will spread the bad news to more than 20 people.[4]

Although these figures really hurt, think about what the Internet can do with bad news. As Jennifer Harshman noted on Suite101.com:

> Now, it is possible to share a customer service nightmare faster, and with more people. A dissatisfied customer may still tell the "bad customer service" story about a dozen times, but he's not telling one person over the back fence. Now, he could be telling thousands of people each time he recounts the story. Utilities such as Twitter, Facebook, MySpace, discussion boards, Internet forums and chat-rooms make it easy to tell the world about an infuriating experience

with a company's rude or lazy employees. In the interest of protecting their friends and family, they might just pass along the warning, which could mean falling profits for that company.

What is worse for businesses than this word-of-mouth "badvertising" is that the words aren't passing from mouth to ear once or twice and then disappearing. Words that pass from person-to-person aren't found by others down the road. Now, Angry Joe Customer's words stay posted on the Internet, accessible to any searcher or surfer who comes along, and they can do damage years after the bad customer service experience has happened. The employee who cheated a customer or refused to honor a guarantee may be long gone, but the complaint posted on a website might still be there, doing damage to a business for years to come.[5]

As a recent *Bloomberg Businessweek* article noted, "Technology is aiding the uprising, empowering consumers to do much more to make themselves heard. Now, with the proliferation of online video, they can be seen as well. 'You could only get the point across so much with text,' says Blackshaw [Pete Blackshaw, executive vice-president of Nielsen Online Strategic Services]. 'As soon as you start adding sight, sound, and motion, you've got a whole other level of [emotion].' More consumers are equipped with mobile Web devices that can find executive e-mail addresses and phone numbers anytime, from any place."[6]

Furthermore, the proliferation of consumer-oriented blogs like consumerist.com means that a customer complaint and a breach of trust travels a lot farther than it once did. That customer you didn't satisfy yesterday is the one writing to us *today*, sharing his or her negative experience with 20,000 other readers. In other words—that one customer you pissed off . . . might very shortly become 10,000 people boycotting your store.

Of course, the solution is simple. Companies! Stop treating your customers like crap. Stop foisting one-sided contracts upon them. Stop tuning out and automatically switching into automaton head nodding mode when a consumer voices a complaint. Stop making like you're doing us a favor by selling us something, as opposed to the other way around. In other words, start conducting your business as if you have a personal bond to each and every one of your customers. Then we can close up shop.[7]

THE Q WORD

Overcoming the tendency to treat customers poorly—and the costs of doing so—will require a new focus on quality service. In fact, providing quality service leads to market expansion and even makes premium pricing possible. In a Forum Corporation survey of 2,374 customers from 14 organizations, more than 40 percent listed poor service as the number one reason for switching to the competition, while only 8 percent listed price.[8] And, according to the Strategic Planning Institute's Profit Impact for Marketing Strategy (PIMS) database, companies rated highly by their customers for service charge on average 9 percent more than those rated poorly.[9]

In the 1980s, the term *quality* primarily applied to manufacturing. When people discussed quality, they were referring to the workmanship of a product and to the number of defects found in products coming off the assembly line. Companies were able to differentiate their products and their organizations based on manufacturing prowess. It has finally become clear, however, that while the manufacturing process is critical, it is only part of the quality equation. Due to global competition, companies have placed so much emphasis on, and have made such great strides in, the production process that it is very difficult to differentiate products solely on the basis of workmanship. The difference between products is often so infinitesimal that more is needed to win the loyalty of the marketplace. As discussed in Chapter 1, there will be growing emphasis on intangibles as a way to satisfy customers.

This emphasis is even more critical in the services industry where products are often intangible, precise specifications cannot be set, and the production and consumption of services are inseparable. Here, quality is defined universally as meeting and exceeding customer expectations—in every step leading up to, during, and after the sale. Customers feel that cost is measured not only in dollar outlay, but also in psychological costs such as convenience, in the cachet of the organization and of the product, and in the risk associated with the acquisition, which is discussed in greater detail in Chapter 11.

Since superior client service is as much a philosophy as an activity, it is important to discover just what kind of culture produces the mind-set necessary to exceed customer satisfaction. Ask yourself:

- Does my organization make policy changes to benefit its employees or the client?

- Does my company take clients for granted because they've "been around" for a long time?
- Do my company's employees do their best work only after the competition has made inroads?
- Do our employees know that customer satisfaction is their top priority?
- Are my company's policies geared to the best interests of our clients or to profitability?
- How well do I really understand my clients' businesses? How much do they know about mine?
- Do I know why clients are happy or unhappy with my company's services? What steps have I taken to find out?
- Am I accessible when my clients need me?
- Do I treat my clients differently now than when I was courting them?
- Am I so concerned about losing clients that I fear making innovative suggestions that might rock the boat?
- Do I encourage and reward employee performance that is in the best interests of clients?

THE LONG-TERM CONSEQUENCES OF YOUR ACTIONS

If organizations want to deliver service excellence, employees must learn the value of long-term customer relationships and understand the consequences of not properly servicing them. They must abandon the view that clients represent immediate sales transactions and a quick buck. Instead, they must view clients as long-term relationships, keeping in mind the potential business that these relationships will bring over the years. They must learn to see themselves through their customers' eyes rather than focusing inwardly. They must go beyond a selling role, offering value-added advice that recognizes their clients' ongoing needs. And, focus must be placed on expanding relationships with a few clients instead of living in a turnstile—searching for new prospects one day only to lose them the next day due to poor service.

According to *Bloomberg Businessweek*, the top 10 customer service champs in 2010 are L. L. Bean, USAA, Apple, Four Seasons Hotels and Resorts,

Publix Super Markets, Nordstrom, Lexus, The Ritz-Carlton, Barnes & Noble, and Ace Hardware.[10] Another example of a company that takes the customer service lesson to heart is Amazon (which ranked 11th in the Bloomberg 2010 listing just referenced). Referring to an article in *The Consumerist* (consumerist.com) entitled "Amazon Sends 'Best Customer Service E-Mail I Ever Received,' " focus.com says, ". . . we see that one reader sent an impassioned plea for help to Amazon CEO Jeff Bezos. Not only did Bezos read the note, he actually told a support rep exactly what to say on his behalf and personally saw to it that the complaint was addressed. While this particular response was somewhat on the humorous side, Amazon has continually been ranked high in customer service for their willingness to deal personally with complaints or problems."[11]

TAKING A HOLISTIC VIEW

Many organizations that market their services to clients through separate business units give the impression that these units represent entirely different companies; they forget that clients view them as one company. When an existing client receives a call from a representative of another division and is treated as a first-time buyer, the result is that the client thinks the organization is disorganized and ungrateful for their business.

Furthermore, when organizations fail to think about the needs of their customers and fail to tailor services to meet those needs, they are providing inadequate levels of service. For example, a good travel agent who is planning a client's vacation will book the flights, arrange for airport transportation, select the hotels, reserve a car rental, and arrange itineraries. In this way, the agent deals with all the specifics of the vacation, sparing the client time and trouble.

This kind of holistic approach aids in building long-lasting customer relationships. When a company fails to approach client problems this way, it is providing a disservice. For example, when individuals are ill, they often undergo tests to determine what is ailing them. When specialists fail to coordinate their findings, it becomes the responsibility of sick patients to be their own health advocate, adding a needless burden at an already difficult time.

A holistic sales philosophy can also be embraced by an organization. If there's a problem, clients assume that their salesperson will know the go-to person in their organization for answers. When a customer has a question or a problem, it's a mistake to say, "I'm in sales, speak to someone in service" or "The person who originally helped you isn't here now" or "Since the merchandise was purchased from a different branch, it has to be returned there." When organizations view themselves as customer-centric, they strive for lifelong customer loyalty.

THE ROAD TO QUALITY

According to the book *Delivering Quality Service*, there are 10 factors that customers use to measure service quality:

1. Tangibles—Appearance of physical facilities, equipment, personnel, and communication materials
2. Reliability—Ability to perform the promised service dependably and accurately
3. Responsiveness—Willingness to help customers and provide prompt service
4. Competence—Possession of the required skills and knowledge to perform the service
5. Courtesy—Politeness, respect, consideration, and friendliness of contact personnel
6. Credibility—Trustworthiness, believability, honesty of the service provider
7. Security—Freedom from danger, risk, or doubt
8. Access—Approachability and ease of contact
9. Communication—Keeping customers informed in language they can understand and listening to them
10. Understanding the customer—Making the effort to know customers and their needs.[12]

These 10 critical factors will be used as the framework for the discussion that follows.

TANGIBLES

Customers develop their first impression of your organization through such things as the look of your website, the way their phone calls are handled and the advertisements that your organization runs. When they visit you for the first time, they notice such things as the attractiveness of your building and whether people are friendly and appropriately dressed. They notice whether the technology you use is cutting edge or obsolete, and they gauge whether your business proposal was professionally prepared. After they buy a product, customers judge you by the service they receive and the ease of understanding your billing.

Pride in your work. Carelessness such as spelling the client's name wrong, preparing a report without checking the accuracy of the data, sending e-mails with typos, or providing estimates with addition errors leaves a bad taste in your client's mouth. Everything must be read and proofread before it goes out the door. When cover letters or e-mails contain typos, clients lose confidence in your ability to deliver; they fear that lack of care and precision may carry over to the quality of your product or the work you do for them.

It's not enough to be on only when you're onstage. Some people feel that a proposal can look sloppy as long as the final product is high quality; that being late for meetings is acceptable as long as they are timely when it's "really important"; that an implied promise doesn't have to be kept, but "real" ones do. They believe that as long as they're properly dressed for client meetings, they can look scruffy with clients after hours. The fact is, trust is the result of accumulated impressions and experiences, and a client's lack of confidence in one area can easily spread to another.

The small details. There's no way to overemphasize the point that every impression is an important one. In *Customers for Life*, Carl Sewell and Paul B. Brown point out that clients look at everything in your organization as a sign of its quality. They ask themselves, "If that's how they take care of their restrooms, how'll they take care of me?"[13] If the flip-down trays in an airplane are dirty, are the airplanes properly maintained? Clients notice if phone calls are answered promptly and whether the person addresses their question or directs them to someone who can. They learn to trust people who confirm meetings, offer directions and parking information before a first visit, and go out of their way to provide favorite restaurants and places to visit during an overnight stay. And they appreciate congratulatory notes on a job promotion, the birth of a child, or even a postcard from a vacation. The expense of an item is not as important as the care behind the gesture.

Providing what the customer needs. Customers don't buy products; they buy solutions. Never tell a customer that your product is best until you know how they plan to use it. Rosabeth Moss Kanter wrote in *Harvard Business Review* that "products derive their meaning and value only from the uses to which customers put them."[14] Many companies are so close to their products that they provide "generic" competitive comparisons and wrongfully conclude that their products are best for everyone. It's important to first determine how products will be used and to compare only those particular features that address specific customer needs. Kanter went on to explain that a "senior executive was widely quoted as saying, 'if customers don't like our solutions, they have the wrong problems.' "[15]

Friendship should never be a substitute for quality. Knowing your clients and nurturing your relationship with them is good business, but friendship should never be substituted for good work. Some people believe they can provide inferior products or cut corners if they wine and dine their clients. If your products are inadequate, or if you don't address your clients' needs, being nice doesn't matter.

Pricing. As Sewell and Brown said in *Customers for Life*, "You can shear a sheep for many years, but you can only skin it once."[16] As a general rule of thumb, don't charge clients for anything in which you are not adding value. According to an article in *Manager's Journal*:

> All too often, "the client is charged for the conversation in which he explains the problem to the senior partner. . . . The client is charged for the senior telling the junior what the client told him. . . . The client is charged for the junior calling the client to clarify some points. . . . The client is charged for the senior reviewing the work of the junior. . . . The client is charged for the time the senior uses to explain the work to the client. . . . The client is charged for all the time it takes the involved lawyers to figure out how much time they should bill the client for the work. . . . The client is sent the bill, and two months later, the client is sent another bill for xeroxing, telephones, delivery, etc. . . ."[17]

A client treated this way will soon be looking for a new attorney.

Stay within budget. Be sure to get approval before you spend a dime of your clients' money. Submit a written estimate and manage expectations by updating it if the scope of the work changes. If it exceeds budget, make sure that you promptly notify your client in writing. Even when changes that increase the cost of projects were requested by clients, notify them; they may not realize the cost implications of their requests.

RELIABILITY

When customers see advertisements, read product literature, or hear product claims made by salespeople, customers expect the assertion to be truthful—without fine print. They want to know that if your organization promises merchandise can be returned if it does not provide complete satisfaction, they can return it without a hassle. Customers want to know that you will keep your word. When you make a promise such as "You'll have it by Friday" or "I'll get back to you early next week" or "I'll put it in the mail today," they want to know it will happen. Furthermore, customers want to know that you can follow directions, that work will be performed right the first time, and that the service will be satisfactorily delivered every time.

Be organized. It is a mistake to fall behind on your paperwork because your focus is on increasing business. Misunderstandings often develop because client discussions were not confirmed in writing. In addition, clients want you to have their information at your fingertips; they do not want to hear "I'll get back to you" because you don't remember the details about their account or can't locate their files under the clutter on your desk. Finally, clients want record keeping to be up to date, and they want to be billed promptly, not three months after work is completed.

Be prepared for meetings. Go into meetings with formal agendas and goals. Don't wait till the 11th hour to finish your work, only to fumble around during a presentation because you don't have the materials ready. Make sure that you have rehearsed your presentation, that your computer is compatible with the projector, that you have an extra lightbulb for the projector in case the original one burns out, that the group next door won't be noisy, and that you know where the light switch and thermostat are located.

Provide service "above and beyond the call of duty." In *Close to the Customer*, James Donnelly points out that "there are some conditions in every service encounter that operate primarily to dissatisfy customers when they are present. However, the absence of these conditions does not create or build strong customer satisfaction . . . that is, when they are not present, the best you can do is achieve no dissatisfaction among customers."[18]

This concept is known as expected service—it involves a level of service that is expected and taken for granted. For example, no customer will ever get excited if you show up on time, if a project is produced within budget, or if billing is accurate. But if you're late for a meeting, go over budget, or produce billing errors, you can be sure your customer will get irritated. It's like being responsible for payroll. No one ever says thank-you if a paycheck is correct, but hold on to your seat if it's wrong.

On the other hand, according to Donnelly, there are conditions in every service encounter that, when present, can build high levels of customer satisfaction. However, if these conditions are not present, they will not dissatisfy the customer. (Said another way, while the absence of an action goes unnoticed, action can result in satisfaction.) For example, if you brought in your car to be serviced and the mechanic not only fixed your problem but also found something else wrong and fixed it at no charge, you would be pleased. But if the mechanic didn't address the problem, you would never know that it existed. Other examples include a doctor's office calling you up a week after a procedure to see how you are feeling, a teacher calling a parent to find out how a former pupil is doing, or a computer technician following up two weeks after addressing an issue to see if you are experiencing any problems.

Donnelly says that it is important to "concentrate first on identifying and then eliminating the causes of dissatisfaction because, as we mentioned, these are what cause customers to leave. . . . Having eliminated opportunities for dissatisfaction, you can devote resources to satisfying and delighting your customers after you have determined that such opportunities exist and what they are."[19]

How do you balance making the right investment in service while maintaining a strong bottom line? According to McKinsey research of companies with the best customer service records in 10 industries, "one key is to minimize wasteful spending while learning to invest in the drivers of satisfaction."[20]

RESPONSIVENESS

Customers want to know that their business is valued and that you'll be helpful and responsive to their needs. They don't want to see three people chatting behind a desk while they wait in line. They don't want to be told that you don't have the time to meet with them as promised because a more important customer called for help.

> An all too common mistake of online retailers is to assume "since we're online, we don't need a support number." In lieu of phone support, web retailers typically direct all questions or concerns to an opaque form that most people, perhaps rightly, assume will never get answered by anyone. Refreshingly, clothes and accessories retailer Zappos.com gets it right in this regard. In addition to online support, Zappos not only provides a phone number, but displays it prominently on its contact page and encourages customers to call no matter what their problem is. Such forthrightness shows customers that the company has nothing to hide, and is in fact eager to assist in any way necessary.[21]

Timeliness. Time is one of our most valuable resources. Lateness is a sign of disrespect. Think about how you feel when you have a 10 o'clock meeting and your appointment arrives twenty minutes late—without an apology. Of course, there are situations when it's impossible to be on time—planes are delayed by weather, children and spouses do get ill, cars are caught in traffic. When such delays occur, your response is key. Notify your appointment when you are running late. By the same token, customers appreciate regular updates if there are project delays or delays in fulfilling an order.

It is also important to answer customer requests in a timely and responsive fashion. According to the *Journal of Services Marketing*:

> The perceived value of time is key in evaluating customers' waiting experiences. Time, then, like money is a scarce resource to be allocated among competing uses. When two customers who value their time differently experience the same service wait, they are paying different prices. . . . Expectations of waiting for service are also related to the amount of choice that the individual perceives he or she has in the situation. Lack of control creates stress which may intensify if continued. . . . When customers feel the purchase decision

is forced on them, as in buying necessities and making routine purchases, the lack of control over the situation can make waiting time unbearable.[22]

There are a number of ways to ease the burden of waiting. For example, theme parks such as Disney World use entertainment to make waiting time part of the positive experience. Waiting can also be made more comfortable by acknowledging how long the wait will be: "This plane is fourth in line for take-off." Waiting is also made easier when concern is displayed. The idea is to ease the perception of delay. For example, if a report is taking longer than expected to produce, even as the result of changes requested by the customer, offering it in sections makes the waiting period easier. The customer knows that progress is being made.

Make certain that your company's policies do not cost you customers. Companies often place policies and procedures ahead of customers. When employees are told to follow the rules or else, when they aren't given leeway to use common sense, customer relations—and company reputations—suffer. Everyone can recount experiences that caused frustration. For example: You buy a new refrigerator and are told that it will be delivered Tuesday between 1:00 and 5:00 p.m. Because you and your wife work, and you don't want to take a personal day, you request a shorter delivery window—to no avail. As a compromise, you ask if it's possible for the dispatcher to call your cell phone when the prior delivery is complete. This will enable you to leave the office and run home in time. This request is also denied.

Or, take the story Jim Donnelly tells in *Close to the Customer*:

> I was browsing in the fabulous Water Tower Place, a collection of some of the finest stores in the world. I spotted a sweater in the window of a department store that I wanted very much. Unfortunately, I was informed by a salesperson that the store was out of stock in all sizes and would not be getting any more in. Disappointed, I left the store. As I walked past the window display and took one more glance at the sweater I wanted so much, I was delighted to see that it was my size. Excited, I returned to the store and found the same salesperson.
>
> "It might be a bit hard to reach," I said, "but the one in the window is my size." "Oh sir," the salesperson informed me, "we never take anything out of the window." "Never?" I asked. "Do you mean that

that sweater will be in the window for the rest of my life?" She informed me that it was company policy not to take anything out of the window.

I pleaded that since there were none in stock in any size and no additional stock was coming in, all this policy could possibly result in was one lost sale and more disappointed customers like me. And she could avoid all of these problems by selling me this sweater. I've had to learn to live without the sweater.[23]

Unfortunately, when employees are forced to choose between doing right by customers or doing what management wants, they often do the latter. That's why management must empower employees to break the rules when it's in the best interests of customers. For example, if the cashier on the express line has no one waiting, he should be able to take the next person on an adjoining line with more than the limited number of items. When employees are empowered to make such judgments, they learn to spot problems and act on them.

Resolving customer problems. When customers call with problems, many employees simply transfer them to someone else without identifying them as the right person. They forget how frustrating it is to be bounced around like a hot potato. In these situations, employees should be encouraged to remain on the phone with the customer until their problem is resolved or the right person to help them is found. Employees could also take the caller's number, do the legwork, and then promptly reply with an answer. Employees should remember that they represent the entire organization, and that customer satisfaction is everyone's responsibility.

Nobody likes calling up a company's support line and having to jump through hoops to get their problem solved. Yet sadly, many companies build friction into their support systems by forcing customers to remember arcane account or customer numbers, e-mail addresses and passwords (that were most likely forgotten moments after they were created) before being helped. Far better in this regard are companies like USAA, which strive to make customer service as easy as possible on the customer. According to MySanAntonio.com, comments like "you guys are too easy" are made frequently to the company's 13,000 support representatives, which (not coincidentally) constitute roughly 60% of the company's work force.[24]

Accepting blame when a problem occurs. Instead of pointing fingers at another part of their organization or even blaming the customer, employees must learn to acknowledge problems and fix them as quickly as possible. After problems are satisfactorily resolved, the cause must be uncovered, not to cast blame, but to make sure they're not repeated.

In fact, the way a problem is handled is a telling sign as to how much you care about the customer. Surveys show that you can win back between 54 percent and 70 percent of customers by satisfactorily resolving their complaints. Indeed, about 95 percent of dissatisfied customers will become loyal customers again if their complaints are properly handled. But be careful; do not assume that you are hearing all of the complaints. According to a Technical Assistance Research Programs study, "On average 1 in 4 customers is unhappy enough with customer service to leave an organization. But of all those that are unhappy, 26 out of 27 will not complain."[25] Indeed, a study by the U.S. Office of Consumer Affairs reveals that consumers don't complain because they believe it is a waste of their time and effort (no one wants to hear about their problems); moreover, they report that they do not know how to complain, especially where to lodge complaints.[26]

COMPETENCE

Customers want to know that employees are properly trained. They want employees to know their own product lines, be able to answer questions, and know their organization well enough to address customer problems. Customers also want to be certain that employees are up to date about new product developments and advances in their fields. It is important to note that when a customer is considering a major purchase, simply answering the customer's questions is not enough.

> To close large sales worth tens or hundreds of thousands of dollars, a firm's customer service staff needs to build and foster *relationships* with customers. It was largely this practice that ranked Jaguar third on *BusinessWeek's* "Customer Service Champs" list in 2009. While car dealers often rush to have you sign, Jaguar prioritizes your comfort **above** the immediate sale. Even if it takes weeks or months, they would rather you walk off the lot feeling confident in your decision than spend money before you were comfortable doing so. Other companies can emulate Jaguar's approach by being supportive,

proactively anticipating your customer's concerns, providing information you think will be helpful (as opposed to shamelessly promotional), and the like.[27]

Trainees. Many companies use the term *trainee* to describe the orientation process by which employees learn the company philosophy, product line, competitive offerings, and so forth. Employees shouldn't feel that once they have completed their initial training, they should stop learning. It's just as important to remain current two years after joining the organization as when you start. In fact, employees should never stop learning.

Product knowledge. When employees cannot answer simple product questions, customers assume the employees haven't been properly trained or don't care about the impression that they give customers.

Product training for employees can be accomplished through such methods as formal training programs, working directly with customers to discover firsthand how products are used, or working at laboratories where they gain hands-on experience with competitors' products or with your company's soon-to-be-announced products.

COURTESY

Remember that every client wants to feel special. No one likes to be treated like a number or to receive form letters addressed to "Dear Customer" when they've been a loyal client for years. When clients experience poor service because they are considered "small" or when meetings are canceled because a high-priority client calls, the client relationship is in jeopardy. Every client expects employees to be courteous, to know their personal nuances, and to answer questions in a clear and non-condescending manner. Perhaps most important, clients do not want to be taken for granted.

Respect. Be courteous to everyone you work with, not just the person who signs your check. No one wants to spend time with someone who makes them feel uncomfortable or inadequate. Furthermore, never underestimate the influence that some employees might have because of their access to the boss.

Admit fault. Poor service is all too commonplace, but that does not make it acceptable. Customers deserve an apology every time they receive less than adequate service. For example, an airline captain who apologizes for a delay and adds, "Sorry we are late in arriving, but our policy is safety first," soothes the ire of a late passenger. When was the last time a dentist apologized for keeping you waiting? Or the maitre d' of a restaurant apologized because your table wasn't ready and offered you a complimentary glass of wine? Don't be afraid to admit mistakes. Sometimes "I'm sorry" or adding a simple "Thank-you" goes a long way. No one is perfect and your customers appreciate someone who is straightforward and sensitive to their needs.

Use your clients' products. Clients want to know that their suppliers are loyal. Don't insult a client by using a competitor's product. Doing so says that you lack confidence in them, and it may raise the question whether you are deserving of their business.

Be careful about hiring clients' employees. Never hire a client's employee unless the client approves it in advance. Even if you handle the situation tactfully, you may find that your new hire, while competent, has a poor relationship with people in his or her former organization.

Use special care with out-of-town clients. There is nothing worse than traveling out of town to visit a client and being anxious to leave as soon as you get there. For example, be careful not to ask the client to confirm your return travel arrangements as soon as you arrive. Moreover, when you visit a client, make it clear that you are available for as long as they need you. Last, try to arrive the evening before a morning meeting to ensure that you are not late or exhausted because you left at the crack of dawn.

Be a good sport. If asked to join activities when visiting a client, do so. And if you play tennis or golf with them, be a gracious winner or, more important, a good loser.

Don't react when you're angry. Every relationship has its ups and downs, and as adults, it's important to know how to manage every situation. Don't let your emotions get the best of you by sending an e-mail or making a call when you're angry; you may live to regret it—count to 10.

Let your client say thank-you. Sometimes a client may want to say thank-you for a job well done. This may include inviting you to dinner or picking up the tab for a drink. Don't make them feel uncomfortable by insisting that you foot the bill. And accept thanks for a job well done graciously, not disparaging your own achievements.

CREDIBILITY

Companies view the reputation of their suppliers as an indication that they will live up to their guarantees. They also prefer working with a company with longevity because of the likelihood they will remain in business; no one wants to be in the middle of a large project with a company that goes out of business or to buy a product from one that won't be around to support it.

When to walk away from a sale. There are many times when it is appropriate to walk away from a sale. Don't accept business unless you can handle it properly. Do not sell your services if you are not 100 percent sure that you can satisfy your client's needs. Never perform a service if you feel that the client won't receive sufficient value for their money. Lastly, never give away business just to get your foot in the door because you may come to resent the client at a later point.

Honesty. Honesty isn't the best policy; it is the only policy. There are two forms of dishonesty: the first is marked by a conscious attempt to deceive, whether by being outright misleading, exaggerating your claims, or withholding information; the second is unintentional, often the result of an honest mistake or a misunderstanding due to poor communication. Both are equally damaging and should be avoided at all costs. After all, it takes a long time to earn confidence and trust, but both can be quickly destroyed if you do not live up to your claims. (Chapter 10 is devoted to this subject.)

Integrity. People do business with those who have a high degree of integrity. They avoid suppliers who charge different prices for the same merchandise. They avoid suppliers who discuss another client's business with outsiders, whether that involves divulging confidential information or making disparaging remarks. They avoid suppliers who hijack other people's ideas or who exploit a relationship by overselling.

Loyalty. Every salesperson has dual loyalty—to clients and to the organization to which the salesperson belongs. It is important that your first loyalty be to your organization. That doesn't mean, however, that you shouldn't be an advocate, fighting for those things that allow you to serve your clients better. It does mean that, even though you may have occasion to be unhappy with your company or boss, you should never discuss those problems with your clients. Never say, "It's not my fault, I only work here" or "What do you expect from my company?" or "If you saw what really goes on here, you would never do business with us." All are inappropriate comments that will make your clients feel uncomfortable with you.

Living the high life. It is never appropriate to put on special airs for clients; as a general rule, clients want to work with suppliers who are similar to themselves. Learn all you can about the culture of your clients' organizations. Try to find out what the office environment is like, how they dress, and what's really important to them. Set your tone by theirs. Trying to impress your clients can backfire. If clients perceive you as someone who squanders money and lives the high life by their standards (for example, by working in extravagant offices or driving expensive cars), they may come to feel that they are supporting your lifestyle.

Gifts. Many companies have policies prohibiting gifts from vendors. Don't put clients in an awkward position by violating their company policies. A client should use your services because of the value that you provide—nothing else.

SECURITY

Clients should not have to think about security—during any stage of the business relationship. They want to know that they can confide in you and never come to regret it; that any information they give you will not get into the hands of their competition; and that you respect privacy laws. They also want to know that you are taking the necessary electronic precautions to protect information through such things as encryption and disaster recovery.

Confidentiality. Once you breach a confidence, even of a friend, your relationship is permanently damaged. No matter how much you apologize or how often you assure them that it won't happen again, there will always be an element of doubt. This applies to personal information or information about their organization; moreover, to avoid suspicion, avoid breaching your own organization's wall of confidentiality. Once you violate your own organization's confidentiality, even in a small way, clients will begin to wonder if you will do the same to them.

Technological security. Today, information critical to the running of a business operation has grown exponentially. And, sharing critical documents with outside vendors has become routine. For example, a direct marketing firm may house a company's lists on their computers or a service organization may prepare a company's payroll. Since these records are not in clients' hands but are critical to their businesses, they want to know that you take proper security precautions, back up files, retain files in different locations, maintain privacy protection, and have a comprehensive disaster recovery plan.

Safety. No client will fault you for having facilities in disadvantaged areas, but they do expect you to ensure their safety when they visit. This may mean having someone meet them at the airport to show them the best and safest way to your office or having ample security in the parking lot.

ACCESS

In an increasingly competitive marketplace, customers ask themselves many questions before renewing long-term commitments. For example, they ask: When I tried to reach my supplier, was it hard to get through to them? Are their hours convenient? Do they have a toll-free number? Do they check their e-mail on a frequent basis? Did they return my calls promptly? Are they conveniently located? If I had a problem and my primary contact wasn't there, did they provide a back-up person to help me? When they went away on a business trip, were they accessible if absolutely necessary?

Be available. Make sure you don't put off client meetings because you are too busy with other clients, and be sure to always return telephone calls promptly. When that is not possible, have someone return the call for you, asking whether someone else can help. This assures your client that you care. Furthermore, when meeting with clients, make sure you give them your undivided attention and avoid constant interruptions. Your mind must be on their meeting, not somewhere else.

When you have to be away for an extended period of time, prepare your clients for your absence. Let them know who is handling their account and summarize the work being performed in your absence. Reassure them that, if necessary, your office can and will reach you.

Be there when you are needed. There are some people who always seem to be around when things are great, but who disappear during tough times. Be a foul weather friend. Be available, even reach out, when clients need you: when they are having personal or professional problems and can use a sounding board; when there is a sickness in their family and they need advice or need to let off steam; when they lose their job and need names to call and ideas to pursue or an office to hang their hat in while they're in transition. You can't do these things effectively and sincerely if you expect to get paid back; you must do them because it makes you feel good.

COMMUNICATION

Look for better ways to communicate with clients. Ask yourself if you use language that your clients understand. Do you focus on your clients' needs or discuss things that are most important to you? Do you keep clients informed about new happenings? Do you speak to senior and technical management with the same technical jargon?

Too close to the forest. Because we have a thorough understanding of our products, we often forget that our customers don't. We forget the problems we faced when we first began using the products. Be careful to explain things to your customers, take time to show them how things work, and gauge the response you receive. Even more important, remember how frustrating it can be to deal with the unfamiliar, and be careful neither to intimidate nor to speak down to customers because they ask fundamental questions. A little patience and empathy can go a long way toward educating your customers to the benefits your products provide.

Presenting to your client. Clients do not buy your products or services because of their features; they buy them because they offer solutions to the clients' problems. Try to present the benefits of new products or services in person; it allows you to answer questions and highlight features that your clients will find most interesting.

Reporting—formal and informal. Be in touch with your clients on a regular basis. One of the ways this can be achieved is through conference reports. Since misunderstandings and miscommunication lead to client losses, written confirmations of your discussions give clients an opportunity to correct misunderstandings. Furthermore, you can use these reports to follow up on outstanding items that need to be pursued and to ensure that everyone in your organization is on the same page.

Another important way to communicate with clients is through progress reports. On a regular basis, summarize the projects that you are working on for each client. It's a good way to manage expectations, let them know the scope of your activities, and highlight obstacles. Such reports provide a good forum for follow-up discussions.

It is also important to keep clients informed about events in your own organization. When they hear about new hires, new product introductions, employee dismissals, new pricing changes, new client gains, or even mergers through the press or through the grapevine instead of directly from you, clients may wonder about your relationship with them.

Out of sight, out of mind. It is important to maintain continual contact with your clients. It isn't enough to get an assignment, disappear, and show up later with a completed work product. Instead, establish key milestones, or benchmarks, and gain approvals at every juncture. This prevents the client from becoming anxious; it ensures that you are moving in the right direction (and allows the client to change course before completing an activity); and it helps reinforce a client's appreciation of you and your work.

Furthermore, make sure your clients know you are thinking about them—out of sight should not mean out of mind. Be proactive: offer fresh ideas even when they aren't requested and forward information that may be of interest, but be careful not to waste your clients' time or overload them with unnecessary information.

Managing uncertainty. Uncertainty creates dissatisfaction. A client may not really know how you are going to tackle an assignment, who will do the work, how long it will take, how much it will cost, or whether it will work. Although the process may be very familiar to you, it may be unfamiliar to a client. Keep clients informed, don't make assumptions, make sure you provide complete information, and be sensitive to their needs. Let clients know the work you are doing behind the scenes; they aren't mind readers. Sometimes clients can be reassured by providing estimates or best guesses; remember that clients are accountable to others in their organization and must provide them with answers.

Managing expectations. A good precept to follow is to underpromise but overdeliver. Always try to do just a little more than the client expects. This can best be accomplished if you understand how expectations are created. Sometimes they are based on hearsay; for example, a client may get a rave review about you or your organization from friends. Expectations can also be based on advertising claims or on a prior experience: "Vendors have always provided me with terrific service." Other times they are the result of personal expectations.

Once you understand how expectations are created, you can manage them:

- Carefully examine the situation for all possible problems before making promises about timing, costs, product performance, or service.
- When marketing intangibles, fully describe your end product so clients know what they will receive (and can avoid surprises).
- If clients request changes that translate into additional costs, be sure to spell them out as they are incurred to minimize the shock when the bill arrives.
- Explain tactfully that delays in receiving approval may translate into delays in the final delivery.
- When you know of delays or problems, don't wait till they compound; bring problems to the client's attention at the earliest possible moment.
- Be conservative in your estimates rather than promising the world and falling short on your promises.
- Don't be afraid to be human—to say that you can't deliver when it's not possible.[28]

Promises. Be careful about promises made. "You can't promise your customers sunny weather, but you can promise to hold an umbrella over them when it rains."[29] Problems arise when promises can't be met. There are no degrees of promises; every promise is equally important because the person who is disappointed by your failure to keep a promise is likely to think: "If they can't be counted on for small things, I sure won't trust them on large ones."

Surprises. Customers don't like surprises. Make sure to let customers know about problems, even small ones, before they discover the problems themselves. Even though your intentions may be admirable (for example, you may be working to resolve a customer issue and spare them needless worry), if customers discover the problem themselves, they'll wonder if there are other problems you're keeping from them.

UNDERSTANDING THE CUSTOMER

Just as you cannot develop a long-term friendship with someone you don't know well, you cannot develop relationships with customers unless you first understand their needs. Do you spend your time dominating discussions or actively listening? Do you understand your customers' political sensitivities? Are you flexible in delivering your services to your customers or are you set in your ways?

Knowledge of customer's company and industry. It's very important to learn as much as you can about a customer's company and industry. This includes understanding the corporate culture, especially its nuances; knowing what criteria are most important to the customer in making decisions; understanding former vendor relationships; and learning why this customer chose to do business with you. Many people wrongly assume that if they are doing work with one company within a particular industry, others are similar. They also wrongly believe that all industries are the same; that if you can develop an advertisement for a consumer products company, you can do the same for an industrial concern. There is no shortcut to working successfully for your customer; it is essential to know as much as you can about each company and each industry. Moreover, taking the time to discover why customers use some of your products and not others, how they use your products, and if they are taking full advantage of what your products offer allows you to learn how you can be of greater assistance to them and perhaps even improve the products themselves.

The knowledge you build about a company or industry over the years provides a significant advantage over potential competitors. Customers recognize that trying to teach someone else the nuances of their organization will be costly. This gives existing suppliers a significant advantage over new entrants.

Identify those things that are most important to the customer. Given that the only thing that matters is customer satisfaction, it is very important to understand what matters most to them. Provide as many opportunities for feedback as you can; for example, conduct account reviews, periodically meeting with your customers to discuss the relationship and how it can be improved; hold focus-group sessions; conduct online surveys; establish dealer councils; set up 800 numbers.

Anticipate customer needs. In today's intensive business climate, it isn't enough to be responsive to your customers' needs; you must be able to anticipate them. One of the best ways to accomplish that is to proactively search for new ideas, both from inside and outside your industry, and then find ways to adapt them to your organization.

Listening. Pay attention not only to what your customers say, but also to things left unsaid. Listening helps you uncover their wants and needs, allows you to identify new product opportunities, and prevents misunderstandings. Make it easy for customers to complain to you, and let them know when you act on their recommendations. It is also important to respond to unfounded concerns, explaining why you are not moving forward on changes they requested.

Objectivity. Organizations retain outsiders to serve as their eyes and ears, giving them a clear picture of what is happening, a picture not colored by position or politics or personal gain. To do this, it is critical to maintain objectivity at all times. In addition, because of your role as an outsider, their employees, distributors, or customers may feel more comfortable confronting you than your customer when faced with an issue.

Make your customer look good. Your job is to make your customers look good—to stay in the background and let them take credit for good work, even if you did it. Avoid making reference, even indirectly, that the work would never have been completed without you. Your role is not to be a star but to create one by whispering ideas into their ears. You were hired to help them do a job, and you succeed when they succeed. Their way of thanking you is by continuing to ask you to do work for them.

CONCLUSION

Treating each client as your only client brings far more long-term rewards than the "love 'em and leave 'em attitude." Not only will you improve market share and reduce your marketing costs, but you will also improve employee morale. In the end, you'll feel good about yourself and know that your clients feel good about you.

Being responsive to clients today but falling short tomorrow because you are not changing with the times is bad business. Chapter 6 discusses how organizations can continually adapt to an ever-changing marketplace.

6

CHANGE . . . WINNING IN THE FAST LANE

BUILDING AN ORGANIZATION THAT ADAPTS WELL TO CHANGE

The future . . . is coming toward us like enormous waves of change. Set after set they are getting bigger and coming faster. . . . Things will never get back to "normal" because unpredictability and change are normal. There is no going back. Get used to it. Change will be followed by more change. That's one thing that isn't going to change. The waves in this ocean won't flatten out, they're only going to get bigger and come at us faster.

—Robert J. Kriegel and Louis Patler,
If It Ain't Broke . . . Break It![1]

We are living in a time of unparalleled change, turbulence, and uncertainty that is transforming our lives at work and at home. According to Ad J. Scheepbouwer, CEO of KPN Telecom based in the Netherlands, "We have seen more change in the last ten years than in the previous 90."[2] For example, in the course of a few weeks, social media became the catalyst for changing the destiny of several Arab nations. Furthermore, the sheer volume and speed of information are having a significant impact on the way companies are structured and how decisions are made. The "ivory tower" supported by large staffs has disappeared from best practices, while the significant reduction of middle management and tales of large layoffs due to outsourcing and downsizing have become commonplace. New technologies have quickly become part of our everyday lives: TiVo and Netflix, microwave ovens, e-mail, and social media have eliminated fixed viewing times, hours in the kitchen, and days of waiting for a response. "When you think about it, aspects of your life change all the time. Fashions change. Your children grow older. Your hair will probably get grayer or thinner. Seen in this light, it would actually be odd if everything except your work changed."[3]

The speed of new developments that seemed to have reached the upper limits has not abated. In fact, according to a *Fast Company* article in 2001 by Seth Godin:

> In five months, Napster went from having 1 million to 10 million users. Eleven months later, it had 80 million users—the most successful technology introduction of all time. And then it essentially went out of business. (Now it's back again—maybe.) . . .
>
> Successful businesses hate change. . . . People with great jobs hate change. Market leaders seek out and cherish dependable systems. But upstarts and entrepreneurs love change. Turbulence scrambles the pieces on the game board; entrepreneurs get a chance to gain market share and profits. And since there are always more competitors than market leaders, there's a huge demand for change. More innovation! More competition! More change! It won't go away. It will only get worse.[4]

In a world in which change is an everyday occurrence, business as usual is a guaranteed recipe for failure. To succeed, today's company must go beyond coping with change; it must embrace change. Rather than react to change, today's employees must learn to anticipate it. Those who cling to the past will meet change with apprehension and anxiety. Only those prepared to meet the challenges of change will be rewarded with unparalleled opportunities. The payoff will go to those employees who are not only committed but also ready to lead the effort.

WE MUST CHANGE THE WAY WE VIEW CHANGE

If all you ever do is all you've ever done, then all you'll ever get is all you ever got.[5]

—Unknown

In years past, management could choose from among six strategies to overcome resistance to change. These strategies, described in a *Harvard Business Review* article, were (1) education and communication; (2) participation and involvement; (3) facilitation and support; (4) negotiation and agreement; (5) manipulation and co-optation; and (6) explicit and implicit coercion.[6]

The first strategy, education and communication, encourages people to embrace change by presenting the benefits prior to implementing the change. The theory goes that by explaining the rationale behind change you help people accept it—and its effects. The article warns, however, that "some managers overlook the fact that a program of this sort requires a good relationship between initiators and resistors or . . . the latter may not believe what they hear. It also requires time and effort, particularly if a lot of people are involved."

The second strategy hinges on participation and involvement of employees in the change process itself. The article warns, however, that the "participation process does have its drawbacks. Not only can it lead to a poor solution if the process is not carefully managed, but . . . when the change must be made immediately, it can take simply too long to involve others."

The third strategy, facilitation and support, requires management support for employees who are facing change because, as the article notes, change efforts "can be time-consuming and expensive and still fail." The fourth approach, negotiation and agreement, involves offering incentives to employees who are against change. Here, the article warns, the greatest problem tends to be cost.

Manipulation and co-optation, the fifth approach, according to the article, requires managers to resort to "covert attempts to influence others. Manipulation, in this context, normally involves the very selective use of information and the conscious structuring of events . . . [but] if the people feel they are being tricked into not resisting, are not being treated equally, or are being lied to, they may respond negatively." The sixth strategy is explicit and implicit coercion. Employees are threatened, either explicitly or implicitly, with penalties for failure to accept change.

Although these solutions may have worked yesterday, they may not meet the test today. The first three strategies require time, an asset no company can waste in today's competitive marketplace. Conversely, when companies rush to implement change, as evidenced in the last three strategies, they may end up creating animosity, increasing anxiety, building resentment, damaging trust, and hampering competitiveness.

There are three factors that render yesterday's change management approaches obsolete. First, change is no longer an occasional but rather an everyday occurrence. Change has become so constant that companies can ill afford the length of time between the generation of an idea and its implementation; as soon as new approaches are introduced, they start becoming obsolete. Just as manufacturers search for faster ways to bring new products to market, companies must search for better and faster ways to introduce change to their organizations. They must create a working environment where employees renew themselves every day.

Second, the way companies are managed has itself changed. In an age in which the workforce is becoming empowered and layers of management are being dismantled, companies can no longer afford to have a few chosen people making all the decisions for the company. In the past, once decisions were made by management, employees were expected to conform. Today, such attempts will reduce employee commitment, something empowered companies cannot afford.

Third, according to Seth Godin:

> Stable times force us to think of our companies as machines. They are finely tuned and easy to copy, scale, and own. We build machines on an assembly line, focusing on how to make them cheaper and ever more reliable. If your company is a machine, you can control it. You can build another one, a bigger one. You can staff it with machine operators and train them to run it faster and faster.
>
> In times of change, this model is wrong. Our organizations are not independent machines, standing in the middle of a stable field. Instead, we work for companies that are organisms. Living, breathing, changing organisms that interact with millions of other living, breathing, changing organisms.[7]

In an interview with *Fast Company*, Peter Senge provided further thoughts on the change process. He said:

> The company-as-a-machine model fits how people think about and operate conventional companies. And, of course, it fits how people think about changing conventional companies: You have a broken

company, and you need to change it, to fix it. You hire a mechanic, who trades out old parts that are broken and brings in new parts that are going to fix the machine. That's why we need "change agents" and leaders who can "drive change." . . .

In our ordinary experiences with other people, we know that approaching each other in a machinelike way gets us into trouble. We know that the process of changing a relationship is a lot more complicated than the process of changing a flat tire on your car. It requires a willingness to change. It requires a sense of openness, a sense of reciprocity, even a kind of vulnerability. You must be willing to be influenced by another person. You don't have to be willing to be influenced by your damn car! A relationship with a machine is fundamentally a different kind of relationship: It is perfectly appropriate to feel that if it doesn't work, you should fix it. But we get into real trouble whenever we try to "fix" people.[8]

In his best-selling book, Senge states, "People don't resist change; they resist being changed."[9] In order to reduce the time needed to introduce change, rather than secure employee buy-in, companies try to force change—an approach that often backfires. In fact, the authors of *Management by Participation* say that "considerable research has demonstrated that, in general, participation leads to commitment, not merely compliance."[10]

In sum, companies must tap the potential of their organization by encouraging employees to be catalysts of change. Instead of being "forced" upon an organization through change management techniques, change must be willingly embraced by each individual and become part of every employee's mind-set.

Reacting to rather than embracing change will be on the tombstone of many companies in the 21st century. In order to succeed, change has to occur as new ideas are born. Companies must move forward in a synchronized way, with leaders alternating the top position as the operation demands special talents; the motion should be like that of a soccer team positioning itself for the score.

FALLACIES ABOUT CHANGE

According to an IBM study that interviewed 1,130 CEOs, general managers, and senior public sector business leaders from around the world,

"Organizations are bombarded by change, and many are struggling to keep up. Eight out of ten CEOs see significant change ahead, and yet the gap between expected change and the ability to manage it has almost tripled since our last Global CEO Study in 2006."[11]

One of the reasons why many change management efforts fail is that the process is often misunderstood—leading to solutions that exacerbate rather than solve problems. Until change management is viewed as a continual process requiring commitment, learning, and understanding, it will be difficult for managers to lead their organizations into the future. Some of the fallacies that result in failure to bring about change are:

> *"The best way to address tomorrow's problems is to see how they've been handled in the past."* People like to define future events based on history. The problem with that approach is that the future contains too many events for which there are no precedents.

> *"I don't have the time to focus on trivial things."* Many companies focus on large problems to the exclusion of small ones—even if they can be easily remedied. They fail to understand the cumulative impact that small problems can have on a company. They forget that, as Peter Senge says, "For almost all of our collective history as a species, the great threats to our survival have been sudden dramatic events: a volcano erupting, a saber-toothed tiger attacking, or an army marching over the hill and wiping out our tribe, for instance. All that has changed. Today, the major threats to our survival as a species are slow, gradual processes. They are systematic phenomena that unfold gradually the way environmental decay has. We have no idea how to deal with systematic threats because all of our notions of ensuring our survival have to do with getting rid of external threats, with fighting something—with fixing our attention on an adversary." This runs counter to a modern world in which threats are systematic and require, according to Peter Senge, "learning to use the tools and methods of systems thinking and translating them into action."[12] Today, it is necessary to focus on the small changes that will enable us to advance as a unified company—with every employee moving in tandem.

> *"Let's have a meeting and think about change."* You shouldn't think about quality only when you're in a meeting addressing quality; you

shouldn't think about learning only when attending a seminar; and you shouldn't think of change as a once-in-a-while occurrence, a separate function apart from everyday activities. Change is as much a mind-set as an activity. It is not a special program or an event, but something that must be incorporated into everything you do.

"Let's send them to a seminar to learn what it takes to be successful." A critical component of change management is education. The American educational focus, however, has always been on specific skill sets; today, when skills become obsolete every few years, we must devote as much effort to learning how to learn as we spend focusing on learning specific skills or techniques. For example, an article in *Harvard Business Review* says:

> Most people define learning too narrowly as mere "problem solving," so they focus on identifying and correcting errors in the external environment. Solving problems is important. But if learning is to persist, managers and employees must also look inward. They need to reflect critically on their own behavior, identify the ways they often inadvertently contribute to the organization's problems, and then change how they act. . . . Put simply, because many professionals are almost always successful at what they do, they rarely experience failure. And because they have rarely failed, they have never learned how to learn from failure. So whenever . . . strategies go wrong, they become defensive, screen out criticism, and put the "blame" on anyone and everyone but themselves. In short, their ability to learn shuts down precisely at the moment they need it most.[13]

"The best way to stay on top of your industry is to study the competition." Too many companies are consumed by their competition. It is just as critical, however, to concentrate outside your field or industry and apply those principles to what you do. If you spend all your time following in your competitors' footsteps, you may catch up, but are unlikely to move ahead. It is, according to Kriegel and Patler, "a strategy that automatically puts you in second place trying to catch up, at best gaining a small, short-term advantage."[14] Benchmarking your approaches, technologies, and processes against best-of-breed companies gives you an opportunity to leap ahead of your competitors.

"Visions and dreams are soft issues; we should focus on hard goals." The difference between a dream and a goal is that the dream provides meaning, while the goal provides an interim milestone. Visions motivate us to change the way we perceive our roles, and they inspire learning. When you follow a dream or strive to make a vision a reality, you think long term and "out of the box." The problem, according to Kriegel and Patler, is that "goals . . . limit you. . . . When we live and die by short-term numbers, it's easy to lose perspective. Everything is exaggerated. Small victories are cause for celebration and small setbacks become huge catastrophes. Minor annoyances take on major importance. As a result, the mad-dash rat race to make the short-term numbers hinders our creativity, our motivation, our spirit."[15]

"If we don't change our first-line employees, we will never be successful." To succeed, a company must require change at all levels of an organization; it must change the company's culture, encouraging continual learning. Unfortunately, according to Peter Senge, a strong proponent of the learning organization, "There is a tendency in the United States, especially in the quality movement, to assume that the changes that need to take place should occur down low in the organization. The idea that people at the top need to lead the change by changing themselves is novel to many U.S. managers. . . . [In America, low-level workers get the most training, mid-level employees get a little less, and the top level gets a] briefing. In Japan, by contrast, it is exactly the opposite. This is very significant symbolically. The leaders are the learners."[16]

"We don't need employee commitment in order to succeed." Employees, forced to accept change, will give it no more than lip service; they just go through the motions. They quietly resist change by such techniques as mumbling under their breath and learning slowly; they may even sabotage efforts to bring about change. In an article in *Quality Progress*, Brooks Carder notes, "If an individual publicly announces that he favors something, but he doesn't entirely believe what he has said, he will be in a condition of cognitive dissonance. To resolve this dissonance, the individual will change his attitude to be more congruent with the statement he has made. However, if he is coerced to make the statement, his attitude will not change. Under coercion he can justify his statement by the coercion."[17]

CHANGE . . . WHY BOTHER?

"If I [Peter Senge] stand back a considerable distance and ask, 'What's the score?' I have to conclude that inertia is winning by a large margin."[18] It is very easy to look at a situation and ask, "If it isn't broken, why fix it?" After all, *inertia* creates comfort, and changing requires breaking old habits, which creates discomfort. The article in *Quality Progress* mentioned earlier notes:

> Managers' habits resist change, are based on education and training, and are embedded in the culture of their organization. . . . These habits produce enough short-term successes to justify continuation year after year. . . . For instance, if you hold enough people accountable, some will succeed. This is sufficient to maintain the habit of holding people accountable. If you set enough goals, some will be reached. This is sufficient to maintain the habit of setting goals. . . . [Indeed,] management methods that achieve short-term success, perceived or real, will often establish management habits, in spite of the fact that the long-term consequences of these management habits can be destructive.[19]

The major reasons, in addition to inertia, for resisting change are:

- *Procrastination:* We all have a tendency to postpone the difficult or uncomfortable. Unless you create a sense of urgency, there's always time to think about change tomorrow. (Procrastination is discussed at length in the next chapter.)

- *Lack of motivation:* Unless the personal benefits are clear, most people will decide that change isn't worth the effort.

- *Fear of failure:* If change requires learning a new skill, change may be avoided simply because we are not emotionally ready to deal with a potential setback.

- *Fear of the unknown:* What we don't know frightens us. The very thought of leaving our comfort zone and facing uncertainty creates enough anxiety and paralysis to avoid change. People are more comfortable with the known—even if it is not functioning well.

- *Fear of loss:* We all worry that a new way of doing things may reduce our job security, power, or status.

- *Dislike of the initiators of change:* It is much more difficult to accept change when we lack confidence in or distrust the people initiating the effort.
- *Lack of communication:* If we do not understand why change is required, misunderstand the initiator's intent, or receive our information in bits and pieces, we are more likely to resist it.

In a companion study to their Global CEO Study, IBM surveyed more than 1,500 change practitioners worldwide. In this study, *Making Change Work*, IBM notes, "An overwhelming 92 percent named **top management sponsorship** as the most important factor for successful change. Rounding out the top four success factors were **employee involvement** (72 percent), **honest and timely communication** (70 percent), and **corporate culture that motivates and promotes change** (65 percent)."[20]

THE ONLY THING WE HAVE TO FEAR IS FEAR ITSELF

One of the most destructive forces in a company is caused by fear. Just as pollution damages the environment, fear is toxic to companies. Fear destroys creativity, shatters loyalty, and discourages people who want to "do what's right." While some managers use fear to stop an activity, this tactic never inspires anyone to perform at their best.

When people believe they lack control, they become fearful—even if imagined. Fears arise over things that are concrete and immediate, such as loss of a job, as well as over things that are more ephemeral and long term, such as embarrassment or damage to one's career.

When people play it safe rather than sailing uncharted waters, they limit opportunities and often put off decision making. For example, Lee Iacocca once noted that the "key to decision making is that at some point you have to rely on your gut instincts, which causes lots of sleepless nights for people who want to play it safe. . . . Unfortunately, research shows that the overwhelming majority of Americans (85 percent) are reactive and static, not action- or dynamic- or instinct-oriented" as a result of this desire to play it safe.[21]

Moreover, fear instills a real sense of powerlessness, discouraging people from openly questioning things, challenging the status quo, or confronting someone when they think something is wrong. When people are afraid to make suggestions or say what's on their minds, or feel that speaking up is a waste of time, innovation and creativity die. A nationwide *Industry Week* survey of employees in 22 organizations revealed that "70% of them say they 'bit their tongues' at work because they feared the repercussions of speaking out. And 98% of their responses indicate that fear has negative effects on them or their work."[22]

Fear also causes people to withdraw, cover mistakes, and misrepresent facts. It teaches them to keep things close to the vest and discourages them from sticking their necks out because trying something new may leave them open to criticism. It makes employees hesitant to discuss problems with others, for fear they will leave themselves open to ridicule.

In fact, according to studies, companies that promote fear destroy creativity, commitment, and confidence. The result is a workforce that has been described by Judith Bardwick as: "Narcissistic: I'm watching out for number one. Paranoid: I think everyone is out to get me. Territorial: I'm grabbing my turf and surrounding it with barbed wire. Rigid: I'm hanging on to what I know. Cynical: I'll believe it when I see it. Political: I'm keeping my eyes open."[23]

At the same time, fear causes some employees to procrastinate or go into automatic pilot, while others go into superdrive, running around making themselves look busy for fear of losing their jobs. It reminds me of the white rabbit in *Alice in Wonderland* who said, "I'm late, I'm late for a very important date. No time to say hello-goodbye. I'm late! I'm late! I'm late!" Only this time it's no fairy tale.

Fear is instilled in employees in many ways, including taking away someone's work, slowly but surely, until the person feels useless; excluding them from communications or from important discussions; cutting them out of the information loop; micromanaging their decisions while looking over their shoulders; openly criticizing, insulting, or challenging their competence or ridiculing them in public; giving them impossible deadlines; or threatening to transfer or fire them.

Kathleen D. Ryan and Daniel K. Oestreich have described the cascade of techniques in their book *Driving Fear Out of the Workplace*:

> *Silence*—pausing and allowing the pause to continue, especially if it is accompanied by direct, deadpan, or cool eye contact, can be extremely intimidating. . . .

Glaring Eye Contact: "The Look"—Some people can look at others with sufficient power to wither the brightest flowers of confidence. This is more than just eye contact. The look is a testing, evaluative glare. . . . Combined with silence, the look is a powerful way to shut down communication—all without saying a word.

Brevity or Abruptness—This behavior is what one research participant described as "short, sharp answers" to questions or comments, using words that have a clipped, cold feel to them.

Snubbing or Ignoring People—This behavior separates people into castes: "I'm up here. You are down there." It can take the form of simply not talking to people, leaving them out of meetings important to their jobs, or reminding them of their "place" . . . put-downs, in-crowd conversation, sitting in the power seats, turning one's back on someone at the meeting, stubbing out a cigarette in front of someone at the table. In general, making sure everyone knows they are very, very important.

Insults and Put-Downs—These represent the commonly cited fear-provoking interpersonal behaviors: cutting remarks, direct or implied, that attack a person's credibility, self-esteem, or integrity. They often take the form of labeling, making jokes at someone's expense, ridicule or sarcasm, and racist, sexist, and other discriminatory remarks of all kinds. The impact of these comments is a combination of both fear and anger, permanently engraving the remarks in people's memories.

Blaming, Discrediting, or Discounting—These behaviors place responsibility for the problem on someone else. The process is one of labeling or fixing blame in a way that traps or targets the other person.

An Aggressive, Controlling Manner—People described this autocratic behavior as demanding, intense, "my way or the highway," . . . This type of behavior easily blends with a micro-managing, high surveillance approach to controlling people, such as requiring time logs for every task. Sometimes this behavior is calculated and manipulative. It is at this point on our behavior scale that abrasive behavior can become abusive.

Threats About the Job—Comments like "I'll remember this," "You are undermining me," and "I can replace you" put the employee's job security on the line. Threats can be either implied or direct. Performance criticisms related to a particular project can include an unstated threat of job loss. . . .

Yelling and Shouting—Next to put-downs and insults, this category, the loud voice or loud argument, was the most frequently cited interpersonal behavior that causes fear. Sometimes, people said, someone's voice was loud enough to be heard "all the way down the hall" or "all over the building," as if the venting was intended to widely publicize a failure and to humiliate the employee. . . .

Angry Outbursts or Loss of Control—This behavior represents an explosion. It is the point at which people throw things in their offices or resort to exaggerations.

Physical Threats—Physical threats are only one step away from patently criminal behavior.[24]

When this kind of environment is allowed to flourish, things get ugly. It is much like the picture William Golding painted in *Lord of the Flies*, where civilized children became savages to protect themselves. In the same way, people will do just about anything to save their hides, including finger-pointing and engaging in witch hunts. In these organizations more time is spent covering up tracks than working. Passing the buck and putting everything in writing become cultural norms. No one challenges the status quo, goes out on a limb, or reports problems for fear of being labeled a troublemaker. Everyone spends their lives in meetings and on committees in order to avoid decision making. People avoid responsibility like the plague. Inaction is justified as not rocking the boat or as maintaining the status quo. As time marches on, minor disturbances grow into major problems. And perhaps most important, in an age of rapid change, the inaction, procrastination, or wasted time that results from fear keeps employees from learning skills that are vital to a company's success.

This kind of behavior will prevent many companies from becoming market leaders. According to Jack Welch, former CEO of General Electric:

> The individual who typically forces performance out of people rather than inspires it: the autocrat, the big shot, the tyrant [is no longer useful]. Too often all of us have looked the other way . . . [because these types of managers] "always deliver"—at least in the short term. And perhaps this type was more acceptable in easier times, but in an environment where we must have every good idea from every man

and woman in the company, we cannot afford management styles that suppress and intimidate. Whether we can convince and help these managers to change—recognizing how difficult that can be—or part company with them if they cannot, will be the ultimate test of our commitment to the transformation of the Company and will determine the future of the mutual trust and respect we are building.[25]

LEARNING . . . K THROUGH LIFE

In a turbulent business environment, organizations must renew themselves every day. When people are forced to think about change in the world around them and in their work environment, the general tendency is to reject what they see out of hand. People either ignore the signals, discount the relevance of the message, or end up shooting the messenger. Indeed, it often takes a crisis to create the sense of urgency required to alter thinking, modify strategy, or embrace change, but by the time the crisis is recognized, the damage is done. It is like the "motivational speech I heard years ago. An indignant employee was saying, 'But how can they lay me off? They need me. I know my job inside out. I have thirty years of experience' Answer: 'No, you don't. You have one year of experience repeated thirty times.' "[26] The danger for America is that, like most civilizations that have fallen, we will not recognize the crisis we face until it is too late.

For business, the challenge is to create an environment that draws its employees' viewpoints closer to those views needed to succeed in the marketplace. In order to survive, businesses must become learning organizations.

ESTABLISHING THE LEARNING ENVIRONMENT

In order to prosper today and in the future, companies must view change as a source of opportunity. Everyone should be encouraged to embrace learning and continuous improvement rather than allowing fear of failure to dominate. To accomplish this, companies must foster an environment of trust, loyalty, and commitment—those qualities that encourage people to learn rather than covering their tracks and playing the blame game.

Furthermore, in this new environment a new kind of leader will emerge. Walter Kiechel III, who has written extensively on this issue, presents the following two examples.

Neal Thornberry, a professor at Babson College and an expert on so-called self-directed work teams, uses the term "unleader" in summarizing what successors to today's managers will and won't do. The unleader will take team development as his primary charge. He'll be an expert in adult learning, of course, understanding that different team members learn in different ways. But he will also know the ins, outs, ups, downs, and general convolutions of group dynamics—how teams form, reach agreement or fail to, act in concert or fall apart. So armed, he'll be equipped to help the team along, mostly by asking questions: "Have you considered the legal aspects of this?" . . . If he does his job right, he'll end up serving not as facilitator . . . but as a catalyst.

Jim Kouzes, a consultant with the Tom Peters Group, [who] offers an only slightly fanciful version of correct managerial technique in the learning organization: Subordinate calls up and says, "I have a problem." Manager replies, "That's terrific, just why I hired you," and hangs up. Subordinate tries again, maybe a couple of times, and gets the same response. If the subordinate finally convinces the manager he needs help, the assistance will largely take the form of more questions: "If this problem is solved, what will the solution look like? Let's generate some ways to get there. What are the strengths and weaknesses of each approach? So which one did you choose?" . . . You're teaching people a problem-solving process.[27]

Once the organization embraces this new management approach, every small success becomes a springboard for additional success, not a capstone. In other words, rather than relaxing once a goal is reached, employees strive to do even better tomorrow.

In the learning environment, everyone looks forward to the next challenge. It is much like the response of James Michener when "asked to name his favorite book among those he had authored. 'My preference, among the thirty-five books I've written,' he said after a long pause, 'is always the next one. I'm an old pro. And the job of an old pro is to move on to the next task.' "[28]

ACCEPTING THE RISKS THAT ACCOMPANY CHANGE

In learning organizations, risk is understood and opposing views are not only tolerated, they are encouraged. The slogan of these companies could reflect the old adage: Nothing ventured, nothing gained. Kriegel and Patler expand on that thought by saying, "Risk taking is natural. In fact, it is unnatural not to take risks. Can you imagine a baby thinking, 'I don't know if I should try to stand. I know I'll fall. I know it will hurt. Maybe I'll wait a few years until I'm bigger and stronger'? If that were the case we'd all end up on our hands and knees."[29] Many companies discourage risk taking by reprimanding people for errors and stigmatizing those who try something new and fail. Instead, management should present problems as learning opportunities, praising innovative attempts even when they fail. After all, the less "pain" associated with risk taking, the more employees will try something new.

Companies can stimulate learning by rewarding messengers rather than shooting those who bear bad news. Messengers aren't the problem; they are a vital part of the solution. To ensure that employees feel free to openly discuss company challenges, organizations should celebrate people who raise issues and then address them. Companies should also applaud people who admit mistakes rather than sweep them under the rug. This encourages people to resolve problems before they get larger. In addition, hiding mistakes only compounds errors because decisions are then based on faulty information.

Although risk taking and admission of mistakes is important, organizations must also learn by them. Joe Paterno, coach of the Penn State University football team, once replied when "asked . . . how he felt when his team lost a game, . . . that losing was probably good for the team since that was how the players learned what they were doing wrong."[30] Paterno's comments highlight the advantages of a learning environment. Soichiro Honda, founder of Honda Motor Company, reinforces that idea when he says that "many people dream of success. To me success can only be achieved through repeated failure and introspection. In fact, success represents the 1 percent of your work which results only from the 99 percent that is called failure."[31]

Not only can an organization learn by its mistakes, but individuals can as well. Management must promote personal growth through constructive feedback. In fact, in an open environment, one where there is honesty and trust, people request feedback and then follow up on the suggestions offered.

Open and honest communication is an essential element in creating an atmosphere of learning and change. After all, people are more likely to embrace change if they understand what it is and why it is required, and if they are prepared for the change, rather than surprised by it. It is useful for senior management to communicate their support for change and to provide road maps that contain milestones that make the journey clear. If a visionary leader communicates the long-term need for change, employees buy in more quickly.

Changing to a more open and trusting environment requires letting go, unlearning many management practices of the past. That is not easy and does not happen quickly. It requires managers to leave behind many skills, sources of status and power, and implicit assumptions about the workplace that were formulated during past experiences. Dr. Tineke Bahlmann notes that "learning only happens in a simple structure . . . without too much hierarchy, where there is room for individuals, where a collision of opinions is cultivated, because only then emerging strategies and creative interactions with the environment can happen."[32]

LEARNING TO LEARN

Learning is key for instituting the kind of change that will make companies competitive both today and in the future. The more you learn, the more you are open to change; the more people are open to change, the easier it is for the company to forge ahead. The first thing research into this subject area reveals is that learning takes many forms—a one-size-fits-all philosophy is not an appropriate strategy. Alan Mumford explains that "researchers have identified four types of learning styles: activists, who learn best from activities while they are engrossed in them; reflectors, who learn from activities which they have had the chance to review; theorists, who benefit from activities when they are offered as part of a concept or a theory; and pragmatists, who learn best when there is a direct link between the subject matter and a real life problem."[33] It is important to keep these learning styles in mind when constructing formalized training programs. It is also critical to know your employees' optimum learning style, so that the informal learning takes place during meetings, feedback sessions, and on-the-spot training.

Recognizing that people learn in different ways, companies might want to recognize teaching models that have proven successful with children.

Lucia Solorzano noted several learning styles in a report in *U.S. News & World Report*: " 'Manipulative' learners [who] . . . need to get more physically involved in their lessons to remember them. Hands-on projects, such as model building or play-acting, are useful learning tools. [While] 'visual' learners . . . retain information best by seeing it. Films, educational TV and museum exhibits help them learn. 'Informal' learners . . . thrive in less structured study arrangements. Beanbag chairs may make a better workplace, for example, than a desk and straight-backed chair. 'Walkman' [iTunes] learners . . . use background noise as a screen for better concentration. . . . 'Dyadic' learners . . . work best with a partner, rather than alone or in a group—small or large. . . . 'Mobile' learners . . . need to move about and take breaks while studying."[34]

There are, of course, numerous other factors involved in learning. For example, some people learn on a need-to-know basis, finding the time and concentration only when necessity drives them. Some systematically assess the gaps in their knowledge and skill base and then take courses to fill in the void. Others use free time for reading, highlighting and filing away material, while others attend lectures or go to conferences. For some, learning involves active participation, doing things by trial and error. Others learn by exchanging information and debating issues with colleagues. Some spend a great deal of time observing and collecting information through constant assessment of their environment; they are always open, looking beyond their boundaries and then contrasting what they see in one place with what they see in another.

All of these methods, including the ones described below in greater detail, are effective.

CURIOSITY

Curiosity and learning are part of human nature. Children are notorious question askers, wanting to know everything about the world around them. They ask questions ranging from why the sky is blue to why there is no sun at night. But as we grow older, we are inhibited by a fear that we will look stupid if we ask questions. Even more dangerous, we begin to assume that the things we have already learned are set in stone. The problem is, as the Greek philosopher Epictetus said, "It is impossible for a man to learn what he thinks he already knows." That is why it is important to re-examine what we take for granted, regaining that childlike ability to question and requestion. We must not allow old information to cloud our judgment, and we must learn to abandon the familiar to discover and savor the new.

MAKING DATA MEANINGFUL

Data is meaningful only when it is attached to ideas. For example, it is not enough to collect financial statistics without recognizing the context in which they exist. It is the accumulation of data coupled with the connections that we draw between different kinds of information that provides knowledge. Therefore, it is critical to have diverse interests because in order to make data relevant, you make connections between what you already know and the new concepts that you are learning. Without that knowledge base, you might lose interest because you don't know how to apply the data.

There are a number of methods for helping people make connections between seemingly unrelated concepts. Metaphors are a very good way to explain the unexplainable, and an analogy is yet another powerful tool. Keep in mind that, as Richard Wurman says, "Facts are only meaningful when they relate to a concept that you can grasp. If I say an acre is 43,560 square feet, that is factual but it doesn't tell you what an acre is. On the other hand, if I tell you that an acre is about the size of an American football field without the end zones, it is not as accurate, but I have made it more understandable."[35]

SEEING PATTERNS

Take the time to see emerging patterns in the world, rather than seeing events in isolation. When you have two things to compare, you can see differences; when you have many, you begin to see patterns. People learn when they look at the things that are happening around them, draw conclusions, and then apply what they learn. Any fact in isolation is a bit of data; a lot of data is information; a lot of information is the beginning of knowledge. When employees see the big picture, they make connections and learn.

ACTIVE PARTICIPATION

Active participation is a more powerful learning device than spoon-feeding. Not only are we more likely to remember something when we discover it ourselves or learn through trial and error, but we are more likely to value it. We file away what we hear, but we test what we discover, which makes us more likely to value it. Abstract concepts do not lead to action the way experience does.

THE SOCRATIC METHOD

One of the best ways to learn is through question-and-answer dialogue, a form of conversation that was used by Socrates as he taught his disciples the principles of logical thought and analysis. Socrates was using a formal version of the oral tradition typical of most primitive cultures. As Peter Senge points out, "Most native American cultures just sat in a circle and talked for hours or even days. No purpose. No leader. No agenda. Just talk. Then the group would disperse and people would go about their work attuned to what everybody else was doing and thinking. Dialogue let them understand collectively a deeper pattern of reality than any one person could understand."[36]

One of today's equivalents is the "brainstorming" session, in which employees get together to look at issues and suggest ways of tackling them. If facilitated properly, such sessions become free and open forums for inspiring out-of-the-box thinking. Through such exchanges, companies can help employees broaden their view of the world. And that understanding, in turn, translates into an acceptance of the need for change.

REFLECTION

Learning requires more than the accumulation of knowledge. It is not enough to collect information; we must absorb it, internalize it, and connect it to concepts that we already understand, thus "owning" what we learn before we use it. Anyone can memorize two plus two equals four—without thinking that two oranges and two apples are four pieces of fruit. Learning takes place after we have time to think about what we are told, make patterns out of information and finally test the ideas.

Companies that push employees to continuously work at peak levels and generate creative ideas on command will never foster the kind of environment in which creativity and innovation flourish. Unless we have time to step back and reflect on our activities, we will never know whether we are moving forward or just creating motion. Senge points out that "in the west we have a cultural predisposition toward action to the exclusion of thinking. . . . In a Japanese organization if you were to see someone sitting and doing nothing, you would never think to interrupt because obviously that person is thinking. It's perfectly acceptable, however, to interrupt an active person. In the west, we are exactly the opposite."[37]

PLAY

Sometimes learning requires us to abandon preconceived notions about how to solve problems. Playing games provides the freedom to think in more original, innovative ways. Jeremy Campbell writes that "under the guise of play, new forms of behavior can be invented with impunity and thus it becomes an inspiration to innovation."[38]

Formal play is also a useful way to build relationships and stimulate communications between employees. For example, participation in a company volleyball or softball game can provide camaraderie that generates new thinking. Furthermore, if these relationships span cross-functional lines or operating units, they also help break down artificial barriers and disseminate information about other areas of the company.

MENTORING

Sometimes it is easier to learn from observing others than from reading books, attending lectures, or through trial and error. For example, one can learn nuances about leadership not found in books because some subtleties can't be expressed on paper. Learning how to manage employees is easier when you can emulate a role model and, even better, receive constructive feedback from that person. For example, learning proper etiquette in certain business situations, dealing with a difficult employee, or responding to an irate customer are all unique situations that may get lost in the translation: you have to be there. It is much like the old apprenticeship system that once governed the learning of skill sets. In those days, a blacksmith was trained by watching another blacksmith, then by helping him, and finally by doing the job under close supervision.

ORGANIZATIONAL LEARNING

Not only must management promote opportunities for employees to learn and grow, they must also introduce new ways of operating that encourage learning and enable change; examples are discussed below.

REDUNDANCY

Ikujiro Nonaka wrote in the *Harvard Business Review* that "to Western managers, the term 'redundancy' with its connotations of unnecessary duplication and waste, may sound unappealing . . . [but deliberate] redundancy is important because it encourages frequent dialogue and communication," which spreads knowledge throughout the organization.[39] For example, assigning two groups the same problem may seem like a waste of time; however, there are numerous advantages to such a process. If they both come up with the same answer, you can be confident that the solution is probably right. If they come up with different solutions, the arguments over them throw new light on the project—and often lead to a third solution that is better than either of the originals. "In this case it is not that one wins and another loses, but they take the best angle from each team to derive the best product."[40]

COMPETING AGAINST YOURSELF

Companies that experience great success often stick to the same "game plan" rather than re-examine what they do. The problem is that if the marketplace shifts, they will be left behind. One method to overcome complacency is to develop a task force to brainstorm how they would compete against themselves. This forces employees to look at their organization from a different perspective and factor these findings into their current plans.

CONTINGENCY PLANNING

Unexpected events will always occur, and in fact, they occur much more often and with much greater rapidity than expected. Therefore, companies must prepare for their eventuality. Christopher Knowlton says in *Fortune* that "you can't control the unexpected, but you can control your response to it. Practitioners of Aikido, a form of martial arts, know that they may get thrown if they resist an attacking force. So they learn to blend with the force and use an attacker's energy for their own advantage."[41]

One of the ways that an organization can prepare for that eventuality is to embrace a "what-if" mentality. This encourages employees to think out of the box and explore the unexpected. What are the most likely scenarios? How will we react to the situation? Where do we have control? What are our options? Knowlton points out in the same article that "war gaming helps Shell prepare for the unexpected . . . they study and debate detailed scenarios developed by the planning department that sketch reasonable but contrasting alternatives for how the world may look in ten years. Each region and each operating company [then] uses [these scenarios] to formulate strategy."[42]

COLLECTIVE INSIGHTS

The more information shared across a company, the more everyone learns. No one unit of the company or single person should hoard information. Nonaka said in his *Harvard Business Review* article that "in an economy where the only certainty is uncertainty, the one sure source of lasting competitive advantage is knowledge. When markets shift, technologies proliferate, competitors multiply, and products become obsolete almost overnight, successful companies are those that consistently create new knowledge, disseminate it widely throughout the organization, and quickly embody it in new technologies and products. These activities define the 'knowledge-creating' company, whose sole business is continuous innovation."[43]

In the article, Nonaka goes on to explain that there are different types of knowledge and that knowledge has to be built upon before it can benefit an organization. He says that "the centerpiece of the Japanese approach is the recognition that creating new knowledge is not simply a matter of 'processing' objective information. Rather, it depends on tapping the tacit and often highly subjective insights, intuitions, and hunches of individual employees and making those insights available for testing and use by the company as a whole."[44]

This tacit knowledge, as he explains, is not often easily shared:

> Explicit knowledge is formal and systematic [so] it can be easily communicated and shared, in product specifications or a scientific formula. . . . Tacit knowledge [however] is highly personal. . . . It

consists of mental models, beliefs, and perspectives so ingrained that we take them for granted, and therefore cannot easily articulate them.

Sometimes, one individual shares tacit knowledge with another. . . . They become part of her own tacit knowledge base . . . [but because that] knowledge never becomes explicit, it cannot be leveraged by the organization as a whole. . . . [In another case,] an individual can also combine discrete pieces of explicit knowledge into a new whole. For example, when a comptroller of a company collects information throughout the organization and puts it together in a financial report, that report is new knowledge in the sense that it synthesizes information from many different sources. But this combination does not really extend the company's existing knowledge base either.

In the knowledge-creating company, all . . . these patterns exist in dynamic interaction. . . . First she learns the tacit secrets. . . . Next, she translates these secrets into explicit knowledge that she can communicate to her team members. . . . The team then standardizes this knowledge, putting it together into a manual or workbook and embodying it in a product. . . . Finally, through the experience [they] enrich their own tacit knowledge base. . . . This starts the spiral all over again.[45]

EVALUATION TECHNIQUES

Over the years, many approaches have been developed to help evaluate the performance of an organization. They can provide ways to learn, grow, and change.

Best practices. The process of measuring best practices entails examining various companies in order to identify novel management approaches that can be transferred to your own company. Moreover, because the companies are often in unrelated areas, findings are evaluated objectively, are adopted with less disruption, and don't place people on the defensive. A good example is GE's Best Practices project, which asked the question, "What's the secret of your success?"

The answers were surprisingly similar, as explained in a *Fortune* article:

Almost every company [studied] emphasized managing processes, not functions; that is, they focused less on the performance of individual departments than on how they work together as products move from one to the other. They also outhustled their competitors in introducing new products and treated their suppliers as partners. . . .

The implications of the Best Practices study were earthshaking. GE realized it was managing and measuring the wrong things. The company was setting goals and keeping score; instead, says business development manager George Zippel, "we should have focused more on how things got done than on what got done." . . .

The Best Practices findings [were turned] into a course . . . [that] teaches three essential lessons. The first is that other companies have much to teach GE. . . . Second is the value of continuously improving processes, even in small ways, rather than taking big jumps. . . . The third lesson is that processes need owners— people whose responsibility and authority reach through the walls between departments.[46]

Benchmarking. Benchmarking requires examining organizations that perform similar functions to determine if they do them as well as, or better than, your company does them. One approach consists of measuring a specific function, for example, marketing, against the marketing groups of other organizations. What software applications show promise? How satisfied are customers with the level of service provided? What are their customer-retention strategies? Benchmarking allows an organization to focus on improving one aspect of a business in very specific ways.

Performance measurement. How do you measure customer satisfaction? How do you solicit customer feedback? How effective is your call center? Do callers get through to someone knowledgeable quickly? Do employees do everything possible to help customers? One element in building an environment marked by continuous improvement is visible and reliable measurement and reward systems. Measuring and rewarding employee performance promotes a culture in which performance, rather than just showing up, matters.

Studies. By participating in comparative studies, you can compare specific characteristics of your organization against other organizations. Moreover, even the process of filling out a survey can teach employees where attention is required.

Customer surveys. Learn from customers by using them as beta sites and soliciting their input on the likes and dislikes of your products and service. Formal or informal surveys also provide valuable information on their wants and needs.

CONCLUSION

Creating a learning organization serves a number of purposes. First, learning helps employees remain sharp and enthusiastic, increasing their value to the organization. When new skills are practiced every day, organizations become more efficient and people are more willing to accept additional responsibility. Second, learning leads to greater fulfillment and loyalty because employees are more challenged, knowing that their skill sets are cutting edge. Third, and most important of all, employees open to learning embrace change. As such, they become catalysts for the rest of the company.

The message is that learning and change go hand in hand. Without learning, change is slow and costly to implement, something no organization can afford today. Chapter 7 discusses the impact that time, a valuable resource and a fixed commodity, has on companies today.

7

WHEN FAST ISN'T
FAST ENOUGH

BUILDING AN ORGANIZATION
THAT RESPONDS WITH SPEED

Standing next to a conveyor belt as beautiful creamy white cakes roll by, [Charlie] Chaplin sprays on the frosting, adds a rose or two, puts the cake in the box, and puts the box on a shelf. Everything is working fine and he is enjoying himself immensely. Then the belt speeds up. In his haste to keep up, he begins moving with the famous Chaplin hyperspeed. As the cakes fly by him, the icing gets sprayed all over, the roses look like Rorschach's ink blots, and the cakes go ker-plop! on top of each other, forming a sweet white mound on the bakery floor. Chaplin foreshadowed our current "modern times." We used to laugh at this scene; now we live it.

—Robert J. Kriegel and Louis Patler,
If It Ain't Broke . . . Break It![1]

In years past, companies had abundant resources at their disposal. They could be squandered without having a significant impact on success. For example, if some employees weren't doing their jobs effectively, there were others around who could get the work done. If marketing programs missed the mark, everyone shrugged and developed new ones. If you had problems to solve, you had days to contemplate solutions. In fact, if you floundered half the time, there was usually enough slack in the system to still achieve your goals. Because of the tremendous resources available, there was little emphasis on allocating them properly. Everyone seemed to have time and money to burn.

Times have changed. WOW, have they changed! According to Harry Emerson Fosdick, "The world is moving so fast these days that the one who says it can't be done is generally interrupted by someone doing it."[2] Where once, you waited a week to have a roll of film developed, today digital photography gives you instant gratification. Where once, you made corrections to a report before lunch and were lucky to get it back before a day went by, today you can make corrections in seconds. It seems like yesterday that we waited two days for a letter to arrive in the mail, where today we get frustrated if an e-mail takes longer than 30 seconds to transmit— so much for patience. Given the tremendous value placed on time, we use cell phones, tablets, and laptop computers to maximize our time on the road; and we look to ATMs, 24-hour grocery stores, and even online grocery shopping to make life more convenient. The emphasis on speed permeates every aspect of the world we live in. For stock traders and foreign exchange dealers who make decisions based on real-time information, a second can be a lifetime. In the world of health care, time can mean the difference between life and death. For a busy accountant or attorney, lost time represents money; for a sales representative, it translates into lost sales opportunities; and for a new-product introduction, it can determine whether a product is a major success or an also-ran. For example:

> Innovation once took years to result in new technologies and marketable products. The use of radio waves to detect metallic objects and enable long-distance communications was first theorized in 1904. Three decades later, the theory resulted in the first practical application of radio detection finding. By the beginning of World War II, the United States, United Kingdom, France and Germany had their own versions of radio detection and ranging—what we now call "radar." Radar opened the door for the accidental discovery of using microwaves for cooking and in 1947, the first microwave oven was installed in a Boston restaurant.
>
> Contrast the evolution of the microwave oven with Google. The Internet juggernaut didn't invent search technology, but did see the need for a better means for organizing and finding Web-based

information. Founders Larry Page and Sergey Brin initially took their
concept to Yahoo founder Jerry Yang, then the master of the nascent
Internet, offering him a way to provide a better search service to his
millions of users. Yang was impressed by the idea, but didn't see the
practical application. He told the Google boys to prove themselves
independently; the idea that Yahoo would simply buy Google if it
showed signs of commercial success. We all know how that story
played out.[3]

In fact, in many cases, time has become more than a scarce resource; it has
become a competitive weapon. As Rupert Murdoch, chairman and CEO of
News Corporation, once said, "The world is changing very fast. Big will not
beat small anymore. It will be the fast beating the slow."[4] There are many
ways that time can be used as a competitive weapon. First, companies speed
new products to market to gain a competitive advantage. For example,
several years ago, "Big Words, a Web-based textbook seller, spent just
$50,000 and took just one month to set up relationships with more than 25
publishers. It then put up a Web site, ran ads in eight college newspapers
in California—and wound up selling books to students at more than
250 universities across the country. 'Before the Internet,' says Weintraut
[J. Neil Weintraut, general partner, 21st Century Internet Venture Partners],
'a company like Big Words might have achieved sales at 8 or 10 universities
at launch time. But Big Words reached 250 in one month. That's fast.' "[5]

Second, time can be used to differentiate products and improve service
delivery, increasing customer satisfaction. For example, "A commitment
to speed explains the success of Progressive, a fast company in an industry
that's undeniably slow: insurance. The company boasts that it settles
auto-insurance claims before competitors know that there's been an
accident."[6] According to *Fast Company*:

> At Progressive, claims reps perform their inspections right after an
> accident, instead of waiting several days to visit customers. Eliminating
> delays generates substantial cost savings. Vehicles that get
> inspected sooner get repaired sooner—which means that Progressive
> pays fewer storage-lot and rental-car fees. And by enabling reps to
> focus on the real work of inspecting accidents—instead of sitting
> behind a desk juggling paperwork and fielding customer complaints
> about delays—Progressive hires fewer reps than it would otherwise.[7]

Another example of using speed to create product differentiation is seen in the eyeglass industry. "Eyelab sought to reduce the long waiting time (normally one week) required to deliver custom-finished eyeglasses to consumers. It did this by transferring manufacturing from a single, centrally located laboratory to mini-laboratories at each of its retail outlets. Today, every Eyelab store has lenses, frames, grinding equipment, and technicians who are able to provide customers with eyeglasses within one hour. "[8] Unfortunately, the advantage they gained was short-lived. Today, most shopping malls have two or three companies providing the same speedy service.

PICKING UP THE PACE

Business is moving faster than it ever has before. And if you can't keep up—as a company, as a team, as a leader—you will be left behind.

—Katharine Mieszkowski, *Fast Company*[9]

Time compression is having widespread effects on the production of goods and services. One area where speed is especially critical is in distribution; after all, customers aren't happy if you can produce something faster but can't deliver it to them more quickly. This particular challenge pertains to trendy products that are continually sold out before demand is satisfied. Retail outlets that lose sales have challenged clothing manufacturers to find innovative ways to remedy this problem: "The Levi Strauss Company knows each night which style and size jeans have sold that day throughout the country. Levi uses this information to manufacture replacement stock and order replacement material. Other clothing companies such as Benetton and The Limited have also adopted Quick Response Systems that link their suppliers, manufacturing plants, distribution centers, and retailing outlets."[10]

Speed, however, is only the latest method of gaining competitive advantage. Over the years, companies have used other strategies to gain an edge. At one time, the primary form of competitive advantage was price; those who made goods cheaper through mass-production techniques were the first winners. The next generation of winners offered choice through innovation and design. The emphasis then turned to quality. In this stage, engineering and manufacturing prowess won the day. In the 1990s, companies learned to make and deliver products and services faster and better in order to succeed. They reduced the time between anticipating a need and meeting it, exceeding the expectations of the customer. In the 21st century, the latest method of achieving competitive advantage is through innovation as well as by exceeding total product satisfaction—from the shopping experience, to value, to after-sales service.

The growing importance of speed is clear:

> By being the first to enter a new market, the business gains an advantage over its actual and potential rivals. This is true whether the business is seeking to develop new geographical/demographic markets or segments for existing products, or whether it is seeking to introduce new products to its existing market segments. If the business is first into a market, so the thinking goes, it can establish what the military thinkers would call 'defensible ground.' First, it can capture market share much more easily without having to worry about rivals trying to capture the same customers. Second, when the rivals do come along—as they inevitably will—the first-mover and its management team will have advantages in the ensuing competition, such as familiar products, brand loyalty, the best retail outlets, up-and-running distribution systems, and so on. By beating rivals into the market, the first-mover can consolidate its position and compete more effectively, not only defending its previously acquired share but even continuing to expand.[11]

In fact, according to research conducted for the book *Strategic Speed*, "Faster companies had an average of 40 percent higher sales growth and 52 percent higher operating profit than their slower peer companies."[12] Moreover, people are willing to pay for speed. A perfect example is Federal Express, which "is the result of Fred Smith's recognizing the importance that households and businesses place on fast and reliable delivery services. . . . [Even the] Postal Service admits that Federal Express users are willing to pay 25 to 40 times more for this service."[13]

The question is, how can we exploit everyone's desire for speed to save time? To start, it is critical that time be perceived as a valuable and limited resource. Time cannot be expanded or changed; it is a constant. Unlike money, which flows in and out, and earns different rates of return, time is finite. According to Jeff Levy, founder, president, and CEO of eHatchery, an Atlanta-based e-business incubator, "You can always get more money, but you can never get more time."[14] Although you cannot increase time, it can be better and more effectively utilized. Today, when the efficient use of time often determines success, we must examine how organizations are run, rethink management practices, and challenge the way we allocate time.

In research conducted for the book *Strategic Speed*, they "asked respondents to rank order the efficiency of their company in terms of six phases of strategic action: identifying an issue or opportunity, deciding to take action, creating a plan, executing the plan, assessing the result, and taking corrective action. Regardless of how fast or slow each company was, each rated its efficiency as greater in the upfront steps of identifying opportunities, planning, and decision making; and weaker in executing the plan, assessing results, and making corrections."[15] Obviously, organizational effectiveness is key.

ORGANIZATIONAL EFFECTIVENESS

Large companies need to be protected all right—from themselves. . . . Large companies have proven willing to cut bodies to reduce expenses, but are more recalcitrant to replacing bureaucracy with entrepreneurship. . . . Thus in the now-classic words of the cartoon character Pogo, "We have met the enemy, and he is us." Or, more accurately, the enemy is complacency supported by bureaucracy— the proliferation of unnecessary rules, cumbersome procedures, and non-value-adding administrators that strangle potential innovators with red tape. . . . Bureaucracy was designed for repetition, not innovation; for control, not creativity.

—Rosabeth Moss Kanter, *Harvard Business Review*[16]

In late 2007, The Boston Consulting Group (BCG) conducted a survey of 2,557 executives in which respondents identified weaknesses in their innovation capabilities. "Foremost among them was speed—the time it takes to move from idea generation to initial sales. Fully 52 percent of respondents said that their company was below average or poor at moving quickly enough."[17]

No one would argue that organizations need administrative and policy-making guidance—the original intent of bureaucracy. The problem is that bureaucracies tend to grow, expanding layer upon layer, becoming, as they increase in size, roadblocks to success. Bloated bureaucracies stifle creativity, suppress ingenuity, slow down responsiveness, and crush aspirations. They put paperwork before people and create a thirst for power, leading to personal ambition over team gains. This occurs because bureaucracies respond to power, to those who are bigger, tougher, and stronger. It happens because in bureaucracies, individual employees or individual customers do not matter—their voices are never heard by the people determining policy. In bureaucracies, committees are established for everything, constructing barriers to responsiveness along the way.

Examples of bureaucratic excess are easy to find. General Electric, in a past *Annual Report*, admits that "unfortunately, it is still possible to find documents around GE businesses that look like something out of the National Archives, with five, ten, or even more signatures necessary before action can be taken." The report goes on to explain that the problem with so many layers of approval is that "layers insulate. They slow things down. They garble. Leaders in highly layered organizations are like people who wear several sweaters outside on a freezing winter day. They remain warm and comfortable but are blissfully ignorant of the realities of their environment. They couldn't be further from what's going on."[18]

In organizations that are heavily bureaucratic, procedures are designed to meet internal requirements rather than the needs of the customer; politics—who said what to whom, who is gaining power, and who gets the credit, who the blame—overshadows everything, from clients' needs, to inroads made by the competition, to overall organizational performance. When promotions are earned through political savvy rather than performance, people choose the political solution rather than the best answer; the "show" becomes more important than content; and rumor becomes the primary form of communication. The result is an organization that focuses inward, losing touch with reality.

The truth is that companies cannot compete in a fast-paced world with shackles around their ankles.

BUREAUCRACIES ARE NOT BIODEGRADABLE

According to John Mackey, CEO of Whole Foods Market, "We don't fit the stereotypes. There's plenty of managerial edge in this company—the culture creates it. Whole Foods is a social system. It's not a hierarchy. We don't have lots of rules handed down from headquarters in Austin. We have lots of self-examination. . . . Peer pressure substitutes for bureaucracy. [It] enlists loyalty in ways that bureaucracy doesn't."[19]

The worst aspect of bureaucracies, however, is that they are tenacious; they never seem to go away. In fact, once bureaucracy takes root, it is as difficult to control in business as crabgrass on a suburban lawn. But in today's world, where speed and efficiency make the difference between success and failure, we must replace bureaucratic obstacles with innovation, speed, simplicity, and continuous improvement. Operational units must opt for remaining small. People must get out of their offices and in front of customers. Ad hoc task forces, composed of multifunctional groups, must be set up to tackle issues; ideas must be selected on merit rather than on an individual's place in the pecking order; and activities that do not add value to the client must be eliminated.

Since no bureaucracy will dismantle itself, it is up to management to change the organization. As Michael Dealey once said in *Fortune* magazine:

> The great pyramids of ancient Egypt have withstood the test of time; historic reminders of an era long gone by, they have remained steadfast against the elements down through the ages. Unfortunately, the same cannot be said for a different, more modern pyramid—the traditional structure of the 20th-century multinational corporation. . . .
>
> [It may be time for corporate structures] to look less like a pyramid and more like a spider. This spider has a multitude of legs that are often in motion—sometimes very fast motion. Think of these legs as the corporation's direct contacts with the environment, quickly sensing conditions and adjusting course to stay on track. These "legs" receive, interpret, and deliver information based on their direct interaction with environmental elements, whether they be customers, suppliers, or regulators. The power and strength of the spider lies in its ability to use these interactions not merely to maintain its present equilibrium, but also to influence and clear its path for future success. While many legs may appear to be going in several directions at once, they are all guided by a central nervous system—top management.[20]

Becoming more spiderlike will not be easy for most corporations. The bureaucratic culture is deeply ingrained, a model that permeates government and business and thus is a part of all our mind-sets. To overcome this way of thinking, it will be necessary to pinpoint particular elements of bureaucratic behavior and find ways to eliminate them.

REMOVING RED TAPE

Agile companies have what athletes and soldiers call 'situational awareness.' They put themselves both in a position to observe what's happening and have the wherewithal to act upon intelligence.

—Faisal Hoque, *Baseline*[21]

When people spend all their time on paperwork and reports, reviewing work with superiors, copying everybody on everything, or getting multiple approvals before action can be taken, important activities that make the organization more competitive are put on the back burner. As a result, the organization's ability to respond quickly suffers. General Electric's *Annual Report* also said that the company wants "to liberate employees from the cramping artifacts that pile up in the dusty attics of century-old companies: The reports, meetings, rituals, approvals, controls, and forests of paper that often seem necessary until they are removed."[22] Achieving success requires eliminating the "red tape" that stifles an organization.

Since there is general agreement that red tape makes organizations less competitive, why isn't it eliminated? A major reason is a lack of trust in the capabilities of others. Some people believe they are more competent than their coworkers, or have better business judgment than their colleagues. Others believe that being directly involved in decision making increases their power and personal visibility. Thus, part of the solution for overcoming red tape is to identify, hire, and invest in a high-quality workforce and then enhance their skills through training. This will make everyone more comfortable with the competency levels of their colleagues and less determined to oversee every aspect of their work. Employees must also work toward a common purpose and be rewarded for team gain.

Moreover, hiring the best and brightest people and then developing and retaining them results in stronger personal confidence and increased company loyalty. Employees feel better about their abilities and know that the organization believes in and supports them. When employees feel confident, they are more comfortable making bold moves and rarely second-guess their decisions. Ross Perot once said, "At GM, if you see a snake, the first thing you do is go hire a consultant on snakes. Then you get a committee on snakes, and then you discuss it for a couple of years. The most likely course of action is—nothing. You figure, the snake hasn't bitten anybody yet, so you let him crawl around the factory floor. . . . I come from an environment where, the first guy who sees the snake kills it."[23]

RULES AND PROCEDURES THAT CREATE FREEDOM

Many people find routines irritating because they stifle creativity and create inflexibility, but they can also be time-saving devices that minimize mistakes. For example, doctors use diagnostic routines for their patients, and airline pilots go through checklists prior to takeoff. Edward de Bono explains in *Six Action Shoes* that "in some ways routines provide freedom. If we had to think about every action we take, then life would be very slow and very complicated. Following a routine actually frees us to attend to matters that really need our attention. . . . Instead of having to analyze each new experience, we simply recognize the situation by using a perceptual pattern."[24] In other words, routines save us time by allowing us to do by rote those things that simply have to be done.

Problems arise, however, when procedures and policies fail to provide value. Often, procedures once designed to expedite special tasks become ingrained in the company's operations, remaining in place long after they are needed. *The Wall Street Journal* reported, for example, that IBM cut 34 items from the information required to justify an engineering change. The story went on to report that when the engineers investigated who had needed the information, they "couldn't even find anyone who knew. . . . That's the crazy thing. Nobody even remembered."[25]

There is a tendency to ignore programs or procedures that were effective yesterday but that may no longer apply today. In fact, we continually add new procedures but seldom eliminate old ones. The reason we do this is simple: People are rewarded for new programs, not for eliminating old ones, even when they are no longer required or have become burdensome.

STREAMLINING THE BUSINESS PROCESS

Things don't move faster simply because you demand them to be done faster. Organizations can achieve order-of-magnitude improvements by setting overly ambitious goals that force people to identify the most effective way to get the job done. One way to streamline an organization is to identify and simplify the way work is performed. One practice shown to improve efficiency involves teams that work across functional areas. The problem, today, is that "most companies organize themselves into vertically functioning groups, with experts of similar backgrounds grouped together to provide a pool of knowledge and skills capable of completing any task in that discipline. This creates an effective, strong, confident organization that functions well as a team, eager to support its own mission. Unfortunately, however, . . . a horizontal work flow combined with a vertical organization results in many voids and overlaps and encourages suboptimization, negatively impacting the efficiency and effectiveness of the process."[26]

Organizing along vertical lines reduces speed. When ideas become compartmentalized, information gets hoarded, optimum solutions elude us, and companies waste valuable time. This is made evident by contrasting an individual running a 100-yard race as an individual and as part of a relay team. The members of great relay teams are concerned not only with individual performance but also with properly transferring the baton to team members. In fact, it is possible for a team to have the four fastest runners in the event yet lose the race due to poor baton transfers. Therefore, everyone has to shift their thinking from personal performance to optimizing team performance.

Unfortunately, studies have shown that "95% of the time it takes to produce a product adds no value."[27] The road to organizational efficiency requires exposing and then eliminating the nonessential activities that delay or interrupt processes. There are six ways to improve a business process: The first method is to eliminate the task altogether. The second is work simplification, the elimination of all the nonproductive elements of a task. The third is to combine tasks. The fourth is to change the sequence to improve speed. The fifth is to simplify the activity, and the sixth and last is to do things simultaneously. Activities such as gathering information, transporting a product, inspecting it, correcting mistakes, and storing it until new instructions are received do not add value.

POLITICS DON'T PROMOTE SPEED

How much time and effort is wasted due to internal politics? How much time is frittered away grandstanding during meetings? How many e-mails do people write to cover their behinds? How much time is wasted trying to look busy? Someone once said to me, "I don't mind the volume of work, in fact, I thrive on it. But the politics are draining and debilitating." How much time is spent justifying yesterday's actions rather than making today's decisions? How much time is wasted trying to look good for the boss? How much time is wasted justifying the value that you provide? How much time would be saved if you focused solely on bettering the organization? If you want to reduce politics, you must instill a common sense of purpose focused on adding customer value; a working environment of openness, of trust, and honesty; a climate in which playing politics is a losing game.

TERRITORIAL BARRICADES AND INDEPENDENT FIEFDOMS

Organizations also suffer from inefficiencies caused by segregating people by artificial classes such as functional or operational groups. When organizations create independent groups or silos that separate one group from the rest of the organization, it often leads to inefficiency. Sometimes it results in misunderstandings or lack of communication. Other times it results in destructive competition—knowingly sabotaging the organization to make one's own group look better. For example, one department, during a slow period, won't volunteer support to another that is swamped because their department heads are in competition for resources.

Organizations also suffer when annual departmental budgets are based on previous expenditures rather than on future needs. When organizations operate this way, departments are encouraged to spend money frivolously at year's end rather than supporting another part of the organization that desperately needs the money.

WORKING AT CROSS-PURPOSES

Another source of waste in organizations occurs when parts of the organization work at cross-purposes with one another, each pursuing independent goals irrespective of how they impact others. For example, the research and development group insists on more testing time before a new-product launch while the marketing department argues for an immediate launch. Marketing believes the delay will cost them the first-to-market advantage, while the R&D group is anxious to ensure a 100 percent fault-free product. To make matters worse, compensation and performance evaluations encourage this behavior.

RESISTING CHANGE

One of the biggest time wasters is resistance to change. When management creates strategic plans in isolation or with external consultants, ignoring the employees who will be responsible for implementation of the plans, it becomes more difficult and costly to introduce change. The critical need to manage change, to ensure employee acceptance and commitment is discussed in Chapter 6, which sets forth a detailed new philosophy for change.

SIMPLE MEANS SWIFT

Measuring ideas by their complexity rather than their merit is inefficient and wastes time and money. And yet, all too often, for example, the more convoluted reports are, the more profound they are considered to be. They are often measured by their bulk rather than by the soundness of their recommendations. *The Wall Street Journal* reported the story of "Bob Aguire, owner of Eastern Reproduction Corp. of Waltham, Mass., [who] handed some paperwork in a sealed envelope to a state environmental regulator. 'He hefted it and without opening it, handed it back. . . . He said it wasn't heavy enough.' "[28] Among other forms of needless complexity are convoluted and inefficient communications. Organizations should encourage people to first consider the needs of their audience and then communicate clearly, avoiding acronyms, jargon, and buzzwords.

The virtue of clear and simple communication is evident in the complexity of the following documents:[29]

The Lord's Prayer	57 words
Ten Commandments	71 words
Gettysburg Address	266 words
Declaration of Independence	1,300 words
U.S. Government Contractor Management System Evaluation Program	38,000 words

THE TECHNOLOGY INVESTMENT

Speed can be gained through technology. Many companies spend millions of dollars on hardware and software to increase the productivity of their employees. Far too few organizations, however, make full use of their technology investment. Unfortunately, many fail to introduce it into the organization properly, while their employees are not trained to maximize its use. Companies that acquire the right technology and introduce it in the right manner achieve an order-of-magnitude savings in time and increased productivity.

PLANNING WITH A PURPOSE

Proper planning must be deeply ingrained in organizations that want to become world-class competitors. Unfortunately, even when companies believe in the importance of planning, they fall into many traps that cost them valuable time along the way. For example, some organizations have analysis paralysis: They spend their time setting up task forces and committees to analyze problems, but then never act on the recommendations. Take the example of a company that hired a consultant to conduct new-product research. When the company was asked by the consultant, "How will you respond if the research points in this direction?" they said they did not know. They were then asked how they would respond if the research pointed in the opposite direction, and the answer was the same. The consultant then said that they were wasting their money conducting research without committing to act on the recommendations: Research is not an end in itself, but a means to an end that can only be achieved through action.

Other problems include falling into the trap of saying, "We must ACT NOW! Forget planning." Many companies that claim they don't have the time to plan always find the time to do things over again when their initial actions fail. Other companies are afraid to take a firm stand on an issue and instead set vague goals that can be interpreted many different ways; then they wonder why their employees are working at cross-purposes with each other. Furthermore, there are companies that are unfocused and don't know how to say no. They try to accomplish everything, diluting their resources— and never end up accomplishing anything.

Organizations that are successful in their planning efforts have common attributes. They ensure that the people responsible for implementing the plan are highly involved in the planning process. They develop cross-functional teams to ensure that input is received from employees with different perspectives and experiences. They prioritize activities even when resources are abundant, and they concentrate their critical resources in those areas that provide the greatest returns.

EXTERNAL RELATIONSHIPS ARE CRITICAL

World-class organizations know that, in today's fast-paced environment, spreading your resources too thin places you at a competitive disadvantage. Companies should focus attention on the areas most critical to their business success and tap external resources to supplement their efforts. To do this successfully requires, as is discussed in Chapter 8, building win-win relationships with external organizations. Today, there is no room for lawsuits and petty squabbles, formalities and long, drawn-out negotiations that all lead to mistrust.

MANAGEMENT STYLE— GETTING THE MOST OUT OF OTHERS

According to Warren Bennis, "[Jack] Welch liked to say that despite all the hype, he really only did three things at GE—and all of them were resource related. He picked the right people, allocated the right resources to departments and moved ideas 'at the speed of light.' "[30]

Organizational waste and inefficiency come in many shapes and sizes, some visible and some invisible. Managers should identify new ways to overcome the cultural behaviors that prevent progress, and help employees to function as efficiently as possible. Good managers are like good farmers: They invest in the future by planting seeds and then nurture and cultivate them, knowing that they will soon reap a harvest. And just as great coaches know the best way to optimize player performance, management must learn to build on the strengths of their employees.

In many organizations, unfortunately, management does not operate efficiently. For example, some managers make their motto, "Ready, Fire, Aim"; they act before they think. They waste valuable time running around in circles, putting out fires instead of lighting the fires of innovation. Other managers believe that being busy is a measure of progress. The truth is, there is a difference between motion and movement. Motion is when everyone moves from point A to point B, accomplishing their goals; movement is when everyone runs around, chasing their tails, never getting anything accomplished. Those who manage this way need to learn the difference between their priorities and the hundreds of "urgent" requests that cross their desk every day.

LEARNING TO COMMUNICATE

Poor communication, which creates inefficiency in organizations, is discussed thoroughly in Chapter 4. Managers waste valuable time by not viewing communication as a priority, by not discussing their priorities, by failing to listen to their people's needs or to answer their questions fully, or by sharing information with their employees only on an as-needed basis. This causes people to feel isolated, duplicate efforts, and work at cross-purposes with others. Employees, afraid of going in the wrong direction, move cautiously instead of charging ahead.

Managers should emphasize the importance of time and of how much delays cost the company. They should foster an environment of open and honest communication, where feedback is welcomed. After all, constructive feedback leads to continuous improvement and strengthens employee confidence.

MANAGING INFORMATION

According to studies, "searching for, and handling, information occupies up to 20 percent of your time"; therefore, it is critical that you think carefully about the kinds of information the organization really needs.[31] Moreover, according to another study, "the amount of paperwork that travels across a desk has increased by as much as 600 percent. . . . The average person wastes 45 minutes a day searching for some item on his desk."[32]

The problem with paperwork is that it often keeps employees from accomplishing important activities for customers. Of course, some paperwork is necessary. The question is, which reports are really required? By whom? For what purpose? Is the information ever acted on? How often should the information be collected? Which reports should be eliminated altogether? Managers who examine reporting requirements with those questions in mind will probably find that much of it is unnecessary.

LEARNING TO MAKE DECISIONS

Some decisions require the careful evaluation of alternatives, while other decisions can be made quickly. If you can learn to identify on-the-spot issues and act on them, you can save a great deal of time. An article in *The Journal of Management* notes that researchers have found "that decisions

[are] made faster when their consequences [are] more important." The same article notes that "contrary to intuition, decision makers [take] longer to make a decision with a problem when several alternatives [are] easily rejected, leaving just two, than when all four alternatives [are] of equal quality."[33]

MEETINGS—THE NATIONAL PASTIME

Meetings raise many of the same issues. According to an article in *Business Week*, "the average senior executive spends four hours a day in meetings."[34] It is important to determine which of them are necessary. You may find that many "meetings" can be conducted on conference calls or else require no more than a brief discussion in the hallway.

Managers should ask themselves how much time is wasted when meetings are called at the last minute, requiring everyone to drop what they are doing or reschedule planned events. How much time is wasted when meetings are called without having an agenda beforehand, when meetings drift into irrelevant discussions, or when meetings are allowed to drag on endlessly? Managers should ask why people are allowed to waste others' time by showing up late, why people are allowed to grandstand or railroad their ideas through, or why people stand around chatting when the meeting is over instead of attending to business.

Another way that meetings waste time is by the amount of preparation that goes into them. In some organizational cultures, there is more emphasis on the "show" than on the content. When that happens, tremendous time is spent preparing materials, rehearsing, and revising presentations for an internal audience. For example, *The Wall Street Journal* reported years ago that "Richard Flaherty, manager of the supplies operation, says he used to make 'thousands of foils [slides] at IBM to get 20 that the VP would show at the corporate strategy session. The preparation would start in November, the big presentation would be in March, and it'd be obsolete by April 1.'"[35] Contrast those time-wasted efforts with today's need to squeeze more efficiency into every activity:

> How do people cope in this do-more-faster age? One reaction is to break tasks down into discrete chunks. What was once a one-hour meeting becomes a series of brief conversations in a hallway or in a parking lot. Likewise, tasks that used to get done in relatively uninterrupted large blocks of time become distributed throughout

the day, several days, or even weeks. "It's a strategy of breaking everything down into manageable pieces that you work on whenever you have time," Darrah [Chuck Darrah, an anthropologist and researcher at San Jose State University] explains. "People seize any opportunity to take care of business, because they don't want to let a minute go by unused."[36]

DEALING WITH FEAR AND INSECURITY

Employees cannot do their best work when they are worried about their future, are discouraged from thinking for themselves, aren't respected for their recommendations, don't feel in control of their destinies, or are treated like children. People can't do their best work when they feel that every decision will be scrutinized and second-guessed, and every mistake will be ridiculed. This lack of confidence causes employees to waste more time trying to impress people internally than they spend getting their job done; to play Monday-morning quarterback and second-guess each other rather than making innovative suggestions.

Confidence and security increase employee efficiency and effectiveness. Fear and insecurity have the opposite effect: They cause employees to take on more and more work, trying to look busy so they won't get fired (and then they do it poorly because they don't have enough time to do it all well—if at all). When this happens, employees spend their time on things they know well, not because these things are priorities but because they feel secure doing them. This leads employees to ignore problems, waiting for them to go away rather than fixing them, and then to look for someone else to blame when the problems eventually surface.

This downward spiral can be overcome only when people believe in themselves and their organizations. The result can best be illustrated in a story about a Japanese company. The first department head looked within his group to see whether his employees were at fault. He was happy to find out they did not play a role. The second department head also looked within his department and found out that his employees were at fault. He was happy too because he was able to identify the cause; the problem could be fixed and the company's customers would never be inconvenienced again.

LEARNING TO DELEGATE

Trying to do everything yourself is not good management, it is an addiction. Walter Kiechel III noted in *Fortune* that "if everybody is clamoring for your time, that time is a precious commodity, and by scheduling yourself into too many things, you show everybody how important you are."[37] To overcome the tendency to "do it all," managers must keep in mind that the cost of hiring talented people and then looking over their shoulders is the destruction of the confidence and creativity that these employees were hired for in the first place. Micromanagement—requests for daily itineraries, endless memos, detailed timesheet reports, and insisting that five approvals be obtained before action is taken—creates an environment of mistrust. Some managers fear that they will not be recognized and rewarded if they aren't personally involved in every activity, if the function isn't housed within their department, or if the activity is not conducted within their sights. Those who don't delegate decisions spend their time doing work for others while their own work piles up on their desk. They think they are making themselves invaluable when in actuality they become bottlenecks wasting precious time for the organization.

Good managers increase their efficiency by learning how to trust. They realize that they cannot be everywhere at the same time or be the best at everything. They learn how to delegate to their colleagues and develop strategic alliances with outside organizations.

ACQUIRING THE ART OF DECISION MAKING

Learning to empower your employees can save valuable time for your organization. For example, think about the time wasted by cumbersome review processes. Individuals with new ideas first have to build a case for their recommendation, preparing a written proposal or presentation for management to review. Then, they must set up a meeting, often involving multiple individuals whose travel schedules have to be coordinated, which may take days or weeks. (Of course, before the meeting takes place we have to define if there are any internal politics or personal preferences, and anticipate potential objections.) And then the meeting takes place. When all is said and done, the decision ends up being made in 20 minutes by people vaguely familiar with the situation. The person making the recommendation was obviously closer to the situation, spent weeks or months thinking it through, put tremendous effort into selling it internally, and could have acted on the recommendation by the time the idea was even placed on anybody's calendar.

The problem is that many managers don't believe people should think for themselves. Robert Waterman, Jr., makes just that point in *The Renewal Factor* when he tells the story of "a General Motors executive [who] says that H. Ross Perot saw something that needed doing inside GM and told a GM manager to do it. The man replied that it was not part of his job description. 'You need a job description,' fumed Perot, 'I'll give you a job description: Use your head.' The bemused GM executive said, 'Can you imagine what chaos we'd have around here if everybody did that?' "[38]

PROVIDING TRAINING

Managers waste precious time by not making the proper commitment to and investment in training. Even when some people know they are overworked, they're often so busy that they don't have the time to train anyone to help relieve the load; this leads to a vicious cycle. Or management is apprehensive about taking their best salespeople out of the field for additional training because their absence would lead to a short-term decline in sales; then they end up promoting someone to sales manager, knowing that this individual never received sales management training. Or management sends employees through training programs, never reinforces the training on the job, and is later disappointed when the employees can't perform the new job well.

CONTROLLING EXPECTATION LEVELS

When managers make impossible demands on others, they get less than satisfactory results. For example, I know a manager who asks his employees to take the red eye from Los Angeles to New York, arriving at six o'clock in the morning, and then wants them to come to work directly from the airport. When employees haven't gotten more than a couple hours of sleep, how productive can we expect them to be the next day? Just because someone puts in the time doesn't make that person productive.

On the other hand, managers who set low expectation levels get what they ask for. At the same time, correcting employee mistakes without explaining how it should have been done or allowing employees to shirk their responsibilities all lead to mediocrity.

DEALING WITH PRESSURE

Managers should learn how to manage stress and be in a position to help colleagues cope with their daily job pressures. Managers who lose control by ranting and raving don't accomplish the same results as a rational discussion; worse, this behavior creates an atmosphere in which employees spend countless hours measuring their actions to avoid explosions. Furthermore, working "under the gun" doesn't always increase productivity. *The Journal of Management* reported that experts studying "the productivity of NASA scientists and engineers . . . found that productivity increased as time pressure increased (deadlines shortened)—up to a point. After deadlines became too short, performance declined. . . . Thus, they suggest that the overall relationship between deadline length and performance may be an inverted U-shaped one. Performance increases as deadlines shorten, but beyond some limited increased reductions in deadline length, pressure reduces rather than increases performance."[39]

PERSONAL TIME MANAGEMENT

> *The average American will, in a lifetime, spend five years waiting in line, one year searching for belongings at home or office, three years attending meetings, and eight years opening junk mail.*
>
> —Michael Fortino[40]

Time is short! Where did the time go? The time just seemed to slip away. If I only had more time! We all have heard these statements bemoaning the fact that there isn't enough time to accomplish what we want to do. The truth of the matter isn't that there's not enough time, but rather that the time needed was spent doing something else.

Unless we learn to treat time as personal capital, and invest it wisely, we will never have enough of it—and never achieve the rewards we seek. Given the demands and the time pressures that we face daily, if we want to accomplish our goals, we have to manage time more effectively (for example, become more organized, stop procrastinating, and make decisions quickly). The problem for many of us is that time management requires discipline as well as changing lifelong habits to be successful.

PLACING A VALUE ON TIME

The first step in mastering time management is recognizing that time has value. Adia Personnel Services, based in Menlo Park, California, discovered that employees spend the equivalent of a three-week vacation chatting by the water cooler. In a nationwide survey of 1,104 personnel decision makers, they found that the average employee probably spends 30 minutes or more each day "shooting the breeze" with their coworkers.[41] If employees invested their time wisely, they wouldn't have to stay late to finish their work.

OVERCOMING BAD HABITS

Time management isn't only about saving time, it's also about changing personal habits. Success depends on discipline. For example, how many people go on quick-fix diets only to gain the weight back; they have no desire to change their lifestyle. Another bad habit that wastes time and energy is worrying about things that you can't control. If you can do something to make the situation better, do it. If you can't, worrying won't make it better. Furthermore, people waste a lot of time complaining to others. These behaviors not only waste time, but sap energy. Unlearn bad habits. Look for ways to use your time more effectively. For example, a quick e-mail can replace a detailed memo, walking to the next floor to ask a question, or the frustration of playing phone tag. Go out to lunch 5 or 10 minutes before or after the lunch rush and avoid lines. Reconfirm appointments beforehand rather than arriving only to find out that your appointment had to leave town at the last minute.

LEARNING TO PRIORITIZE

As Peter Drucker said, "It is more important to do the right things than to do things right." Some people keep busy on low priority items. For example, they bounce from city to city, attending meetings even though face time isn't required, or they maintain very elaborate to-do lists, but don't prioritize the items on the list. Instead, each item is addressed in order.

The problem with this behavior is that being busy isn't a measure of success. In contrast, proactive people tackle one thing at a time, focusing on what is important but not necessarily urgent. They avoid getting caught up in busywork or buried in minutiae. In order to ensure that you "do the right things and do them right," set milestones for yourself, measure your progress against your company's long-term goals, and establish and re-establish priorities.

AVOIDING PROCRASTINATION

When you procrastinate, you spend more time focusing on why work will be hard rather than on starting it; you spend more time complaining about the work rather than completing it; and you find it easier to explain why the job isn't done rather than doing it. In the *Baylor Business Review*, Joe Cox and Raymond Read catalog the reasons why people procrastinate. Included in their list are such items as:

> *Fear of failure or rejection*: Procrastination allows persons to avoid risk while still protecting their self-worth . . . by never attempting a task, I cannot fail. . . . *Low self-concept or image*: Many people see their worth only in the ability to perform well. By procrastinating, no effort to perform has been extended; thus there is no danger to self-worth. . . . *Peter Pan Syndrome*: A childlike world without responsibilities or the necessity of doing unpleasant tasks. . . . Hoping someone else will do it . . . *Wishing for things to happen*: . . . If you put it off long enough, it no longer has to be done. . . . *Perfectionism*: This is the unrealistic attitude that if a person cannot complete a task perfectly, there is no reason to start the task. . . . *Inability to say no*: With an overbooked agenda, something must wind up on the back burner. . . . *Adrenaline addiction*: Some people like the rush of last-minute deadlines. . . . *Fear of success*: Some procrastinate because they fear successes. If they succeed, they must continue to accomplish. And, since the pressure to accomplish and beat the previous record is constant, it is thought that success should be avoided. *Lack of skill*: Not having the appropriate expertise or learned skills to effectively handle one's job. . . . *Decision making*: The difficulty some people encounter when trying to make tough decisions causes them to simply avoid making those decisions. . . .

> *Too little to do*: A person learns to accept boredom and inactivity as a lifestyle. . . . *Authority resistance*: Procrastination can be a way of expressing hostility or anger at a superior or an organization.[42]

Almost everyone puts off doing something at some time in life. The problem is when procrastination becomes a way of life. To succeed, you must find ways to break the pattern, choosing specific goals and target dates to meet. If you break big activities into small steps, tasks become less overwhelming and you will gain the confidence to complete them today.

BECOMING ORGANIZED

One of the reasons people accomplish less than expected is because they are disorganized. They run from crisis to crisis, without thinking, and can't find things when they need them most. An article in *Today's Office* reported that "managers and clerical staffs often spend 25–40% of their time searching for information that is misfiled or missing."[43]

Unfortunately, challenging people to get more organized runs up against a bias—organization implies rigid behavior that precludes creativity and innovation. The fact is, being organized buys time for thinking and creating.

CONTROLLING INFORMATION

When was the last time that you cleaned up your e-mail files, computer desktop, hard drive, or desk files? It seems as though people would rather do anything than deal with old things they have accumulated. The problem is, if you never weed out your files, clean up your bookmarks, cancel publications you don't read, ask that your name be taken off mailing lists, you'll always waste time searching for things that you need.

TAKING TIME TO PLAN

Planning for the future saves time. It allows you to consolidate activities, thereby saving time, money, and annoyance. Instead of making several trips to buy office supplies, let everyone know that you make one trip, on the 15th of every month. Or, save the trip and buy online. Instead of stopping at a convenience store every night because you've run out of something, make one stop. Instead of buying clothing and returning most of the items the next day, save the extra trip by making the final decision at the time of purchase. Failing to plan will leave you with no time or energy to tackle your priority items or those things you enjoy most in life.

AVOIDING DISTRACTIONS

"Do you have a minute? I have a great idea." "I have to turn this project in in half an hour. Can you take a look at it for me?" "So, what did you think of the ballgame last night?" "I'll call when I have a really strong investment recommendation, OK?" These are some of the distractions that people face every day.

Remember, you have a choice. You can permit salespeople to walk in unannounced; you can read every e-mail joke; you can let others control your time by dropping everything when they call; you can be distracted by those who don't value their time and try to steal yours; or you can focus on priorities that help you accomplish your goals.

UTILIZING SMALL BLOCKS OF TIME

Just as it is important to manage large blocks of time, it is also important to invest in small increments of time—they add up. How many times have you been kept waiting 10 minutes for a meeting, 15 minutes for the dentist, 20 minutes for a luncheon companion, 30 minutes because a flight is delayed, or 45 minutes commuting on a train? If you added up all these small increments, you'd realize how much time you waste.

Make a conscious effort to invest your minutes wisely. For example, carry reading material, keep a notebook with you to outline that speech you were asked to give, bring along stationery so you can write thank-you notes to family and friends. If you use the time that most people seem to waste, you'll accomplish more—and spend less time and energy fuming over inconveniences that often cannot be avoided.

EMPLOYING TECHNOLOGY TIME-SAVERS

Learn how technology can help you become more productive. Then use it. Never answer e-mail or the phone when you're in the middle of an activity; make hands-free calls from the car when you're caught in traffic; identify software apps that will increase your productivity; use e-mail rather than playing phone tag.

CONCLUSION

> *You know, people are constantly looking at their watches, but they don't really see them. [They are] too busy regretting the past or worrying about the future. So they miss the beauty of little things and, before they know it, the seasons have changed, the children have grown up, and life is almost over. Then they blame me [father time]. "Time went too fast," they say. But I'm here now.*
>
> —Paul Hellman, *Management Review*[44]

Don't think of time only in terms of developing your career and being efficient in business. It also affects your personal life, allowing you to enhance family relationships, improve yourself, become fit, pursue hobbies and cultural activities, find your spiritual side, and give back to the community. Rather than living your life on a treadmill, take the time to smell the roses.

In *Fortune* magazine, Walter Kiechel III says that

> what the workaholic has forgotten, and the would-be manager of time should always keep in mind is what one might be doing outside the office. Possibilities include walking out in the weather of sunlit days and storm: watching the seasons change; seeing children grow and maybe even helping the process along; talking in candlelight, perhaps over a meal . . . and being there to solace a troubled friend, or child, or aging parent. If you consistently choose work over these alternatives, then you really have a problem managing time.[45]

8

PARTNERING . . . ENTERING THE AGE OF COOPERATION

BUILDING A FLEXIBLE ORGANIZATION

In a linear world, things may exist independently of each other, and when they interact, they do so in simple, predictable ways. In a nonlinear, dynamic world, everything exists only in relationship to everything else, and the interactions among agents in the system lead to complex, unpredictable outcomes. In this world, interactions, or relationships, among its agents are the organizing principle. Complexity science in the business realm therefore focuses on relationships: relationships between individuals and among teams; relationships to other companies in their business environment, or economic web; and, ultimately, relationship to the natural environment.

—Roger Lewin, *Business Spirit Journal Online*[1]

In today's competitive environment, companies are complementing their core capabilities with external resources. This allows them to concentrate their limited resources in their core areas; it enables a company to access specialized skills that their existing employees don't possess; it affords flexibility during peak periods; and it provides a company with an objective perspective from external providers. These arrangements take many forms, ranging from complete outsourcing, to partnering, to retaining consultants, to third-party contractors, to freelance personnel. "Today more than 20 percent of the revenue generated from the top 2,000 U.S. and European companies comes from alliances, according to a Booz Allen Hamilton study. HP/Cannon, Intel/Microsoft, Yahoo!/SBC, PepsiCo/Starbucks, Sony/Ericsson and Cisco/IBM are some well-known successful alliances."[2]

In order to optimize any relationship, it's important to learn how to forge strong bonds and build lasting relationships with your partners. The key to success is knowing that formal contracts don't make successful relationships, people do. It requires a willingness to create a foundation on which trust, loyalty, and commitment can be built.

According to Stephen Covey, a win/win mind-set encourages people to see life as a "co-operative as opposed to a competitive arena."[3] Remember, every relationship is unique and must be treated as special. There isn't a single set of rules to achieve success, but there are certain behaviors that should be avoided. For example, partnerships cannot succeed if a partner is kept in the dark and is unaware of key events. Partnerships also cannot succeed when one partner attempts to gain the upper hand or has selfish motives. Furthermore, partnerships cannot succeed if they involve scape-goating; everyone should have a vested interest in the venture's success.

The basic rule, whether you invest in a business, develop a licensing agreement, outsource a capability, or bring in freelance support, is that you get what you put into the relationship. A partnership is successful to the degree that it replaces the traditional "us versus them" mentality with a new "us" that enables everyone to grow and to reach their full potential. "Long gone are the days when some people were hell bent on achieving success at the expense of others; there had to be a 'winner' and a 'loser.' This mind-set is based on 'shortage' mentality, which suggests that there is 'not enough to go around' for everyone."[4]

In the past, conventional wisdom said that multiple vendors increased competition and enhanced performance; that playing one supplier against another was good business. The goal was to win at all costs. "Most people feel good when they get concessions. They give them bragging rights. They're unmistakable proof of a successful hunt. They drag them back to their corporate den and celebrate them with the negotiating equivalent of an end-zone dance."[5] Today, however, the trend is quite the opposite. An article in *The Wall Street Journal* explains that

> companies around the country are cutting back the number of suppliers they use . . . by as much as 90%. They are demanding

higher levels of service and product quality from the survivors. And are willing to pay a premium on the theory that getting things right initially is cheaper in the long run. . . . A decade ago, corporate executives and consulting gurus noticed that Japanese companies often had just a few hundred direct suppliers while their U.S. counterparts often had thousands. And the Japanese tended to have much closer and longer-term relationships with their suppliers, often owning a piece of them.[6]

A good illustration of this management practice is demonstrated in the computer industry. "Dell cut the number of its core PC suppliers from several hundred to about 25. It standardized critical PC components, which streamlined its manufacturing. Dell got faster by making things simpler."[7]

Another article in *The Wall Street Journal* points out that "competition is one way to increase the efficiency of outside vendors, but many in-house lawyers are trimming the list of law firms that they use. Some general counsel say they get higher quality at lower cost by building relationships with fewer law firms."[8] Experience has demonstrated that the only way to build lasting relationships is to begin with honorable intentions, make a commitment, and invest the time and effort with a select few.

Jack Welch, former CEO of General Electric, said it best in a GE *Annual Report*:

Our dream . . . is a boundary-less Company, a Company where we knock down the walls that separate us from each other on the inside and from our key constituencies on the outside. . . . A boundary-less Company will level its external walls . . . reaching out to key suppliers to make them part of a single process in which they and we join hands and intellects in a common purpose—satisfying customers.[9]

Welch is not the only leader sensing the need for strong partnerships. An article in *Small Business Reports* notes that

It will not be sufficient to be big and multinational with the advantages in costs, finance, distribution, and service that large companies possess. Nor will it be enough to be small and entrepreneurial, with the advantages of innovation and rapid customer responsiveness. Our organizations, large and small, will have to increasingly "network" . . . to achieve success. What are the advantages of networking? "It's like having a fighter who can move like a lightweight and hit like a heavy-weight," claims an IBM director. Networking firms will be able to effectively bring both the economies of scale and customer responsiveness to the marketplace—like a battleship surrounded by PT boats, with both power and speed of attack.[10]

WHAT CAUSES RELATIONSHIPS TO FAIL?

According to a *Fast Company* article, "We don't often think about relationships in business. We too often think about transactions. About deals. About tasks and to do lists. Relationships are nurtured over time. Transactions happen in a moment. Good business thinks first about relationships. The relationship between the business and the community in which it exists. The relationship between owners, management, and staff. The relationship with customers and suppliers. The relationship between its actions and its impact on the environment. Relationships are nurtured over time. Transactions happen in a moment."[11]

One of the most successful business relationships of all time was between Warren Buffett and Katharine Graham of the *Washington Post*.

> The most enormously successful partnerships are those built from trust, respect, and mutual understanding. Billionaire investor Warren Buffett is renowned for his stock market prowess, as well as his strategy of betting on the long-term growth of successful companies like American Express and Berkshire Hathaway. Buffett's ingenious ability to understand the stock markets made him a cult figure, but it was also his patience that played a big part in his rise to the top. His unwavering faith in his companies allowed him to see beyond the short-term failures and to the triumph in the long-term. He is famous for the relationships he developed during the course of his life. His companionship and investment with Katharine Graham of the *Washington Post* is one of the most famous business alliances of all time. He met Graham in the 1970s as an investor in The Washington Post Company, her family's newspaper company, where she became the first female Fortune 500 CEO. The relationship became one of deep personal reverence. Graham considered him her closest friend and relied on him for personal as well as business advice. Buffett

made a fortune from his investment in the *Post*. Today, newspaper publishing, television broadcasting, cable television systems, and magazine publishing have been added to the Washington Post Company's numerous holdings. Buffet's investment company's initial $10 million investment in the media empire is now worth $205 million. Buffett still sits on the Board of Directors at the *Washington Post* and is also advisor to Graham's successor, her son, Donald E. Graham.[12]

Clearly, some relationships last. The difference between those lasting more than 40 years and those lasting only a few years sounds a little like the dichotomy between couples celebrating their golden anniversaries and the grim fact that one in two marriages ends in divorce.

How do you ensure that your relationship thrives? A great place to start is learning why some succeed and others fail.

Relationships fail for many reasons; some important ones are:

- *Lack of commitment.* Relationships fail because partners are not equally committed to the venture or to building a lasting relationship. The result is that one partner resents making a greater commitment and getting little back in return.

- *Cultural differences.* Relationships fail when partners, particularly organizations, are unable to adapt their work styles to complement the other's culture. For example, an entrepreneurial organization that thrives on flexibility may have trouble working with a large bureaucratic organization where several layers of approval are required before decisions are made.

- *Poor management.* Relationships fail because management does not value the relationship and make the personal investment required to grow it. Unless management is fully behind the relationship, it will not flourish.

- *Poor communication.* Relationships fail when organizations hinder the transfer of information. Unless there's a philosophy of open and honest communication, people spend their time looking over their shoulder rather than moving the venture forward. Furthermore, the rationale behind decisions may not be fully understood, causing errors, redundancies, and misunderstandings.

- *Failure of individual relationships.* Relationships also fail because the individuals responsible for maintaining them may lack either the interpersonal skills or the personal chemistry needed to nurture these relationships.

According to a McKinsey study, "About 55% of all strategic alliances are deemed successful, and 15% are considered mixed successes."[13] The issues that result in failure cannot be cured by applying Band-Aids; the underlying damage must be properly treated if the wounds are to heal with as little scarring as possible.

THE LEVEL OF COMMITMENT

When new business opportunities are pursued with a vengeance, people often make unrealistic promises and concessions that cannot be realistically delivered. Then, even though no one pushed the "winner" to make concessions, the winner may resent the relationship because it's one-sided. This is similar to buyer's remorse—after bidding too much at an auction, the bidder feels bad about getting caught up in the excitement of the moment.

To avoid these issues, strive for win-win relationships. One key question to ask yourself in evaluating the merits of a relationship is how much your business will be valued by the other organization—you don't want to be considered just a drop in the bucket. Ask yourself whether your partner will consider the venture a priority. This will enable you to judge the amount of time and attention that you can realistically expect your partner to devote to the relationship.

Partnerships get into trouble when one side fails to pay equal attention to the relationship. It is often ironic how hard people work during the courtship of a relationship only to let it fall apart after the deal is sealed. Remember, relationships are built through many small actions—managing expectations, watching your partner's back, being responsive to requests, keeping people in the loop, and being available when you're needed. To ensure that relationships thrive, partners should invest in their "marriage" on an ongoing basis.

If you don't nurture relationships every day, you'll miss the signs if your relationships slowly begin to deteriorate. For example, if a supplier's business is declining, that supplier may not be able to maintain the same level of service to you as in the past. Or due to success, one partner may outgrow the relationship; the value that the partners provide to each other becomes lopsided over time.

Commitment also suffers when one partner feels they aren't getting the attention they deserve. In this situation, renewed expressions of commitment can be helpful.

Customer conflicts are another way to destroy relationships. This occurs if you have relationships with several organizations that compete with one other—they resent the fact that you're working with their competitor.

It is also important to demonstrate commitment during tough times. For example, when an organization receives negative publicity, its partner may worry about being tarnished just by being associated with that organization. The truth is, a good partner will try to withstand the strain.

CULTURE

Another challenge that causes partnerships to fail can be attributed to cultural differences. For example, some relationships falter because their organizations don't share similar goals or a common vision. While one organization may be focused on short-term gains, the other is more interested in building a large, thriving enterprise Furthermore, if the organizations represent different stages in their life cycle, a well-established organization may have the assets to invest for the long term, while the fast-growing start-up may not have the cash flow or profitability to contribute in the same fashion.

The speed with which companies make decisions may also be a factor. For example, while the entrepreneurial partner's success can be attributable to being nimble and innovative, it may conflict with a large bureaucratic organization that smothers its innovative culture.

One General Electric venture, with Huntsman Chemical, was born over lunch and immediately spurred more projects between the firms. Glen Hiner, who was head of GE's plastics and materials business, believed that under the old GE culture, marked by a centralized management system, such an alliance would not have developed: "By the time the proposal had gotten through the process, someone else would have done the deal ahead of us."[14]

MANAGEMENT

An interview with Danny Ertel and Stuart Kliman, members of the Harvard Negotiation Project (HNP), lists skills crucial to managing strategic alliances. "It's not enough for two companies—or tribes—to pose together for the duration of a press conference. They need to forge a strategy for building mutual value. 'Both partners need to be successful,' he [Kliman] says. 'Otherwise, when times get tough, somebody's going to be tempted to make gains at the other side's expense.' "[15]

Management should not force its philosophy or management style onto an exciting new alliance; an alternative would be creating an entirely new organization to "house" the relationship. Another option to consider is appointing an individual—a champion—who'll be sensitive and responsive to the unique nature of the alliance and who'll have the responsibility and accountability for its success.

Another potential obstacle is raised when management neglects to secure buy-in across the organization: "We [headquarters] thought the deal was great, but we couldn't convince our offices to make it a priority." When headquarters is the catalyst for the relationship, success is dependent on building close working relationships at the local level.

Once relationships are established, partners should continue to make sure everyone benefits from the partnership's success. All too often, one partner asks the other to do the impossible, and then further asks them to reduce their bills because the extra costs incurred by their demands weren't budgeted.

Furthermore, partners must avoid haggling. Trust can be damaged when an agreed-upon fee structure is questioned every time one partner finds a lower price somewhere else. Management must be willing to alter company policy if it jeopardizes the relationship—for example, a small business unable to wait 45 days to get paid. Although the business may be afraid to request prompt payment for fear of jeopardizing the relationship, their partner's sensitivity to their needs will bring them closer and benefit both organizations.

EXPECTATIONS

Some alliances are a marriage made in heaven. "An alliance between Seattle-based Starbucks and Purchase, N.Y.-based Pepsico created the popular coffee-flavored drink, Frappacino. The relationship moved Starbucks into the bottled-beverage market while PepsiCo gained an innovative product with a well-branded partner. Each met their strategic and operational goals. A perfect match."[16]

In order to build a successful alliance, organizations should set realistic goals for an alliance from the outset. Partners often get so excited during the honeymoon period that they set expectations too high. Then as reality sets in, and they become challenged with implementation issues, they fall short of their commitments. Furthermore, partners often underestimate the time and effort needed to get to know each other. When unrealistic goals are established from the outset, both partners set themselves up for disappointment—giving naysayers in their organizations an easy opportunity to attack the relationship.

Some relationships fail because of the inability to establish priorities. They try to accomplish everything and end up completing nothing.

Rather than placing all your eggs into one basket, it is more sensible to light some small fires by starting only a few projects at a time. Along the same lines, balance activities so that some projects come to fruition on a short-term basis, while others deliver benefits over the long term. The small wins build confidence and maintain momentum. Many relationships fail over time because management loses interest or cuts off funds before the benefits of long-term projects can be realized.

Some relationships fail because one partner makes unrealistic demands of the other. If partners don't view themselves as equals, the end product may be compromised because "subservient" partners fail to express their true feelings about an issue or problems they see looming.

KNOWLEDGE

Another factor that damages relationships is the inability to learn enough about a partner's business environment to add value. For example, one member of a partnership may not be familiar with the other's industry, organization, or the culture in which that organization operates. Managers must continue to develop their people and remain up to date in their partner's field or risk damaging the relationship.

COMMUNICATION

Some organizations have layers of personnel who serve as filters of information. If you aren't given the information you need to fulfill your end of the partnership, you'll never be able to provide sufficient value to your partner. In turn, your partner will wonder why they spend an inordinate amount of time providing directions, and yet proper action is not taken. This may lead them to question your competence or listening skills. The fact is, getting information third hand, from someone who doesn't fully understand how it is going to be used, is not helpful. Strong and direct lines of communication between those responsible for maintaining the partnership need to be established.

In other cases, information is held back, either consciously (as a power grab) or unconsciously. It stands to reason that when two groups have different frames of reference, they are bound to make different assumptions and arrive at different conclusions.

Last, people are obligated to use discretion in a relationship. When one partner comes into contact with sensitive information, such as new product designs or strategic plans, it is their obligation to maintain confidentiality. Leaks can cause serious damage to a relationship.

INDIVIDUAL RELATIONSHIPS

Strong personal relationships contribute to great organizational partnerships. Changes in personnel, therefore, must be handled with particular care. If a partner "bought into" a relationship because of their confidence in one particular individual, finding the right replacement is critical if that individual leaves. Furthermore, when you promote an individual or an individual leaves, you lose tacit knowledge built over the years, as well as the bonds that person developed with the partner. This issue can be diminished if multiple relationships exist, if information is captured and shared over time, and if a transition plan is set in place.

It is inevitable that personality clashes occur in a relationship. Although it's in everyone's best interest to resolve confrontations, sometimes they cannot be fixed. As a last resort, someone may have to be replaced to protect the relationship. Obviously, this is easier in a large organization that has deeper "bench strength" than in a small organization where choices may be limited.

THE ANATOMY OF RELATIONSHIPS

What is a good relationship? Roger Fisher and Scott Brown said in their best-selling book, *Getting Together*:

> From a dozen officers at the same bank we received definitions of a "good" relationship as diverse as: "A long-standing pattern of doing business." "We have made a lot of money dealing with them." "Great financial potential." "Our president plays golf with their chairman of the board." "They pay their bills; we can trust them." "We have to do things for them in return for past favors." . . . One management consulting firm, for example, keeps track of its clients in terms of the length of the relationship, the amount of money at stake, the number of people involved on each side, and the frequency and extent of communication. . . . For some, the goal of a good relationship is a make-believe world without differences: "We have a marvelous relationship: we agree on everything."[17]

All of the things just mentioned are ingredients of good relationships. People who are good at building successful alliances work very hard to structure win-win relationships. One component of success is searching for areas of opportunity where both organizations benefit. For example, if one organization has an excellent product and the other an excellent distribution capability, both organizations have a vested interest in the success of the venture.

A partnership succeeds in the long run when both organizations work for their common good rather than each trying to gain the upper hand. When partners spend all their time trying to outnegotiate each other, the result is that everybody loses. Moreover, one of the organizations is likely to come out noticeably ahead, leading to jealousy and resentment. In well-intentioned relationships, everyone does their utmost to understand their partner's needs and to satisfy them.

Good relationships are also built by establishing specific goals and objectives. Problems arise when relationships drift along aimlessly. For example, when organizations come together because they admire each other rather than for a specific purpose, they are unlikely to accomplish anything meaningful. A specific venture must be selected, and objectives assigned, to achieve results.

It is also important to recognize that no relationship—personal or business—can be successful if forced. Relationships do not result in immediate returns. They require long-term investments of time, money, and effort if they are to grow and produce meaningful results.

WHEN DOES THE RELATIONSHIP BEGIN?

Relationships begin long before papers are signed and the work begins. They start with first impressions generated during preliminary conversations. The courting phase is when expectations are established and promises made. Never promise more than you can deliver, and certainly don't create unrealistic expectations about what the relationship can attain. The courtship should last long enough to help you determine whether it's more than just an infatuation that will lead to eventual divorce.

The courting phase of the relationship is the best time to explore areas of common ground and have a meeting of the minds. It is important to be honest in establishing expectations with your partner. Although complete honesty may raise fears about clinching the deal, this is when both organizations must think beyond their immediate goals and look to the future of their relationship.

Although exaggerating your expertise, resources, or capabilities may seem harmless, doing so provides grounds for resentment the moment the relationship begins. To avoid this problem, it is important to strike a balance between the challenges that have to be overcome and the opportunities that lie ahead.

Before entering into a more formal relationship, take the time to understand your partner's needs. You must be curious. Spend time learning your partner's philosophy, priorities, strategic direction, culture, and rationale for past decisions. Get to know the people—their backgrounds, interests, experiences, and regional differences. And finally, try to learn why other relationships have succeeded or failed.

Although relationships thrive on good intentions and mutual trust, a letter of understanding or contract should stipulate all the parameters of the relationship, including financial arrangements and other promises made.

CREATING THE RIGHT ENVIRONMENT FOR GROWTH

There are two elements of a relationship that must be balanced to ensure success. The first is the deliverables—the goals, objectives, and strategies that have to be achieved. The other is the process—the way those activities are accomplished and how everyone relates to one another. Very often people overemphasize the importance of results over process. This is clearly a mistake. The success of any relationship should not be evaluated solely on meeting specific goals; it lies in the strength and durability of the relationship built between the partners.

One way to stimulate long-term relationships is by creating a working environment where people are well treated; where integrity, sensitivity, humility, and patience are valued; and where commitments are honored even if circumstances have changed since the promise was originally made. In this kind of environment, people do more than strive for common goals, they learn from one another, and they treat people with dignity and respect even during heated disagreements.

Every partnership should reach beyond the formal bounds of a signed contract with a willingness to do more than originally planned. Partners should promote the philosophy that the relationship was not developed for a single purpose, but for the long haul. This may mean making investments not immediately beneficial to your organization or helping your partner in ways that are tangential to the relationship. Furthermore, it is important to remember that there will be good times and bad. Standard setbacks should be accepted as a learning experience coupled with a willingness to go the extra mile for each other. For example:

> In the mid-1970s, Mattel teetered near bankruptcy. Unable to pay its advertising bills from TV stations and magazines, longtime Mattel agency Ogilvy & Mather took the unusual step of handling those obligations for the client. O&M had little hope of getting its money back any time soon, but the agency decided to play the odds, believing the toy marketer would eventually make good its debts and that the relationship would endure.[18]

The bottom line is that this gamble paid off for both Mattel and Ogilvy & Mather. On August 14, 2002, Mattel announced, "Ogilvy & Mather (O&M) is now responsible for all advertising assignments on a global basis and will be responsible for the global coordination, modification and distribution of Mattel creative materials for all international markets."[19]

WORKING TOGETHER

In every successful relationship, explicit goals and objectives are embraced by those involved in the venture. Then, the goals are clearly articulated to others in the organization, making it easier for everyone to rally behind the cause and work together as a team.

In the book *Team Players and Teamwork*, Bill Fox, formerly division manager at Bell Communications Research, is quoted as using the following sports analogy to explain the concept of teamwork:

> "The 10,000 runners in the New York City marathon race have a common goal or purpose. However, they are not a team. They are, in fact, in competition with each other. Teamwork requires interdependence—the working together of a group of people with a shared objective. More specifically, the only way the runners can reach their goal is by competitive efforts. . . ." Using another track example, Fox argues that "a relay team is a good example of a real team. Each member of the team shares a common goal and they must work together to achieve it."[20]

In many failed ventures, teamwork breaks down; senior managers involved in initiating the relationship "disappear" once the agreement is in place. It's as if a coach were to assemble a team and then tell everyone to play the game without direction. It just doesn't work that way. Relationships not only require the involvement of top management from both organizations, they also require strong peer relationships between organizations. Unfortunately, people don't always recognize the importance of these relationships. Instead, they gravitate to short-term results. Remember, the time spent getting to know your peers on a personal level is not wasted time; it enables you to avoid second-guessing a partner's intentions as well as to spot obstacles down the road. It is important to note, however, that in the long term, successful partnerships are built on accomplishments, not solely on the strength of personal relationships.

In order to facilitate the process of working together, champions should be charged with strengthening the relationship. The champions, from each organization, must be cheerleaders or catalysts, but not the sole owners. They should build grassroots levels of support for the relationship and ensure that barriers are eliminated and the resources required to succeed are available. They should promote and extend the relationship at all levels of the organization so that it receives the necessary support and commitment required for success.

In sum, champions have four primary functions:

1. They must serve as catalysts, ensuring that bonds are built between various members of their organization and their partner's organization. They must be willing to empower others instead of maintaining tight control over the flow of information and doing everything themselves.

2. They must disseminate success stories about the relationship throughout their organization.

3. They must ensure that the needs of the partner are heard and the resources required to succeed are made available.

4. They must simplify the approval process by breaking down barriers and streamlining the decision-making process.

MAINTAINING THE RELATIONSHIP

BUILDING UNDERSTANDING

Knowledge and understanding underlie all successful relationships. In order to work together successfully, everyone must be informed and feel like equal partners in the relationship. In his book *Information Anxiety*, Richard Wurman reminds us:

> Once you see or understand something, you cannot conceive of what it was like not to have seen or understood it. You lose the ability to identify with those who don't know. . . . If you could remember what it was like not to know, you could begin to communicate in terms that might be understood more readily by someone who doesn't know.[21]

One way to ensure that everyone has the information they need to meet their responsibilities is to maintain open lines of communication. It is important to issue timely information about major events, policy changes, or personnel changes within the organization. It is also important to communicate with your partners at the same time you discuss events with your own employees. By opening lines of communication and tearing down external walls, you make it easier for everyone to work together toward a common goal.

An environment should be created where ideas are encouraged, and people feel free to express their opinions; where feedback is viewed as constructive rather than confrontational. Moreover, people should feel that they're contributing to the greater good. That means no one feels hurt if someone comes up with a better idea than the advice they offered. It is a supportive environment, where risk taking is encouraged, where responsibility is accepted, and where mistakes are treated as learning experiences if the venture doesn't pan out.

BEING PREPARED FOR PROBLEMS

No matter how well partners communicate, every relationship will experience setbacks along the way. Failures are not the time to point fingers or reassess the value of the relationship. In fact, a process for resolving difficult issues should be established early in the partnership before a problem looms over your head. If you accept the premise that problems are natural in every relationship, you'll find it less troubling to deal with them when they emerge. But remember that, as Fisher and Brown have said:

> Giving in does not build a good working relationship. It may avoid arguments, but it also eliminates the opportunity to learn how to talk through problems and to become skillful at reaching solutions. Without such skills, a relationship will be too weak to survive problems that are bound to come along. It is not enough to solve the immediate problem. We have to think ahead to the effect that this transaction will have on the next one, and the one after that.[22]

Debate must be encouraged, and problems must be brought out into the open rather than swept under the rug. Partners must feel comfortable raising difficult issues before they turn into major conflicts; dealing with problems expediently will help strengthen the relationship in the long run.

When trying to resolve problems in a relationship, keep in mind that force or pressure tactics should never be used to resolve problems. Diplomatic skills are the best option. For example, an attitude of "take it or leave it" often results in someone who "takes it" only until they can find another partner. It is impossible to maintain a solid, lasting relationship if partners threaten to walk, go over a partner's head, or find another partner whenever a problem arises.

Furthermore, when arguments turn into personal attacks, working together in the future becomes difficult. Efforts to wear someone down by acting like a spoiled child erode respect. And playing games—or allowing them to be played—is always destructive. While these tactics may achieve short-term victory, the price you'll pay is lasting resentment. The proper way to resolve these issues is through discussion and win-win agreements.

TEARING DOWN WALLS

Customers and suppliers must be willing to tear down the walls between their organizations and share the required information to get the job done. The more that organizations think of themselves as "us" rather than "them," the greater success they will realize. This can be accomplished by providing a monetary incentive to achieve their mutual goals.

DECISION MAKING

There are two rules that are critical in decision making. The first is to avoid unilateral decisions; the second is to avoid forcing decisions on your partner.

There are a number of reasons why people violate these rules. They feel that their decision is in the best interests of their partner; they believe that they are best qualified to make the decision; they believe that if they don't seize the moment, the opportunity will be lost; they believe that their partner would have agreed with their decision anyway; they believe that the decision is not really that significant; or they're so excited that they take the plunge before thinking.

Remember, unilateral decision making is a mistake. When a partner feels that they are being cut out of the decision process, no matter how insignificant the matter, they will wonder if other decisions are being made without them.

HANDLING TRANSITIONS

Continuity is such an important ingredient in a relationship that managing transitions must be made a priority. If relationships are not built across levels, employee turnover can bring partnerships to a halt. When a new person is brought in to manage a relationship, each partner should be involved in the selection process or at the very least, notified of the change before it takes place. Furthermore, the new individual should understand the nuances of the relationship before assuming the role to avoid being considered a detriment by the partner while learning on the job.

There are a number of things you can do to help ensure continuity in a relationship:

- Choose individuals with long tenure to be the chief liaisons with your partner.
- Insist that all "relationship managers" have a right-hand person who is well known to the partner and intimately familiar with the relationship.
- Set up a transition period when individuals are promoted or rotated into other positions: See to it that they remain in contact with the partner and with their replacement during the transition.
- Make sure the new individual honors all of the predecessor's commitments.

MAKING IT HAPPEN

Today's lean organizations cannot survive without strong alliances to supplement their core capabilities. The result is an age of cooperation, which brings unexpected rewards. But cooperative arrangements also bring responsibilities; for example, each partner must grow and expand their capabilities so they can maintain their end of the partnership, both now and in the future.

In the final analysis, the value of any partnership depends on the nature of the relationship. "A 72 year longitudinal Harvard study exploring what makes for 'a good life' offered no more surprising or compelling conclusion that the most important thing in life is the quality of our relationships. Nothing else—not money, not achievement, not recognition—came close to determining the quality of our lives."[23]

Good relationships in business don't just happen. They are the result of honesty, integrity, respect, commitment, trust, confidence, and openness. In any healthy relationship, partners create an environment that encourages continuous improvement, risk taking, a long-term perspective, and of course, win-win relationships. Clearly, the stronger these attributes are, the more enduring your partnerships become.

As in partnerships, win-win relationships are at the heart of networking, one of the most powerful skills a person can master in this new age. Unfortunately, many people treat networking like a game of bumper cars in which progress is measured by the number of people they run into rather than by the quality of the underlying relationships created. The truth is, great networkers believe that by helping others, they'll eventually end up helping themselves. Chapter 9 discusses the potential of networking and how to increase your effectiveness in this critical area.

9

NETWORKING

The successful networkers I know, the ones receiving tons of referrals and feeling truly happy about themselves, continually put the other person's needs ahead of their own.

—Bob Burg, *Endless Referrals: Network Your Everyday Contacts Into Sales*[1]

Looking for a job? Need some personal advice? Looking to make some new connections? Perhaps you should try networking. Today, people network through social media sites, by joining clubs, going to lunch with friends, attending conferences, joining industry associations, and going to alumni dinners and reunions. People network with church members, school buddies, and through community organizations. Do these activities help? Are these activities worth the time and effort? Do some efforts pay off better than others? In other words, are there right ways and wrong ways to network?

Those who know how to network swear by it. Experienced networkers claim they can reach anyone in the world with only six interactions, an idea known as "six degrees of separation."

In 1967, American sociologist Stanley Milgram devised a new way to test the theory, which he called "the small-world problem." He

randomly selected people in the mid-West to send packages to a
stranger located in Massachusetts. The senders knew the recipient's
name, occupation and general location. They were instructed to send
the package to a person they knew on a first-name basis who they
thought was most likely, out of all their friends, to know the target
personally. That person would do the same, and so on, until the package
was personally delivered to its target recipient. It only took (on
average) between five and seven intermediaries to get each package
delivered. Milgram's findings were published in *Psychology Today*
and inspired the phrase "six degrees of separation."[2]

Research identifying common characteristics of successful entrepreneurs
notes that they "spent significant time developing new contacts and
managing old ones (about 50 percent of the day)."[3]

Unfortunately, some take the position that "doing everything" is better
than "doing less." They treat networking like a game of bumper cars in
which progress is measured by the number of people they run into rather
than by the quality of the underlying relationships created. Simply put,
handing out *more* business cards at a meeting or adding *more* Twitter
followers, *more* Facebook friends or LinkedIn contacts is "notworking."

Others treat networking like a personal marketing campaign dedicated
to spreading the word about themselves and their needs, while ignoring the
needs of their peers. This "me-first thinking" not only won't work, it's
actually counterproductive.

Still other people join affinity groups merely for personal gain, but it
doesn't take long for people to learn that these folks are not givers, but
takers. These "notworkers" don't understand the importance of building
long-lasting relationships; instead, they'll reach out to others only when
they need something. And then they're surprised when their requests
produce little.

Successful networking occurs when people come together based on
mutual respect and common interests, then voluntarily provide support for
others with no strings attached. They believe that by helping others, they'll
eventually end up helping themselves.

Those who network properly say that it provides significant benefits.
On a business level, networking can serve as a great source of information,
new ideas, referrals, leads, new hires and can even become a valuable form
of market intelligence. On a personal level, networking can be a wonderful

source of emotional support or career advice; it can help you find someone who can be objective about a business challenge; and it can lead to long-term relationships. The possibilities are endless.

THE UNDERLYING STRUCTURE

According to business literature, networking can be defined as:

- "A pattern of human interactions characterized by a process of information exchange usually leading to other human interactions and/or material, service, information, monetary or spiritual exchange." (Richard Haight)[4]

- "An organized method of making links from the people you know to the people they know, gaining and using an ever-expanding base of contacts."[5]

- "The lines of communication, the alternative express highways that people use to get things done. In crisis and in opportunity, the word spreads quickly through these people–power lines."[6]

Networks are not formal groups operating under formal rules. They tend to be polycentric rather than monocentric, shaped like a spider web, where connections are made laterally, up and down, or across to other networks. Networks can be extensive or simple—the strength of the relationships among their members varies and is visible only to the individuals involved.

Networks are not hierarchical: No one is in charge, and the group does not depend on any single individual for its survival. Participation in networks is optional, and members treat one another as equals rather than as superiors or subordinates. Networks have no boundaries, formal agendas, or prescribed sets of rules; membership varies greatly as networks expand and contract at various times; and the life cycles of networks vary enormously.

A network is built on a foundation of mutual trust and support among members. Participants in a network come together because of common interests and objectives, and they voluntarily give of themselves (primarily through a barter system) because they know that by helping others, they may end up helping themselves. Conversely, people who join groups merely for personal gain are not really networking—they are takers. It doesn't take long for others to learn their true motives.

You should limit the number of groups that you join—favor those that might help you achieve your goals personally and professionally. As Casey Stengel once said, "If you don't know where you're going, you might end up somewhere else." Avoid joining organizations merely because they are prestigious groups whose names you want to place on your résumé.

Ask yourself if you are networking for purely selfish reasons or whether you are prepared to give as much as you receive. If you network only for personal gain, you may end up wasting your time—and the time of the other members. Before you begin networking, accept the fact that networks may not offer immediate rewards; they require patience, commitment, and an investment in time and effort.

It is best to meet people with like interests and those who believe in win-win relationships. These people can be found almost anywhere—on social networking sites, at professional and trade associations, conferences, seminars and trade shows, software user groups, office parties, community organizations, and health clubs. Networks can include business and school alumni, customers, vendors, airplane acquaintances, fellow commuters, school buddies, and family friends. To demonstrate how expansive social media has become, Facebook recently confirmed that it now has 800 million active users.[7] LinkedIn has officially reached the milestone of 100 million users.[8] And Twitter, as well, recently reported that it has 100 million active users, half of whom tweet to the site daily.[9] All three sites continue to grow at phenomenal rates.

BUILDING RELATIONSHIPS

Networking can result in close or casual relationships. Give both types a chance. They serve very different and important purposes. It is important to note that electronic tools, such as social media, enable you to maintain relationships with hundreds or thousands of friends.

> Electronic tools can increase the number of active connections each person can maintain . . . the kind of relationships that go with knowing who each person is and how each person relates socially to every other person. [British anthropologist Robin Dunbar has offered the number of relationships that a person can maintain.] No precise value has been proposed for Dunbar's number, but a commonly cited approximate figure is 150.[10]

The challenge is to know the benefits of both close and casual relationships and to balance them carefully. When you network with people similar to you, which usually results in close relationships, it's easier to ask them what they would do if they were you. They may travel in similar circles of friends, hear what you hear, and react to situations the same way you do. Moreover, they have a better understanding of what makes you tick and will be there for you if you need them. Close relationships, however, require more time and effort; meaning that you can develop only so many strong ties.

In casual relationships, by contrast, people don't expect the same level of effort and commitment from you. Casual relationships provide access to people of diverse backgrounds and specialty areas. They serve as bridges to new groups of people, offer greater objectivity when discussing personal issues, and may offer an entirely different perspective when presented with a challenge. Therefore, they can provide access to people different from you, as well as insight or information that you or your associates may not have heard.

This kind networking is summed up best in *Corporate Networking* by Robert Mueller: "If we confine our networking only to those whom we know personally (or position) we miss the 'other world' out there of friends of our friends. This is the exciting, potential scope which networking offers when conducted in a conscious and determined way."[11]

TURNING TALK INTO ACTION

The first step in developing a network is to identify and document the special characteristics and personal strengths of the people you meet. Learn all you can about them. For example, identify whether they exhibit a special skill, have subject matter or industry expertise, are a good source of competitive intelligence, have a strong network, or seem like wonderful people.

The next step is to categorize the members of your network (using keywords) on both a personal and a professional basis, so that you can easily identify whom to call if you or someone in your network requires assistance. For example, decide who is good with details and who views things conceptually. Who has big company or entrepreneurial experience? Who has government, nonprofit organization, or family-run business know-how? Who has experience with booming growth companies, with turnaround, downsizing, or merger situations? Who provides brutally "honest" opinions and who provides more tactful feedback to avoid hurting your feelings? On a personal level, you can categorize people by their knowledge and experience of travel, fashion, cooking, fitness, social media, technology, nutrition, cars, health, gadgets, financial planning, etc.

The final step is to identify your own personal strengths to determine how you can help others. This can't be stressed enough. After all, networking is a two-way street. People who believe that networking is all about taking are making a serious fundamental error. Rewards and successes go to those who learn to trust others, are willing to assist others, and recognize the rights of others to make demands on them. Any attempts you make at networking will fail if you offer little and always ask for a lot.

As Regis McKenna, author of *The Regis Touch*, once said, "Word of mouth is probably the most powerful form of communication in the business world . . . Word of mouth is so obvious a communication medium that most people do not take the time to analyze or understand its structure. To many people, it is like the weather. Sure, it's important. But, you can't do much about it. You never see a Word of Mouth Communication Section in marketing plans."[12] What McKenna is discussing is the failure to give networking, and word-of-mouth marketing, the priority it deserves and the opportunities you miss as a result of that failure.

WHY DOESN'T EVERYONE NETWORK?

If networking provides all these benefits, why doesn't everyone network?

PERSONAL BARRIERS

Many people find it difficult to leave their comfort zone and reach out to others, or they don't understand the value of networking. They believe that it is easier to "do it yourself" than to trust others. The major personal barriers to networking usually fall into one of the following categories:

- *Selfishness.* Some people want immediate gratification and are not willing to make the required investment to succeed. For them, it's all about short-term personal gain. They do not extend themselves to others.

- *Myopia.* Some people are so shortsighted that they're not able to comprehend the value of networking. These people are always too busy to network. They fail to realize that networking is significantly more efficient than going it alone.

- *Shyness.* Some people find it too uncomfortable to approach those they do not know or too difficult to deal with the unfamiliar. They prefer to remain in their comfort zone and let others make the first move.

- *Lack of know-how.* Some people do not know the benefits of networking or how to take the first step.

NETWORKING IS NOT AN EXTRACURRICULAR ACTIVITY

The second barrier to networking is being part of an organization that does not support or that even discourages networking.

In this case, a request to attend an external meeting or conference is viewed as a vacation or met with a response such as, "Don't you have any work to do?"

If this is an issue, do your networking on your own time. Reach out to fellow commuters, join Facebook, Twitter, or LinkedIn, attend town meetings, join clubs, meet people at the gym, become active in your college alumni group, or coach a Little League team. And remember, where the situation permits, don't forget to promote the benefits of networking within your organization.

HOW TO MAKE NETWORKING WORK

Networking is a long-term strategy. Networks improve over time as they are shaped and molded by their staunchest members. To be part of a successful network, it is important to follow a few rules.

1. Don't wait until you desperately need a network to begin developing one (for example, looking for a new job). Networks are based on trust, respect, and personal chemistry—that doesn't happen overnight.

2. Join a social network or an industry or professional association to add structure to your professional relationships while expanding your network.

3. If you join a group (such as a trade association), get involved rather than sitting on the sidelines. You receive only as much as you are willing to give.

4. Group get-togethers are not substitutes for one-on-one meetings. Large gatherings tend to have "fixed agendas," making it difficult for members to open up personally. Furthermore, a few members may dominate discussions in large groups.

5. Networks expand and contract. Keep in touch with members of your network on a regular basis or you'll drift apart. (Birthday and holiday greetings, or congratulatory notes, require only a few minutes of your time and will be remembered.)

6. Collecting a lot of business cards and then wrapping them up in a rubber band, only to collect dust, isn't networking. Neither is "friending" lots of people on Facebook or contacts and followers on LinkedIn or Twitter. Keep in mind that your goal is to develop lasting relationships.

7. Networking offers unbelievable potential. For example, in a tough job market, what do you think would be more effective—blindly sending out hundreds of résumés or getting an informal introduction to a potential employer from one of your contacts? Take the time to nurture your network. It can change your life!

SOME RULES FOR ENSURING SUCCESS

Use caution at the outset. In order to establish a relationship, you often have to make the first move. But it is important that your initial gesture be something other than a request. Earlier, I discussed the importance of knowing the strengths of your contacts; the other half of that equation is to know their personal needs as well. If they do not gain personally through the network, they will be far less likely to participate in the future. The best way to meet their needs is to listen to what they say from their perspective rather than filtering the information through your biases.

Be prepared. Keep in mind that you are unlikely to be of assistance if you can't put your finger on the required information. Organize yourself so that you are in a better position to help others. One way to do this is to create a simple database that lists the members of your network and their individual strengths.

Find the right approach. When you need assistance from your network, how do you determine which member to approach? If timing is not critical, you can ask several members for assistance, and you can ask them to ask others for help as well. Also, when making requests, you may get different answers (or perspectives) on the same query. For example, a writer can send a document to as many as five people for review—a subject matter expert, a proofreader for grammar and style, someone outside the field to determine how clearly the information is presented, a member of the target audience, and a member of the writer's own organization to check for internal political sensitivity.

Avoid mistakes. There are many ways to become an unpopular member of a network. Although most people will likely help you, remember that most people do not respond well to pressure. Be careful not to ask people for help without thinking about their ability to respond. You may place them in the uncomfortable position of admitting they cannot help.

- *Use other people's time wisely.* Know what you want before making a request. Too many people make requests before deciding exactly what they need. The result is wasted time and effort.

- *Evaluate the reasonableness of your requests.* Are you asking people to put their necks on the line? Will it cost them a lot of time or money? Would you do it for them if the tables were turned?

- *Respect other people's priorities.* Your request may be your priority and may not seem to be a major undertaking to you, but the people you ask may have a full plate at the moment, which means that, much as they would like to help you, they cannot find the time to do so.

- *Be specific in your requests.* If you're vague, you get something that you don't need. Communicate why you're making the request and ask how they would approach it. This allows them to be creative; moreover, they very well might have a different perspective or might approach the situation from an angle that you haven't explored. Also, be sure you explain what has been done to date so they don't spend valuable time and effort duplicating someone else's efforts.

Pattern Research, a networking organization, has provided examples in their membership manual of the wrong and right ways to ask for something:

Wrong ways to ask for a favor:

- "I am dropping off 50 copies of my 110-page business proposal for you to mail out . . ."
- "Are there any people in your network looking for a smart investment deal?"

Right ways to ask for the same favor:

- "If I wanted to distribute my business plan to some interested network users, how should I handle it?"
- "I have a high-risk real estate deal for people looking for a legal tax shelter. The minimum investment is just $5,000."[13]

Satisfaction guaranteed. When you are approached with a request, keep in mind that if you can't fulfill it, the next best alternative is to recommend someone who can.

NETWORKING PROTOCOL

Networking should not be a haphazard, on-and-off affair. To network successfully, you would be wise to keep the following points handy for review:

- Networking should be a give-and-take relationship. If you do too much for a person without ever accepting something in return, you end up making the recipient hesitant to ask for more, and you imply that the recipient has nothing to offer.
- Don't keep score. Just because you have performed one favor doesn't mean you should expect one in return. Gaining a reputation as someone who keeps score, who is always looking for a *quid pro quo*, will make future networking harder.
- When you do someone a favor, do it without making a big deal out of it. Either do it because you want to help or don't do it at all. Be sure not to act as if you expect something in return.
- Besides giving people exactly what they are looking for, suggest ways to do more. Don't, however, give something extra without first confirming that it's needed. This is a lot like gift giving: You should give people what you know they want, not what you want them to have.

- Do not push yourself on people. You might mean well, but this is the business equivalent of a child's loving a new pet so much that he smothers it.

- Do not try to show off by providing everything you know about a subject or by e-mailing volumes of material when a quick answer will suffice. Don't waste people's valuable time. Information overload is bad business. Quality is always preferable to quantity.

- Do not make promises you can't keep. It is better to say you can't deliver something than to set an expectation and fall short.

- Make sure your telephone call is convenient. People may be in a meeting or working on a critical deadline. Be aware that some people prefer e-mail while others prefer the phone. Furthermore, some people like to be called at the office, others at home. Be conscious of these preferences.

- Do not become too reliant on any one individual. You can destroy the best of relationships by taking advantage of someone's good nature.

- When making requests of others, be considerate. Do not request sensitive information, watch the costs of your requests in both time and money, and make sure your requests are ethical and reasonable.

- When people come to you with a problem they have labored over for weeks, don't solve it for them in seconds. If you do so, you may make them feel inferior. Even better, ask questions that lead them to solve the problem themselves.

- If people provide you with sensitive information, it should be kept private or you will lose their trust.

- Avoid divulging or asking people to divulge confidential information.

- Do not judge other people's requests. What might seem foolish to you may be a priority to them for reasons they are hesitant to reveal.

Those who are successful at networking will tell you that its potential is unlimited. It only stands to reason that the people who benefit most are the "givers"—those who go all-out to help others—rather than the "takers"—those who are merely out for personal gain. The best networkers have learned that, as with anything in life, what goes around, comes around. How about you? Are you a networker, or a notworker?

10

TRUST ME . . .
TRUST ME NOT

BUILDING A TRUSTING ORGANIZATION

Trust is the ultimate intangible. It has no shape or substance, yet it empowers our actions. And its presence or absence can govern our behavior as if it were a tangible force. The belief that we live in a reasonably predictable world is the cornerstone on which cooperation is built, and the basis of our planning and action. Would you cross the bridge, mail a letter, confide in a friend, or work at a job without some trust that the bridge will hold, the letter will be delivered, the friend will keep confidence, or you will get paid for your efforts? Living without some measure of trust would consign us to perpetual fears, paranoia, inefficiency, and even inaction.

—Gordon Shea[1]

Trust is the fabric that binds us together, creating an orderly, civilized society from chaos and anarchy. If we can't trust our husband or our wife, if we can't trust our children, if we can't trust our boss or our colleagues, if we can't trust our preacher or our senator, then we have nothing on which to build a stable way of life. Trust is not an abstract, theoretical, idealistic goal forever beyond our reach. Trust—or a lack of it—is inherent in every action that we take and affects everything that we do. Trust is the cement that binds relationships, keeping spouses together, business deals intact, and political systems stable. Without trust, marriages fail, voters become apathetic, and organizations flounder. Without trust, no company can ever hope for excellence.

There has, however, been a deep, fundamental change in the way we view the world today, and, as a result, trust is no longer fashionable. Few adults can remember a world without cynicism. Where "death do us part" once had meaning, today one of two new marriages ends in divorce and countless others exist in name only. Politicians who were once solid members of the community are dropping out of campaigns due to scandals and irregularities. Employees who once believed in devoting their entire working lives to one organization have seen so many colleagues tossed out in restructurings and outsourcings that those who remain are often left emotionally uninvolved in their jobs. In fact, in 2005, a survey commissioned by the World Economic Forum showed that "public trust in a range of institutions has dropped significantly since 2001. Public trust levels in national governments, the United Nations and global companies are now at their lowest since tracking began in January 2001."[2] In addition, in 2011, *The Wall Street Journal* reported that "In the [Edelman Trust Barometer] survey, which focuses on 'informed' people (defined as those with college degrees in the top 25% of wage earners for their age), only 37% said they trust government to do the right thing, down from 43% last year. Only 45% trust business, down from 51% last year. This subset of Americans now trust business less than the French do and is almost as skeptical about companies as Russians are."[3] The trust deficit has significant implications for employees and considerable financial implications for businesses.

> Left unattended, low trust can exact a high financial price. According to Watson Wyatt's WorkUSA 2002 survey, the three-year total return to shareholders is almost three times lower at companies with low trust levels than at companies with high trust levels. A report by Towers Perrin on employee engagement shows similar findings. "Those organizations that have high employee engagement [which is driven by high trust] have higher revenue growth, lower cost of goods sold, and lower sales, general, and administrative expenses," says Emmett Seaborn, a principal with the Stamford, Connecticut-based consultancy. Simply stated, trust matters, and it matters now more than ever.[4]

The trust deficit is a sea change from the time when a person's word was his bond, when employees worked for one company until they retired, when business deals were made on the basis of "I know your father" or "We've worked with your company before." These were all ways of saying we recognize your values, understand how much your reputation means to you, and know how you conduct business. These values resulted in increased business, stronger customer loyalty, better employee morale, reduced turnover, and higher profit margins.

These old values also decreased the cost of conducting business because people who trust one another share information, listen to one another, and are more likely to accept feedback as constructive, instead of getting defensive. They waste little time playing politics, feel comfortable sharing new ideas, and help one another in order to serve the common good.

If businesses are to thrive in the global marketplace, trust must be more than something that is talked about; it must be at the core of everything that is done. Organizations cannot be jungles where only the fittest survive, living in a state of battle readiness in order to meet the grueling tests of everyday corporate life. If companies are to motivate employees and win their loyalty, they must change the way relationships are constructed. All too often, "we spend a lifetime building a trusting relationship with our friends and families, but we spend thirty minutes in an orientation session with our new employees and expect to have a successful and productive employee. For employees to trust the management, they must know that the management shares the same basic goals in the long run . . . and [that] each will behave in ways that are not harmful to the other."[5]

Just as high levels of trust reduce friction among employees, bond people together, increase productivity, and stimulate growth, low levels of trust adversely affect relationships, stifle innovation, and hamper the decision-making process. Employees in organizations marked by low levels of trust usually operate under higher levels of stress. They spend a great deal of time covering their backsides, justifying past decisions, and conducting witch hunts or looking for scapegoats when something doesn't work out. This keeps them from the free exchange of ideas that results in innovative solutions. The constant need to prove one's worth also promotes short-term fixes rather than long-term solutions.

Low trust in organizations also pushes people to operate with incomplete information, to come up with the most favorable interpretations, and to treat people's suggestions with suspicion. As a result of limited discussion and feedback combined with the speed at which everything moves today, problems are not clearly defined and situations are not thoroughly examined. This means that, all too often, decisions are made out of context, and they are based on inaccurate views of reality, without an awareness of risks.

Furthermore, in organizations marked by low levels of trust, employees have so much difficulty exploring the full range of options or responding creatively to problems at hand that new challenges are avoided. Employees are so afraid of being reprimanded for failure, or torn down and ridiculed by their colleagues, that they shy away from new activities that require new ways of thinking. Their defensiveness and mutual suspicions limit them to the restricted set of alternatives they have all agreed upon, which are designed to minimize their vulnerability. Exploration, innovation, and creativity become dangers in this kind of environment.[6]

Of course, low levels of trust—with all their associated costs in the loss of loyalty, productivity, and innovative thinking—do not happen overnight. However, companies are often slow to see the warning signs because, during boom times, it is more difficult to notice low trust levels. In periods of dramatic growth, promotions are often given to people who achieve goals, without regard to the long-term implications of how they achieved those goals. This mentality encourages employees to solve problems with quick fixes and then maneuver for a promotion before their actions have an effect on the people around them.

Moreover, during high-growth periods, people often focus on the short-term objective of making deals and then moving on. They don't have to worry about taking advantage of a supplier, overselling a customer, or misleading an employee because, by then, the problem won't be theirs; they will have moved on to something else. This misguided thinking leads to many of our long-term problems

TRUST—THE MIRACLE INGREDIENT

According to Gordon Shea, trust can be described as the "miracle ingredient in organizational life—a lubricant that reduces friction, a bonding agent that glues together disparate parts, a catalyst that facilitates action. No substitute—neither threat nor promise—will do the job as well."[7]

In organizations, trust is like love in a marriage: it bonds people together and makes them strong and effective. Trust in a relationship increases security, reduces inhibitions and defensiveness, and frees people to share feelings and dreams. Trust empowers you to put your deepest fears in the palms of your colleagues' hands, knowing that they will be treated with care. Trust enables you to be yourself and maintain your own values without worrying about acceptance. Trust makes colleagues willing to spend time together and make sacrifices for one another. Trust is an expression of faith that makes it easy for colleagues to have confidence in one another's ability to perform well and to know that they will be there if needed. Trust means that promises made will be kept, and it also means that if a promise is not kept, it was probably for good cause. And finally, trust means that a relationship will last not because it is good business, but because the relationship itself is valued.

The dilemma is that in order to be able to trust, you must be willing to accept the risk associated with trusting. When reaching out to people, we always risk the chance of being wrong, but if we never try for fear of failing, we may never experience the satisfaction of being in a trusting relationship.

THE PARAMETERS OF TRUST

Trust is generally defined as a belief in the integrity of another individual. But clearly, there are different kinds and degrees of trust; for example, there are some people you trust enough to confide in, some you may trust with your material possessions, some you trust to help you with a business assignment, others you may trust with your personal safety. But even in these categories, there are levels of trust; for example, you may feel comfortable loaning a friend $10 knowing he or she will pay you back, but you may be less inclined to loan that friend $10,000. And there are people you trust in one area but not in another. For example, while you may trust the mechanic to work on your new car, you may not trust him to babysit your children; while you may trust your closest friend enough to confide your deepest secrets to him or her, you may not trust your friend to pilot you in an airplane.

It's also important to recognize the line between liking someone and trusting them, as Dale E. Zand points out in *Information, Organization, and Power*, "You may have affection for another person but still not trust them. For example, a parent may love a 10-year-old child but not trust him to drive the family automobile. Furthermore, you may trust another and have no affection for them. For example, a passenger in a commercial plane may trust the pilot but have no affection for him or her."[8]

WINNING TRUST

Understanding the meaning of trust allows you to work toward being a trusted and trusting person. The truth is that trust is never guaranteed, and it can't be won overnight. Trust must be carefully constructed, vigorously nurtured, and constantly reinforced. Trust is established over time, gradually, through a long chain of successful experiences. In the early stages of relationships, whether personal or business, we extend ourselves in small ways and observe the responses to our actions. Then we take appropriate action, withdrawing, maintaining our behavior, or extending ourselves a bit further each time until trust is established.

Although trust takes a long time to develop, it can be destroyed by a single action. Moreover, once lost, it is very difficult to re-establish. Our reactions to the betrayal of trust are not very different from our reactions to a death in the family. When trust is violated, the hurt is long and deep. As Friedrich Nietzsche once said, "I'm not upset that you lied to me, I'm upset that from now on I can't believe you."[9] It is only after forgiveness is truly granted, which happens at the end of a long agonizing process, that trust can be regained. Forgiveness allows you to let go of the past and move on to the future.

The destruction of trust does not happen without warning: A friend who was always there when needed begins to return calls sporadically; spouses stop confiding in each other; a company communicates with its employees less frequently, providing less information or holding back information. In the case of a company, the reactions may be a high degree of fear, suspicion, absenteeism, low job satisfaction, decreased commitment, and high turnover. People become risk-averse and withdraw into themselves. More time is spent justifying previous actions than adding value to the organization; more time is spent figuring out how to get things approved than completing the work at hand; and more time is spent figuring out the political implications of doing something than doing what is best. These warning signs are important because the sooner the decline of trust is recognized, the better the chances of rebuilding it.

THE FOUR STAGES OF TRUST

FIRST STAGE: FOUNDATION
History

Reputation

SECOND STAGE: SUPPORT STRUCTURE
The Values on Which Trust Rests

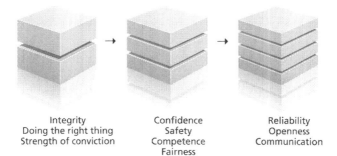

Integrity	Confidence	Reliability
Doing the right thing	Safety	Openness
Strength of conviction	Competence	Communication
	Fairness	

THIRD STAGE: CONSISTENCY

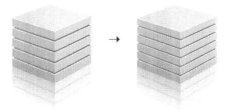

FOURTH STAGE: FROM PREDICTABILITY TO FAITH

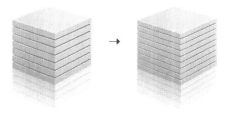

Building trusting relationships is a process that can best be described as stacking layers on a foundation one at a time in such a way that each layer bonds on top of the prior one before another layer is added. In a world where time is a precious resource, where we must often move without having the time to explore all the options, we use shortcuts to circumvent the process. For this reason, an individual's or organization's history or track record is often evaluated to gauge how we may be treated in a relationship. The foundation, or first stage, represents the beginning of a relationship and depicts the history of those involved. We generally start off with some preconceived notion about others. We meet and develop first impressions about people through the friends we have in common; watching how they treat others; the things they talk about in meetings, while commuting, at parties; and general observations during work. We develop first impressions of companies by seeing an advertisement, getting references from people, or reading articles about them on the Internet.

The second stage represents values that lead to trusting relationships, such as integrity, reliability, and openness. Once these characteristics are demonstrated, they form the support structure of a trusting relationship. When these actions are repeated time and time again, the relationship is strengthened and becomes part of the framework of the next phase. The third stage, consistency, enables us to anticipate probable actions. It provides a certain degree of comfort that helps us to maintain the relationship even through difficult times. The fourth stage is faith—as these layers are stacked on top of the other three stages, everything that came before them strengthens the framework. This is the stage at which actions are so predictable that we don't consciously have to think about the relationship. At this phase, trust has become so integral a part of the relationship that we expect it to work. At their peak, relationships imbued with trust are bonded together by a faith so strong that it is very difficult to destroy the relationship. It is at this stage that people allow themselves to become entirely vulnerable to others.

THE FOUNDATION: HISTORY

The past is often the best indicator of the future; we all look for precedents as a key to anticipating behavior. We want to know how someone acted in the past when faced with a similar situation. Last time I confided in her, was she able to keep a secret? Last time he promised he would deliver it on time, did he keep his word? Last time I loaned him money, was it paid back? Last time they sold me a product, did they stand behind it? Last time there was a downturn in the economy, how were employees treated? Last time we presented an idea to management, who took the credit for it? Last time there was a problem in the department, did management support us or look for a scapegoat? Last time we faced tough times, did management stand behind its people or fend for themselves?

Whether you are an organization trying to gain trust in the marketplace or a salesperson trying to gain the trust of a consumer, keep in mind that trust is not won instantly; instead, it is earned by consistent actions repeated over time. Similarly, organizations become trustworthy by repeating their actions over the years. Organizations that institutionalize the value and importance of lifelong customer relationships over immediate sales transactions know that winning an immediate sale is not as important as exceeding customer expectations over time. They know that signing a sales agreement is not the end of the sales process, but the beginning of the next sale. They know that the minute a purchase is made, and the consumer has placed trust in their organization, they must work hard to maintain that trust.

Building a history of trust can differentiate a company and its products from its competitors. Years ago, Xerox Corporation had an advertising campaign that said, "We won't love you and leave you," inferring that its competitors sometimes sold copiers and then were never heard from again.

Organizations that emphasize long, trusting relationships are rewarded in numerous ways. First, there is potential repeat business. Loyal customers may even look for other available products from your company. And once their trust in your organization grows, they may reward you by making larger purchases. Finally, long-term relationships encourage satisfied clients to tell their friends or colleagues about the great products and service that they are receiving from you.

Reputation. The most tangible form of history is reputation. An individual's or organization's reputation is often a key to their probable behavior toward a friend, a client, or an employee; it indicates how they might treat others both now and in the future. That's why, before we enter into a relationship, we ask ourselves if the person or organization is known to be a trustworthy individual or a good corporate citizen. It's why we want to know how they have treated others when the chips were down or when they were backed into a corner.

An impeccable reputation reduces the time that it takes to gain trust with a sales prospect or new client, thus providing a company with a significant competitive advantage. Receiving an endorsement from a credible individual or having other companies refer customers to you is an excellent way to build trust. Indeed, anything that enhances an individual's or an organization's reputation is a shortcut to building trust.

But just as reputations are built over the years, they have to be protected and re-earned each day, or they will soon be lost. Years ago, expressions such as "No one ever got fired for buying IBM," "It's as good as a Cadillac," "It's as safe as money in the bank" not only enhanced the sales efforts of these organizations, but also allowed them to attract new employees. People placed their trust in the product or in the organization because others did so in the past and never lived to regret it. It's important to note that these reputations must be carefully protected.

This means that individuals and organizations must be careful to act in ways that enhance their reputations. For example, an organization whose business is centered in the community or in a tightly knit industry has a vested interest in upholding its business reputation. If its reputation sours, it has no place to run.

Both individuals and organizations must also be very careful to avoid real or perceived impropriety. If they become involved in questionable dealings, they must clear the air quickly, openly and honestly. Unfortunately, once people distance themselves from an inappropriate situation, and it's subsequently learned that they were involved in any way (or if closure is never achieved), a cloud of doubt will shadow them forever.

THE SUPPORT STRUCTURE:
THE VALUES ON WHICH TRUST RESTS

At the start of any relationship, people consciously or unconsciously examine actions rather than words to measure trustworthiness. As time goes by, the more that values such as integrity, fairness, and reliability are evident, the more people learn to trust one another. The more such qualities are recognized, the deeper the trust and, as long as nothing happens to change those first impressions, the stronger the relationship grows. This applies to relationships between individuals, between individuals and organizations, and between organizations. The man and woman trust one another and commit to marriage; the companies enter into a strategic alliance; the job hunter accepts the new position offered by his future employer; the customer buys the product that the organization sells; and the supplier enters into a deal with the buyer. Relationships are built on the values listed below, and these values comprise the second stage, the support structure on which trust rests.

Integrity. There are a number of questions you ask yourself when assessing someone's integrity. Do they have a good value system? Are they honest, straightforward, and nonmanipulative? Do they tell the truth and keep their promises even if circumstances have changed since they gave their word? Do they avoid even the appearance of impropriety, and are they aware that the company they keep can be a reflection on their own integrity? Do they pay as much attention to the spirit of the law as they do to the letter of the law?

The same questions apply to organizations. Do they stand behind their products? How do they treat their employees and vendors? Are they good corporate citizens? Do they satisfy their commitments?

Doing the right thing. Another characteristic we look for when building relationships is whether people or organizations do the right thing not because they're afraid of being caught, but because it's the right thing to do. Do employees do what is politically expedient and beneficial for themselves or what is in the best interests of their companies, their clients, or their colleagues? Do they exaggerate claims to win the sale, or do they present the pitfalls as well as the benefits?

One good way to look at this is to follow the Golden Rule: "Do unto others as you would have them do unto you." Doing the right thing may include giving of yourself, without any expectation of personal gain, or exceeding client expectations even if there isn't any opportunity for additional business. It may mean addressing a problem before it becomes public and you are asked to correct it—even if it represents significant financial exposure.

A good example of the way an organization handles a crisis can be found by examining the actions of Johnson & Johnson during the Tylenol poisonings compared to the actions of Exxon and BP after the *Exxon Valdez* and Gulf oil spills, respectively. Johnson & Johnson's credo says that their first responsibility is to the people who use their products. In 1982, soon as they were informed that Tylenol may have been tampered with, the company launched a public recall and pulled the product off the market; they then developed new, safer ways of packaging it, including warning labels, all at an enormous cost. Exxon made promises about cleaning up the 1989 *Valdez* oil spill and did expend resources to repair some of the damage, but it was later revealed that, after the price tag rose, management had, behind closed doors, decided to limit the effort. In the end, Exxon's decision to cut off funding for the cleanup and to let "nature" repair the environmental disaster cost them much of the public forgiveness they had achieved with their initial efforts. BP's deepwater drilling rig in the Gulf of Mexico was struck by a massive fire in April of 2010 that killed 11 employees and caused the uncapped well to spill millions of gallons of crude into the Gulf and the Gulf Coast ecosystem. Unfortunately, the company underestimated the problem, was slow to react, and most notably, the CEO complained that he just wanted his "life back" when he was attempting to apologize to the Gulf residents for the spill. The lessons are numerous: First, preparing for a world in which things only go right is extremely dangerous. Second, make sure to act quickly and accept responsibility for your actions. Third, accept assistance even if it hurts your ego. Fourth, make every attempt to demonstrate that you've learned from your mistakes and that safeguards are in place so that the event is unlikely to happen again.

People who always want to do the "right thing" sometimes face difficult decisions. For example, how much are they willing to tell a prospective client about their misgivings about their own product? Is holding back the truth to protect another individual doing the right thing? There is no set answer to these questions. Everyone has to draw the line for themselves.

Strength of conviction. Another set of questions to ask yourself when determining trustworthiness is: How ethical are the people or organizations I'm dealing with? Do they have strong values? Do they stand up for what they believe in? Are they afraid to present their opinions to upper management? Do they feel comfortable breaking bad news when it is necessary to do so?

Basically, strength of conviction translates into standing up for the things that you believe in. This may include telling clients what they really need to hear instead of what you think they want to hear. Although they may disagree with you or even fault you for challenging them at the moment, they will respect you for speaking your mind and not being a "yes" person. It may include requesting from your organization the resources that you need to properly serve your clients. It may also include not selling or recommending products or services that are not in a prospect's best interests, even if you are under pressure to increase sales.

The strength of someone's conviction often poses a dilemma to individuals as well. For example, people who have strong convictions are often faced with the dilemma of knowing when to stick to their guns and when it's time to compromise to achieve unanimous consent. On the other hand, those who quickly compromise their ideals or who waffle all the time also cannot be trusted. Gerald Zaltman and Christine Moorman were exactly right when they wrote in the *Journal of Advertising Research* that "the dilemma is that if you always dig in your heels and fight for your ideas, you are considered arrogant. However, if you constantly back off when the client challenges one of your ideas you're considered a pushover."[10]

Confidence. It is important to determine whether the people you build relationships with are comfortable enough to admit their faults and errors. Ask yourself: Do they always have to be right? Do they listen to suggestions? Are they afraid to admit mistakes? If they cause a problem, do they try to find a way to fix it, or do they look for people to blame?

Confidence can be displayed within an organization by the management style that you choose. In *Principle-Centered Leadership*, Stephen Covey says, "Synergy results from valuing differences, from bringing different perspectives together in a spirit of mutual trust. Mistaking uniformity for unity, sameness for oneness, insecure people surround themselves with others who think similarly. Secure people, on the other hand, realize that the strength of their relationships with others lies as much in their differences as in their similarities. They not only respect individuals with different views, but they actively seek them out."[11]

In the same way, only people with an inner confidence can treat trust as more than just another buzzword. The following story about Ben Strohecker, founder and former president of Harbor Sweets candy company, is a perfect example of someone with the confidence to practice what he preaches (the first quoted words are Ben's):

> "To trust, you must first trust yourself enough to let go. . . . The feeling
> I had when I first exposed my financials to all of the employees was

tantamount to jumping into Marblehead Harbor in January. I'd exposed my only remaining secrets. I was administratively naked. I'd already decided the presidential perks I'd been raised with—like private secretaries, personal parking places, and private offices— were not my style. . . . So my only remaining badge of office was my financials—and I let them go." The productive powers of trust have made believers of both Ben Strohecker and his workforce. So much so that when a financial consultant came in to present benefits options to the company's leader, he suggested presenting the ideas to the workers. The visitor responded by saying, "You're crazy. They'll ask for the moon." Some did ask for the moon, Mr. Strohecker acknowledges. But the other employees put them down and said, "What kind of place do you think this is? We don't want to go out of business." [As a result] "They came out with a recommended package that was probably more conservative than what we would have given them."[12]

Ben Strohecker's confidence in his people allowed him to trust them to the point where he could give away authority—and his trust was rewarded.

Safety. When deciding whether to put your trust in someone, you try to discover if they are calm, patient, and logical. You ask yourself whether they have a lot of emotional highs and lows. When conflicts arise, do they act in a caring and responsible fashion? Do they resolve problems and make decisions on the basis of logic, or do they make emotional judgments based on bias, residual anger, or desire to avenge the past?

Companies can demonstrate that they are safe by the strength of their balance sheets, by the length of time that they have been in business, and by their history as a forward-looking organization. Spending on research and development and remaining at the cutting edge over a long period send a strong signal to the marketplace. It's comforting to know that companies that invest in research and development will continue to enhance their current technology, develop new products and services, and be there to serve your needs in the future.

Companies can also demonstrate safety by such diverse factors as the level of employee turnover (a sign of good management and employee satisfaction); whether products have been abandoned in the past, leaving customers out in the cold; or the level of their sales support and the quality of their marketing materials.

Competence. Trust is increased when an individual is believed to be competent. An advanced degree, an affiliation with a well-respected organization or an organization with a reputation for its thorough training, and professional status, all enhance the trustworthiness of an individual to some degree. These are indicators of a limited amount of competence, but they don't guarantee competence. Salespeople can increase their level of trust by demonstrating their familiarity with a product, their ability to address product questions, their prior experience in resolving a client issue, and their in-depth knowledge of the prospect's industry—but nothing is as useful in building trust as satisfactory work.

An organization's willingness to trust its employees depends in part on its estimate of their competence to perform specified tasks. But it is important to remember, as noted in Chapter 2, that people live up to the expectations that we set. The more we trust people to do things right, the more likely they will live up to our expectations.

Organizations that have strong recruiting and education programs have greater trust levels. When organizations are known for aggressive hiring practices and solid training, rather than for throwing employees in the water and watching them swim, trust is enhanced. When employees know that their peers are well trained, they know they can depend on them, that they will receive high-quality information, and that they do not have to fend for themselves.

Fairness. Peter Drucker has said, "The leaders who work most effectively, it seems to me, never say 'I.' And that's not because they have trained themselves not to say 'I.' They don't think 'I.' They think 'we'; they think 'team.' They understand their job to be to make the team function. They accept responsibility and don't sidestep it, but 'we' gets the credit. . . . This is what creates trust, what enables you to get the task done."[13]

How much we trust other people or organizations often has a lot to do with our perception of their fairness; in other words, the belief we have in their objectivity, their lack of prejudice, their impartiality. Are they objective? Do they show bias or favoritism? Do they present both sides of an issue or spin the issue to their advantage? Are they open-minded and willing to listen to new ideas? Do they give everyone the time of day, or are their minds already made up? Do they give credit where credit is due, or do they accept credit for other people's efforts? Do they have reasonable expectations? Do they know when someone tried to do their best and praise them for their efforts, or do they reprimand them for failure to perform? In the face of disagreement, do they respect the opinions of others or do they attack them, embarrassing, reprimanding, or humiliating them in front of others?

Organizations have demonstrated their fairness by such actions as taking back merchandise with no questions asked or promising that if you find the same merchandise for less money, in 90 days, and can present proof, they'll pay you the difference.

Reliability. Another quality we look for when deciding whether or not to trust a person or an organization is reliability. We ask such questions as: Are they dependable? Do they follow through on promises made? If you ask for something, can you consider it done? Are they careful not to overstate what they will do? Do they know that even a perceived promise places their honor on the line? Do they exaggerate sales claims or set impossible expectations? Even though a company may have little direct control over the outcome, a promise made can result in a promise broken. Be wary of promises such as these: the product will be fixed by Tuesday; the service person will be there in an hour; you can expect at least an 8 percent return on your investment; even though I haven't had a chance to look at your tax return, you'll probably get the same refund as last year; take this medicine and you'll feel better in an hour; the product never breaks down the first year.

Organizations can demonstrate their reliability by showing that their interest lies more in building long-term customer relationships than in selling a product; they can enhance your satisfaction by ensuring that the owner's manual is clear, that the service force is well trained, that critical parts are not back-ordered, and that customer complaints are handled promptly.

One way we judge reliability is by determining whether a broken promise was intentional. In *Getting Together*, Roger Fisher and Scott Brown distinguish among the different kinds of unreliability: "People can be unreliable in different ways. They can be erratic, ambiguous, secretive, misleading, deceptive, or dishonest, or they may weigh promises lightly in the face of changed circumstances. . . . Some people run their lives according to well-developed habits and carefully planned schedules. Others are more spontaneous and variable. We often think of the first type of person as being more reliable than the second type."[14]

Openness. Openness in relationships is built upon some existing level of trust. You feel comfortable confiding in people, knowing they would never breach your confidence or use the information against you at a later date. If they respond to that openness as expected, trust is enhanced and intimacy and honesty grow.

As Fernando Bartolome pointed out in the *Harvard Business Review*,

> It is terribly important to get subordinates to convey unpleasant messages. The sooner a problem is disclosed, diagnosed, and corrected, the better for the company. . . . In a hierarchy, it is natural for people with less power to be extremely cautious about disclosing weaknesses, mistakes, and failings—especially when the more powerful party is also in a position to evaluate and punish. . . . Often the motive for silence is at least superficially praiseworthy: people keep quiet about a developing problem while trying to solve it. Most believe solving a problem on their own is what they're paid to do, and in many cases, they're right. Subordinates are not paid to run to their bosses with every glitch and hiccup. As problems grow more serious, however, managers need to know about them.[15]

It is not enough to be totally open and honest with your employees. This philosophy must be extended to your clients and suppliers as well through such behavior as giving advanced previews of future products and sharing best practices.

Secretiveness. The opposite of openness is secretiveness, and it has the opposite effects. Organizations that deliberately build barriers between themselves and their employees or their clients will never develop relationships based on mutual trust. It does not matter whether secrecy is demonstrated by isolating top management from employees, building barbed wire around the boss's office, using one-way communication (top-down), or distancing management from clients by hiding them in an ivory tower.

The problem, according to Gordon Shea, is that "when an organization is secretive, tightly controlled, does not delegate authority, and sharply separates management and management decisions from employees and lower-level managers, it doesn't take much intelligence to recognize that management does not trust its 'underlings' to behave as reasonable, responsible people."[16]

It's in every organization's best interest to get closer to employees, suppliers, and customers. Getting closer to clients requires such actions as involving them in the product development process, aggressively asking them for feedback on the services that you provide, and demonstrating commitment to them by involving top management with their account.

Communication. In Chapter 4, the importance of open and honest communication is discussed in depth. Here, communication is viewed as an essential quality that creates high-trust organizations. Lack of communication is particularly harmful when relevant information is withheld in order to maintain control or gain personal advantage.

Organizations lack trust if employees have to weigh and measure everything they hear—if they can't trust the information that is given them. In organizations marked by trust, employees don't ask themselves: Am I being kept informed? Will they inform me of a decision that may affect me or let me find out by chance? If they are unwilling or unable to live up to a client promise, will they let me know in a timely fashion so that I can inform my clients? Would they intentionally try to misrepresent what I said? Do they tell everyone the same story?

Managers display trust when they openly communicate with their employees and reveal information that they don't have to. Dale E. Zand notes that "a manager shows trust when he seeks counsel from peers, superiors, or subordinates. He increases his vulnerability when he permits them to influence his decisions. He may be seen as a weak leader or some counselors may inadvertently or deliberately mislead him. A manager additionally shows trust when he delegates. He increases his vulnerability when he depends on others to analyze a problem, gather information, or implement a decision."[17]

The opposite of open communication occurs in organizations marked by low levels of trust. In such organizations, managers who do "not trust others will conceal or distort relevant information . . . withhold facts, disguise ideas, and conceal conclusions. [Such managers] will hide feelings that increase exposure to others. As a result, [such managers] provide incomplete, untimely information that inaccurately portrays reality."[18] The problem, according to Zand, is that "when managers withhold relevant information, distort intentions, or conceal alternatives, they introduce social uncertainty and increase the total uncertainty in solving a problem.

Social uncertainty increases the probability that underlying problems go undetected or are deliberately avoided."[19]

These, however, are all problems that can be avoided through the careful use of communication. Effective communication can also have a great impact on trust levels with clients. For example, trust is increased when clients are given advance notice of bad news so that expectations are controlled, when the downside of a product is presented along with its benefits, and when the competition is treated objectively without being denigrated.

The whole picture. Taken together, these qualities form the foundation on which trusting relationships are built. When they become part of a person's or an organization's track record, relationships grow stronger and last longer. They are the basis on which people choose friends and on which people select organizations to buy from and work with.

THE THIRD STAGE: CONSISTENCY

Once people or organizations have repeatedly displayed traits mentioned in the prior section, we tend to increase our trust in them. But at this stage, we have not internalized that trust; it is not a part of our belief system. The relationships we're building will have to stand the test of time. As we get to know the person or organization better, we begin to see patterns of behavior as well as their actions toward others, actions they are likely to repeat.

Furthermore, we look for patterns that are regular and consistent because the more predictable people are, the higher the degree of comfort we have with them. In order to establish this, we ask ourselves: Do they encourage an activity one day and prohibit it the next? Do they feel strongly about their ideas today and abandon them tomorrow? Are they reliable one day and scatterbrained the next? Do they have the strength of their convictions, or do their moods blow in the wind? Is it possible to anticipate their responses to a request or a new suggestion? Do we know if our actions will win praise or criticism? If the chips are down, will the individual or the organization be in our corner? Are their actions consistent with their words, or do they send mixed messages?

You can't verbally abuse someone one day and expect that acting with kindness the next day will erase all memories of the previous day. If you say things you later regret, for example, attacking the individual rather than debating the issue, excusing yourself does not make up for your actions. "I was angry at the time, I didn't mean it, I had other things on my mind" does not suffice. You must be consistent in displaying respectful behavior to maintain and grow trusting relationships.

Organizations demonstrate consistency by treating customers and employees in the same way and by standing behind the products and services they market. They do not introduce a new product with a big splash today only to abandon it tomorrow, nor do they enter and divest themselves of businesses so fast that they make consumers afraid they won't be around to service them tomorrow.

Consistency is also demonstrated through continuous product quality. One organization that has competitively differentiated itself this way is McDonald's. You know that when you have a McDonald's hamburger anywhere around the world, it will taste the same, making you feel at home.

There is a caveat here. Companies must grow and change to be successful. Indeed, it is important to introduce new and improved products to stay ahead of the competition. This seems antithetical to consistency. In these cases, the way that product transitions are managed is critical. After a while, the consistency that an individual or company demonstrates becomes expected. We assume they'll behave a certain way each time. Our trust grows and the layer is added to the one before, becoming, again, part of the history of the relationship.

THE FOURTH STAGE: FROM PREDICTABILITY TO FAITH

Now that consistency is established and bonded to the earlier attributes, thus becoming a part of an organization's or a person's history, we have a strong sense that we can predict what the person or the organization will do in the future. As a result, we do not question and worry about promises made: we trust them and are comfortable with our belief in them.

The problem is that any time organizations or individuals make claims, no matter how small, and they do not deliver, they shatter the comfort zone created by our trust and lose predictability. In fact, as Fisher and Brown have pointed out, "If conduct is unpredictable, we may think the person is untrustworthy. If a person is untrustworthy, we begin to question his honesty. Once we have thought in terms of honesty, that concern spreads to other areas. . . . A company that has been (perhaps unavoidably) late in shipping its products finds that customers begin to suspect the quality of the products themselves and sometimes the integrity of the company's personnel."[20]

Once the comfort zone is challenged, anything thought to be predictable in the future may be treated as suspect. In fact, once a claim is made, and not fulfilled, it can impact people's impressions in totally unrelated areas. For example, your company may announce that a new product will be out in May, only to announce in April that there has been a product delay and that it won't be available until the fourth quarter. At the same time, a salesperson may be making "false" claims to a prospect who read about the product delay online. The prospect may then wonder whether all the claims being made by the salesperson are misstated.

However, it is unusual for an individual or organization with a history of trustworthiness, consistency, and predictability to make claims that fail to materialize or to make promises they don't keep. What is far more usual is that they become so predictable that you stop evaluating their actions and allow your faith in them to take over. That decision is often made unconsciously. This stage, which is less defined than the others, is like a web of fine golden cords that make the structure within glow.

Faith enables you to go beyond facts and still feel secure about another person or even an organization. Faith is often a result of someone motivated by unselfish reasons caring about your interests above their own. It's a result of people responding supportively. It's a result of empathy, of someone showing concern. It's knowing that someone would never try to hurt you, take advantage of you in a pinch, or criticize you in front of others. It's knowing that your organization will support you, be available if you need them, coach you, encourage your ideas, and take an interest in your career and in your life.

Faith is strengthened when you put customers' interests in front of your own, not only meeting, but exceeding their expectations. It's strengthened when an organization is clearly more interested in helping prospective clients resolve their business issues than in selling them additional products. It's strengthened when you keep clients informed about new developments that may affect their organization even though the work that you performed has been completed.

CONCLUSION

Trust is in as much need of protection as the air that we breathe or the water that we drink. It is easily squandered and hard to regain. According to Tom Peters, "The essence of managing any company, whether it's IBM or Joe and Harry's Grill, is about caring, listening, trust, respect, and dignity. We talk about international competition, world-class quality, competing in time, quick turnaround, fast response, innovation, and that's the right stuff to talk about. But the other side of the coin is that all of that comes from people who give a damn, who care, who are committed, and who are cared about."[21]

The heart of the matter, as Shea noted, is that "it's time to think of trust as an asset—money in our pockets or in the organization's treasury. We can grasp the real utility of this resource if we view trust as a miracle currency: either it can be accumulated and spent without necessarily depleting our reserves—or it can be lost so that we become destitute."[22]

11

FOLLOWING YOUR CONSCIENCE

A RECIPE FOR PEAK PERFORMANCE

This book began by stressing the importance of intangible factors such as empowering your workforce, creating a work environment that encourages risk and discourages fear, improving business processes and eliminating waste, promoting continuous education and the personal and professional growth of employees, communicating in an open and honest manner, building trust among employees, networking with friends and associates, nurturing long-term relationships with suppliers and customers, working hard to develop an impeccable reputation, living according to sound business ethics, and unifying your organization around a mission and shared values. While many believe these factors are critical for competing in this century, others consider them "soft" issues.

INTANGIBLES: DIFFICULT TO QUANTIFY BUT VITAL TO SUCCESS

The Industrial Age brought us products such as cars, heavy farm equipment, refrigerators, washing machines, and computers—equipment that could be seen, touched, and demonstrated. The Information Age, in contrast, is characterized by intangibles—resources that involve intellect and the ability to gather, analyze, transmit, and synthesize information. In fact, today, such intangibles form the basis of some of the most successful companies. According to an article in *The New York Times Magazine*, "Microsoft's only factory asset is the human imagination."[1]

Just as you cannot measure liquids in pounds or nuclear fusion in quarts, you cannot use yesterday's measurements of success to gauge the importance of a knowledgeable, experienced, and committed workforce; a creative working environment; brand awareness; or reputation.

There is a tendency in this country, however, to believe that if something cannot be quantified, it does not exist. It brings to mind the 18th-century question: If a tree falls in a forest, and no one is there to hear it, did it make a sound? To apply this to management practices: If someone enhances performance in an organization using an approach that cannot be quantified, did the improvement take place?

You won't find these soft attributes in an annual report because they are intangible and difficult to quantify. But that doesn't make them any less important to an organization. These soft issues are all very like the tree that falls in the forest. In the Information Age, however, if we don't believe that there was a sound, maybe it's time to get our hearing checked.

THE ORGANIZATION'S VISION, VALUES, AND BELIEFS MUST BECOME OF PEAK IMPORTANCE

It's time for a new style of leadership. Workers do not respond well to micromanagement or to being treated like cogs in a wheel. In order to increase workforce productivity, management has learned various theories, techniques, and approaches that are believed to motivate employees. But they are all based on the fundamental premise that it is management's role to do the motivating—that is, it is up to management to push employees toward certain behaviors or to control them in a certain way. Management can reward employees by giving them a promotion, a raise, or a pat on the back; they can reprimand, discipline, or fire them; they can create rules and procedures that give selected individuals the authority to make decisions over a minimum threshold. Or, managers can earn the respect of their colleagues through their expertise, their personal integrity, and their ability to foster trust. While reward, punishment, and authority come with an individual's position, the most effective forms of management—respect, expertise, and trust—reside in the person and are earned over time.

Furthermore, it is possible—in fact, desirable—to gain employee commitment through a leader's vision or the organization's beliefs and values. According to research conducted by James C. Collins and Jerry I. Porras, faculty members at Stanford Graduate School of Business, "If you take the visionary companies that we studied going back to 1926—or whenever the companies were first listed—and let's say you had a chance to buy a share of stock in something called 'Visionary Companies, Inc'—the visionary companies have outperformed the general market by 55 times!"[2] Successful leaders know that today's motivational techniques may satisfy employees only long enough to achieve short-term goals. If you supplement today's forms of employee motivation by instilling a belief in your organization's mission and stress the importance of every employee's contribution, you bring about commitment that motivates people forever.

COMPANIES MUST MATCH INDIVIDUAL NEEDS AND CORPORATE VALUES

For today's employee, being part of something special and making a difference in the world, is much more important than the rewards sought by yesterday's "me" generation. According to a survey conducted by PricewaterhouseCoopers, "57% of the class of 1999 graduating business students in 11 countries said that attaining work/life balance is their top career goal. Another survey conducted by High Hopes, Little Trust in 1999 found that the biggest concern among young workers (49% of women and 45% of men) is not having enough time for their family and work."[3] Further evidence that students just entering the workforce are more interested in a good work-life balance than in money is also found in another study. According to a 2009 Universum student study that polled more than 60,000 students in American undergraduate and MBA programs, "67 percent of undergraduates and 58 percent of MBA students consider work-life balance to be their No. 1 career goal, more important even than compensation."[4]

The new breed of employee wants to work for an organization that they can feel proud of—one that contributes back to society; an organization that has values and viewpoints compatible with their own; an organization that is oriented toward the long haul, working toward the prevention of ills, not just curing the symptoms; an organization that cares about morals and ethics and doing what is in the best interests of its clients; an organization that doesn't dominate their lives and allows them ample time to spend with their families; and one that cares about the impact that it has on the environment. Employees want this because they recognize that such an organization will also care about them.

What is the impact of such a philosophy? What happens when you really love what you do? When you really believe in a cause? When you really care? When you feel part of something special and are doing something good for people? When you know that every action that you've made has had an impact? And when you know your efforts won't be forgotten? You become passionate about what you are doing, you can't wait to get out of bed and go to work in the morning, and you feel good about other people's successes. This generates a spark, an excitement, and an energy that becomes contagious. Employees become so committed that friends talk to them and their minds drift to work, they come in to work on the weekend to pursue their ideas, and they tirelessly fight for causes they believe in—not because it's in their own best interests, but because it's right. This kind of commitment is happening, and those organizations that unleash it are winning.

When there is a crisis, companies can count on everyone pitching in. When sacrifice is required, everyone is willing to step forward. When management needs that little something extra, people can't wait to step up to the challenge. People don't have to be cajoled, they don't have to be threatened, and they certainly don't have to be bribed. They only have to be asked.

BEING ALL THINGS TO ALL PEOPLE IS
A GUARANTEED RECIPE FOR MEDIOCRITY

Everyone talks about sticking to their knitting, but many companies don't know what their knitting is. According to a *Fortune* magazine article, "Focus means figuring out, and building on, what the company does best. It means identifying the evolving needs of your customers, then developing the key skills—often called core competencies—critical to serving them. It means setting a clear, realistic mission and then working tirelessly to make sure everyone—from the chairman to the middle manager to the hourly employee understands it."[5]

IF YOUR ORGANIZATION ISN'T FOCUSED, SOMEONE IS
PROBABLY UNDOING SOMETHING YOU JUST COMPLETED

In order to be successful, an organization must focus its efforts on those factors that are critical to its success. If you randomly select 50 people in your organization and ask them basic questions about the direction and priorities of the company, how similar would their answers be? When employees don't know where the company is heading, they can't be expected to sacrifice themselves for the benefit of the organization. They won't get excited about what they're doing, or put down their swords and stop the political bickering, and they won't be passionate about their careers or the future of the organization. Unless you get common answers to the most basic questions, you foster waste, redundancies, inefficiencies, confusion, and anxiety.

When you look at successful small corporations today, many of them have something in common. People have a common sense of purpose, and believe in the founder's vision. They maintain their individuality, but strive for team gain. People care more about the organization winning than about who gets the next promotion, and they know that resources are limited, so they concentrate them on critical areas rather than squander them.

THERE IS A DIFFERENCE BETWEEN MOTION AND MOVEMENT

Once you've determined the critical success factors that will lead you to your destination, it's important to set milestones to ensure that you keep heading in the right direction. You should always keep in mind that there's a difference between motion and movement. Motion is getting from point A to point B—working on those things that will do the most to help you achieve your goals. Movement is recklessly expending time chasing your tail; working hard at things that keep you busy, but have low payoff; maintaining very elaborate to-do lists, but never looking to see which activities are important to the success of the organization; trying to accomplish so many things and spreading yourself so thin that your actions don't have a meaningful impact. Ask yourself whether those activities that are closest to you at the moment are the most important or just the most urgent. Otherwise, you'll spend all of your time putting out fires rather than lighting them.

FLEXIBILITY IS CRITICAL—
ORGANIZATIONS SHOULD BE BOUNDARYLESS

Organizations must remain flexible in order to succeed; they must create an organizational structure and operating style that permit them to take advantage of new opportunities. Many companies, for example, utilize contract employees or often outsource functions to complement their internal resources, accessing specialized skill sets that are not available or adding extra people during peak periods; gaining objective viewpoints from people with multiclient experience; and discovering new trends that may affect their business.

In the past, conventional wisdom said that multiple vendors increased competition and enhanced performance; that playing one supplier against another was good business. Today, conventional wisdom is quite the opposite. As organizations focus more of their efforts on areas that are critical to their success, they will rely more on external resources, outsourcing, strategic alliances, and building strong external relationships. The only way to ensure that those relationships will last is to start with honorable intentions, make a commitment, and expend the time and effort so that everybody wins.

IF EVERYONE SPENDS TIME TRYING TO GAIN THE UPPER HAND, EVERYONE LOSES

Optimizing partnerships requires building balanced relationships. To do this, keep in mind that contracts don't make successful relationships, people do. A partnership is successful to the degree that it replaces the traditional "us versus them" mentality with a new "us" that allows everyone to grow and to reach their full potential. People who are good at building successful alliances work very hard to structure win-win relationships. One key element to make this work is the search for overlapping areas of opportunity where both organizations win. For example, Nokia announced a very complementary relationship with Microsoft to drive sales. "Nokia fully expects, and plans, to do what Microsoft and its handset partners have so far been unable to do: make Windows Phone 7 a must-have mobile platform."[6] A partnership will succeed in the long run when both sides work together for their common good rather than each trying to get the upper hand. When greed takes over, partners spend all their time trying to outnegotiate each other and both end up losing. Moreover, in these situations, one of the organizations is likely to come out noticeably ahead of the other, ultimately causing jealousy and resentment.

PLANTATION MANAGEMENT DESTROYS PRODUCTIVITY

Treating people fairly must extend beyond your suppliers to those who work with you. Every individual should be given the opportunity to reach his or her full potential. When managers don't abide by this philosophy, employees show little initiative on the job, but are highly motivated outside of work; they put in time but no energy; they spend more time working on their résumés than on the activities at hand. According to The Conference Board, a New York-based private research group, in a 2007 survey of 5,000 U.S. households, "more than half of all respondents said they dislike their current jobs, compared to less than 40 percent in a similar survey conducted 20 years ago. These days, the lowest levels of job satisfaction are among younger workers, the survey found. Only 39 percent of respondents aged 25 and younger said they liked their current jobs—the lowest level in the survey's 20-year history—compared to 45 percent for workers between 45 and 54."[7] A management style that produces these results obviously won't be enough to compete successfully in today's global economy.

In fact, the result of this plantation-style management is already causing a disastrous collision between the needs of businesses and the demands of today's workforce. "Forty percent of 4,285 full-time private-sector employees surveyed by CareerBuilder.com said they had difficulty staying motivated in their current jobs, and 24 percent said they didn't feel loyal to their current employers."[8] Furthermore, according to MetLife's 9th Annual Study of Employee Benefits Trends (conducted in 2010), small businesses (fewer than 500 employees) may now face a new challenge—employee retention. There has been a significant decline in employee loyalty. According to the study, "In November 2008, 62% of small business employees reported feeling a very strong sense of loyalty toward their employer, but in 2010 that number dropped to only 44%. In fact, 34% of small business employees surveyed would like to work for a different employer. In contrast, small business employers' perceptions of that loyalty remained essentially unchanged over the last few years with 54% currently believing that their employees feel a strong sense of loyalty to the company."[9] Employees want to work someplace where they can make a meaningful contribution; where procedures, policies, and protocol are never more important than results; and where building bonds between people is considered as important as the bottom line.

According to W. E. Odom, former chairman of Ford Motor Credit Company:

> Today, the good managers are doing everything that they can to tear down the walls and destroy boxes. Today, they try to manage through empowerment, not intimidation. Not by seeing people as problems, but by getting people to solve problems. Not by telling people what to do, but by enabling people to make decisions. Not by devising elaborate financial models, but by providing people with the tools and incentives to think. Not by demanding allegiance, but by treating people with respect and dignity. In other words, managers today are placing an increasing amount of trust in their employees, and earning trust in return.[10]

PEOPLE WILL LIVE UP OR DOWN TO YOUR EXPECTATIONS

Companies that search for the best and brightest people must learn that their efforts shouldn't end when those people join the organization. To retain these employees, companies should invest heavily in them, both personally and professionally. Today, employees demand trust and respect. They want their input solicited, their strengths utilized, and their contributions valued. Furthermore, they want and should be given challenging new responsibilities that stretch their potential.

Managers who act in this way are far more likely to achieve superior performance from their employees. In fact, "formal psychological research as well as a large amount of casual empiricism by others leave no doubt that the power of expectation alone can influence the behavior of others. This total phenomenon is called the Pygmalion effect."[11] Studies have shown that the IQ scores of children, especially on verbal and information subjects, can be raised "merely by expecting them to do well. . . . A study showed that worker performance increased markedly when the supervisor of these workers was told that his group showed a special potential for their particular job."[12]

The opposite is also true: Employees who feel like helpless drones perform that way. Employees who believe they are essential to the success of the operation will always rise to the occasion by accepting greater responsibility, ultimately increasing their productivity.

THERE IS A DIRECT CORRELATION BETWEEN THE WAY EMPLOYEES ARE TREATED AND THE WAY THEY TREAT CUSTOMERS

As a leader, keep in mind all the costs, including the hidden ones, of mistreating employees. Among those costs are employee resignations, with the accompanying loss of key skills and customer knowledge; employees who voice discontent, thereby hurting morale; employees who use every possible "sick day" or constantly show up late; and employees who become apathetic, producing only enough to avoid being fired.

Dissatisfied employees who spend much of their workday expressing dissatisfaction and unhappiness create an air of dissension, depressing those around them, hindering concentration, and lowering everyone's spirits. Apathy is often so subtle that you may not even realize the problem exists. When investigators examined this phenomenon in 2010, they found: "The number of actively disengaged workers increased from 3 percent to 24 percent in organizations that have laid off employees, Gallup researchers found Watson Wyatt's Employee Engagement Index declined 9 percent for all employees from 2008 to 2009. More importantly, among top-performing employees, engagement dropped a much steeper 23 percent."[13] The implications of these findings are dismaying, and the ramifications for productivity and service quality are even more disheartening.

FOR EVERY ACTION, THERE IS A REACTION

Not only is it important to recognize that every action toward an employee inspires a reaction, but that actions toward employees rarely impact only those directly involved. If you compare a corporation to the human body with its complex and interdependent systems, you will understand why change in one area affects the whole. Every action provokes a reaction, especially when people have long-established relationships with others in the organization.

JUST AS CAPITAL EQUIPMENT REQUIRES MAINTENANCE TO PROTECT ITS VALUE, CREATIVITY REQUIRES NURTURING

Creativity makes a difference at every level and in every type of organization—whether in creating new products and services, managing an advertising agency relationship, or finding ways to solve long-standing problems that seem unsolvable until someone with imagination throws an old ball with a new twist.

This means that organizations must first analyze the internal climate, norms, and personal biases that inhibit creativity and then create an environment where new ideas are welcomed and allowed to flourish; where ideas are evaluated on their individual merits rather than on the status of the person introducing them; and where people look for "the good" in every idea, trying to add value to it rather than shooting it out of the sky.

An article in *Industry Week* noted that organizations that understand the need to foster creativity "regard new ideas as wild flowers. They know you do not plant seeds for wild flowers; you find them by searching in many places. They concentrate on preparing the conditions for wild flowers to grow as they push for incremental change everywhere."[14]

PROGRESS REQUIRES MISTAKES

According to an article in the *Harvard Business Review*, "Wise executives worry more about invisible mistakes—failing to take risks, failing to innovate to create new value for customers."[15] They know that when people aren't making mistakes, they're probably not trying anything new. Everyone should recognize that being right all the time is an enormous barrier to innovation. When organizations foster a risk-averse climate, creativity will be stifled. Making mistakes, and then learning from them, is an important stage in the learning process. Employees need confidence and assurance that experimentation resulting in failure won't have repercussions.

ORGANIZATIONS SUCCEED BECAUSE OF THE EFFORTS OF MANY, NOT THE STRENGTHS OF A FEW

In the past, senior management made decisions and employees implemented them. Today, however, the world is quite different. According to William J. O'Brien, former chief executive officer of Hanover Insurance Company in Worcester, Massachusetts, "The fundamental movement in business in the next 25 years will be the dispersing of power, to give meaning and fulfillment to employees in a way that avoids chaos and disorder."[16]

This will be particularly necessary in a world of rapid change, in which large bureaucracies with multiple levels of approval delay the rapid response needed to succeed in an ever-changing world. Change is fast and fierce. The speed of new developments that seemed to have reached the upper limits has not abated. In fact, according to a *Fast Company* article in 2001 by Seth Godin:

> In five months, Napster went from having 1 million to 10 million users. Eleven months later, it had 80 million users—the most successful technology introduction of all time. And then it essentially went out of business. (Now it's back again—maybe.) . . .
>
> Successful businesses hate change. . . . People with great jobs hate change. Market leaders seek out and cherish dependable systems. But upstarts and entrepreneurs love change. Turbulence scrambles the pieces on the game board; entrepreneurs get a chance to gain market share and profits. And since there are always more competitors than market leaders, there's a huge demand for change. More innovation! More competition! More change! It won't go away. It will only get worse.[17]

IF THE ORGANIZATION DOESN'T LIVE IN THE HEARTS AND MINDS OF ITS PEOPLE, IT DOES NOT EXIST

Titles should all but disappear in organizations. "Organization charts in a company neither define relationships as they actually exist nor direct the lines of communication. If the organization does not exist in the minds and hearts of the people, it does not exist. No chart can fix that. An organization's function is simple: to provide a framework, a format, a context in which people can effectively use resources to accomplish their goals."[18] Organization charts build walls between people, stifle communication and creativity, and are often the cause of internal politics, jealousy, and resentment.

EVERYONE CAN MAKE A DIFFERENCE: CASTE SYSTEMS STIFLE EXCELLENCE

" 'Oh, come off it,' you say, 'a business enterprise needn't be one happy family to succeed. Aren't plenty of slave ships making good time?' Some are. But companies seething with class discord pay a penalty in drag," according to David Sirota of Sirota Alper & Pfau.[19]

It is important that employees at all levels communicate regularly, share innovative ideas, and solve problems together. Caste systems create obstacles to success. When people socialize only along status lines, when they use jargon their colleagues can't understand, when management distances itself by creating impressive executive floors and establishing perquisites such as parking spaces, private dining rooms, and flying first class, its actions lead to suspicion, increase personal distance, and create an air of unapproachability.

BUREAUCRACIES ARE NOT BIODEGRADABLE

Peter Drucker once said, "Elephants have a hard time adapting. Cockroaches outlive everything."[20] Bloated bureaucracies crush aspirations, stifle creativity, suppress ingenuity, and slow down responsiveness. Unfortunately, once bureaucracy develops, it is as difficult to control in business as crabgrass on a suburban lawn. It causes people to thirst for power, value personal ambition over team gain, and put paperwork before people.

In bureaucracies, employees "don't matter" because they are single voices, and individual customers "don't matter" because they are never heard by the people who determine policy. People choose the political solution rather than the best answer. Promotions are earned through political savvy rather than performance; the "show" becomes more important than content; and rumor becomes the primary form of communication. This causes organizations to focus inward and lose touch with reality.

To succeed, bureaucratic obstacles must be eliminated, and speed, simplicity, and continuous improvement emphasized. Operational units must remain small. People must get out of their offices and in front of customers. Ad hoc task forces, composed of multifunctional groups, should be set up to tackle issues; ideas should be chosen based on merit rather than on an individual's place in the pecking order; and activities that do not add value to the client should be eliminated.

WASTE NOT, WANT NOT

Today, a minute can be a lifetime. Time is a precious resource that cannot be replenished: it is a constant that cannot be changed. Unlike money, which can earn different rates of return, time is finite. You cannot get more time, but you can manage your time more efficiently. In past years, growth was so plentiful and resources were so abundant that we didn't have to face the consequences of waste. Today, this isn't the case; we can't make up for lost time by throwing resources at problems. Your organization won't be competitive in the future if your competitors build products using fewer people, and aggressively market their products while yours are still in the testing stage; if innovative ideas are tied up in the approval process; if creativity is stifled by procedures; if employees are more comfortable procrastinating rather than working; and if precious time is wasted in countless meetings.

People are not willing to wait for something when a better alternative is within reach; they won't pay more to make up for ineptitude; and they won't be sympathetic when their success depends on others' efforts. Just as car manufacturers design aerodynamic racing cars with as little wind resistance as possible, companies that want to finish first have to expose and then eliminate all of the nonessential business activities that add drag rather than value.

IF YOU'RE NOT MOVING AHEAD, YOU'RE FALLING BEHIND

In a world in which change is an everyday occurrence, business as usual is a guaranteed recipe for failure. To succeed, today's company must go beyond coping with change; it must embrace change. Rather than react to change, today's employees must learn to anticipate it. Those who cling to the past will meet change with apprehension and anxiety; those prepared to meet new challenges will be rewarded with unparalleled opportunities. The rewards will go to employees who are not only committed—but ready—to lead the effort.

According to a past Coca-Cola *Annual Report*, "We don't view the future as preordained, but as an indefinite series of openings, of possibilities. What is required to succeed in the middle of this uncertainty is what the Greeks called 'practical intelligence.' Above all else, this 'practical intelligence' forces adaptability and teaches constant preparedness. It acknowledges that nothing succeeds quite as planned, and that the model is not the reality. But it also teaches that choice and preparation can influence the future."[21]

It's very easy to look at a situation and determine that since nothing is obviously wrong, it should be left alone. After all, inertia creates comfort, and change requires breaking old habits, which creates discomfort. In order to prosper today and in the future, however, businesses must seize change for the opportunities it offers. As part of that effort, leaders should encourage learning and continuous improvement through experimentation, making it clear that there's no disgrace in trying and failing. This will require fostering an environment of trust, loyalty, and commitment—those qualities that free people to devote time and attention to their work instead of covering their tracks and hiding errors.

EVERYONE IS RESPONSIBLE FOR LEADING CHANGE

Because change is no longer an occasional but rather an everyday occurrence, companies can ill afford the length of time between the development of an idea and its implementation. As soon as new ideas are introduced, they become obsolete. Just as manufacturers search for faster ways to bring new products to market, companies must search for better and faster ways to foster change in their organizations. They must create a working environment where employees change and renew themselves everyday. Second, in an age in which the workforce is becoming empowered and layers of management are being dismantled, companies can no longer afford to have a few select people make all the decisions for the company.

The reality is that people don't resist change; they resist being changed. Executives should aim not at changing their employees, but rather at fostering a spirit that it's everyone's responsibility to change the organization. In addition, in the past, management made decisions and employees were expected to conform. Companies incorrectly assumed that while participation was nice, it was not critical. Today, such attempts will cost the commitment of employees, something empowered companies cannot afford.

THE ONLY THING WE HAVE TO FEAR IS FEAR ITSELF

Just as pollution damages the environment, an air of fear is toxic to companies. When people believe they lack control over what happens to them, they become fearful. And whether their fears are real or imagined or arise over things that are concrete and immediate, such as loss of a job, or things that are more ephemeral and long term, such as personal embarrassment or damage to personal credibility or career mobility, the results are still the same: inaction, withdrawal, hiding mistakes, misrepresenting facts, or procrastination.

According to *The New York Times*, "Every working adult has known one—a boss who loves making subordinates squirm, whose moods radiate through the office, sending workers scurrying for cover, whose very voice causes stomach muscles to clench and pulses to quicken. It is not long before dissatisfaction spreads, rivalries simmer, sycophants flourish. Normally self-confident professionals can dissolve into quivering bundles of neuroses."[22] This response is brought on by a sense of powerlessness, and fear; it makes people less likely to challenge the status quo, confront issues, or openly question things they feel are wrong. A past survey of employees in 22 organizations around the country revealed that "70% of them say they 'bit their tongues' at work because they feared the repercussions of speaking out. And 98% of their responses indicate that fear has negative effects on them or their work."[23] In a time of constant change, fear must be eliminated so that all employees feel absolutely comfortable making suggestions that will better the organization.

UNLESS YOU LEARN SOMETHING NEW EVERY DAY, YOU'RE BECOMING OBSOLETE

Learning is not only an important catalyst for organizational change, but according to an *Industry Week* study, "There is a direct relationship between the amount of training the workforce receives and how committed that workforce is."[24] People today understand that they must accept responsibility for their destinies. The days are gone when it was possible to stay with an organization for life. Employees have job security only to the extent that they continue to grow, providing more value to their current employer and becoming more marketable should they decide to leave. Thus, employees believe that the company that invests in them cares about them. As a result, training provides double value, making the organization more competitive and building employee commitment.

INTERNAL COMMUNICATION IS NOT A LUXURY; IT IS A NECESSITY

Since open and honest communication is essential to creating a climate conducive to learning and change, management must accept responsibility for fostering this kind of environment. Changing to a more open and trusting environment requires letting go, unlearning many management practices of the past. But that is not easy, and it does not happen quickly. It requires managers to leave behind many skills, sources of status and power, and implicit assumptions about the workplace that were formulated during past experiences. In the past, leaders assumed the role of controlling the information employees needed to make day-to-day decisions. Leaders who continue along that path will become frustrated as they lose the confidence of employees whose desire for timely, customized information is not satisfied. Leaders must view communication as an avenue to release the creative genius of an organization, not as a bothersome chore. After all, communication acts as a powerful agent of change, a source of continuous improvement, and a catalyst for moving the organization forward.

In an age of rapid change and abundant information, employees can't be productive by waiting till the end of the month to get a generically written, watered-down newsletter that doesn't provide relevant information. While that may have been satisfactory yesterday, when everything wasn't so time sensitive, in today's global economy, it just isn't enough. Employees are saying that they need information today because it will be obsolete tomorrow; they are saying that it must be tailored to meet their specific needs or they're just not interested.

Where professionals once produced employee communication, laypeople are now developing it. Where it was once broadcast from the ivory tower, it is now transmitted through the grapevine. Where the purpose of internal communication was once to report on the completion of an event, it now plants seeds that will grow into new ideas. Where communication was once infrequent, it is now constant. Where there was once lag time in reporting an event, communication is now instantaneous. Where formal mass communication was once commonplace, customization and personalization are now the norm.

COMPARTMENTALIZATION OF KNOWLEDGE
BUILDS WALLS BETWEEN PEOPLE

Employees must know and understand how their actions affect others in an organization, and they must be held accountable for the impact their decisions have on other parts of the organization. Problems occur when employees become so focused on achieving their own departmental goals that they optimize their own personal interests at the expense of the organization. When employees don't share information, efforts are duplicated, deadlines are missed, redundancy occurs, rework increases, and interdepartmental relationships deteriorate.

It is everyone's job to encourage communication to flow freely in an organization, breaking down the compartmentalization of knowledge. Communication cannot be stifled because of organization charts or other artificial boundaries created by management. Employees must feel free to contact anyone who has information that can help them accomplish an activity. Management must actively develop forums encouraging employees to get to know people, build shared values, discuss emerging issues, and solve common problems.

THERE IS NO SUBSTITUTE FOR OPEN
AND HONEST COMMUNICATION

Access to information is so fundamental to doing our jobs properly that it must be considered a right, not a privilege. At a time when we must encourage creativity from all of our employees, the information that we share serves as the fundamental building block and catalyst to stimulate those new ideas.

According to Henry Stimson, U.S. secretary of war in World War II, ". . . the only way you can make a man trustworthy is to trust him."[25] But if this rings true, according to a Towers Perrin 2004 study, of 1,000 U.S. workers polled, "just over half (51%) of the respondents believe their company generally tells employees the truth, while almost a fifth (19%) disagree. At the same time, 51% believe their companies try too hard to 'spin' the truth. The survey also shows that employees believe their companies communicate more honestly with shareholders (60%) and customers (58%) than with workers."[26] To ensure that people are not kept in the dark, even unwittingly, management must be committed to open and honest communication throughout the organization. That openness is part of the nurturing environment that spurs creativity, an environment in which there is little distrust, one in which everyone pulls together to achieve a common end. In this environment, new ideas are challenged and constructive feedback is offered.

ORGANIZATIONS MUST BECOME OBSESSED WITH LISTENING

Many management groups spend so much time talking among themselves that they lose sight of reality. Organizations must become obsessed with listening to both their customers and their employees. Many managers isolate themselves from those who have daily contact with customers and, as a result, lose touch with customer needs. Some CEOs appear in their offices infrequently because they spend so much of their time serving on boards or making appearances. Other managers isolate themselves by spending time in meetings with other managers. When employees don't have access to management, when they have to go through layers of secretaries to make an appointment that is later canceled and rescheduled, saying that the company has an open-door policy is meaningless.

CUSTOMERS MUST BE THE CENTERPIECE OF YOUR ATTENTION

Due to global competition, companies have placed so much emphasis on, and have made such great strides in, the production process that it is often difficult to differentiate products solely on the basis of quality workmanship. Now, much more is needed to win the loyalty of the marketplace. Overcoming the tendency to treat customers poorly—and the costs of doing so—will require a greater focus on the customer. In fact, intangibles, such as quality service, have been shown to lead to market expansion and to premium pricing.

The change in emphasis is much more evident in the services industry where products are often intangible, precise specifications cannot be set, and the production and consumption of many services are inseparable.

Here, quality is defined universally as meeting and exceeding the expectations of clients—in every step leading up to, during, and after the sale.

Furthermore, clients must not be viewed as isolated transactions but rather as the potential lifelong relationship that they represent. Every client deserves to be treated as your organization's only client. Companies cannot afford to spend the time and effort that it takes to develop new business only to lose clients shortly thereafter. In fact, companies should be so outraged when they lose an existing client that they immediately search for ways to improve themselves so that it never happens again. Think about the effort of bringing in new clients; the way they are courted; how you accommodate their every whim. Then, when they become clients, the honeymoon ends. Think about your major clients. When they call, everything else is dropped; when they make suggestions, everyone listens; and when they need something done, everyone responds. Now think about all your other clients. We can't accommodate them because it's against company policy; we don't listen to their suggestions because we know better than they do; we can't take their calls because we're in meetings; everything that takes a little extra effort is a bother.

Since superior client service is as much a mind-set as it is an activity, it's important to define the culture that produces superior service. Such a culture is built on the belief that policy changes should be made to make your client's life better, not your own; that your employees do their best work because they care rather than because the competition is making inroads; and that your company's employees know that their first and foremost job is to service clients, never taking their business for granted.

UNLESS YOU LISTEN TO YOUR CUSTOMERS, YOU'LL BE MAKING TODAY'S DECISIONS BASED ON YESTERDAY'S INFORMATION

Just as you can't develop a lasting friendship with someone you don't know well, you cannot develop relationships with customers unless you understand their needs. And that won't happen by magic. Ask yourself if you spend your time dominating discussions or actively listening. Do you understand your customers' political sensitivities? Are you flexible in responding to customers or are you set in your ways?

Because giving customers what they want is the only thing that matters, it's very important to understand what customers consider excellent service. You can accomplish that by providing such opportunities for feedback as conducting account reviews, periodically meeting with your customers to discuss the relationship and how it can be improved; holding focus group sessions; conducting surveys; establishing dealer councils; and requesting feedback through your website and 800 numbers.

In fact, in today's global business climate, responding to customers' needs isn't enough; you must anticipate them. Thus, one of the best ways to improve customer service is to actively search for best practices, both from inside and outside your industry, and then find ways to adapt those ideas to your organization.

TALK IS CHEAP

Having integrity means sticking to your principles, no matter what. It means making sure that your actions are consistent with your words. If it's the last day of the sales month, and the numbers look lousy, are employees still encouraged to do what is in the best interests of the client or are they asked to sell something for immediate gain? Are managers rewarded for the development of their people as well as for the bottom line? Is a promise made to a client kept even though circumstances have changed in such a way that the agreement is now less profitable? The answers to these questions will tell you whether your company values principled behavior over short-term business.

TAKE THE SHORT-TERM VIEW—ONLY IF YOU PLAN TO BE IN BUSINESS FOR THE SHORT TERM

Real leaders provide a legacy for those who follow them; they don't focus only on today's results. They build organizations that deliver service excellence and train employees to recognize the value of building long-term relationships. They help employees learn to see themselves through their customers' eyes rather than focusing inwardly. They teach employees to go beyond the selling role, offering advice and information that provides added value to the buyer and recognizes their ongoing needs. They concentrate on building ongoing relationships with a few clients instead of endlessly searching for new clients and then losing them as they focus on yet new leads.

QUALITY, TRAINING, AND INTERNAL COMMUNICATION MUST BE INTEGRATED INTO EVERYTHING YOU DO

Employees shouldn't think about quality only when participating in a quality meeting; they shouldn't think about learning only when attending a seminar; and they shouldn't think of communication as just a series of activities such as newsletters or brochures. Quality, training, and communication are as much a mind-set as they are an activity.

HONESTY ISN'T THE BEST POLICY—IT'S THE ONLY POLICY

It takes a long time to win confidence and trust, but both can be quickly destroyed if you do not live up to your claims. People do business with those who have a high degree of integrity. They avoid organizations that charge different prices for the same merchandise. They avoid organizations that have a reputation for talking about other clients with outsiders, whether that involves disclosing confidential information or just not speaking well of them. They avoid organizations that claim other people's ideas as their own or that take advantage of a relationship by overselling.

KNOW WHEN TO WALK AWAY FROM BUSINESS

There are many times when the best thing for you to do is to walk away from a sale. Don't accept business unless you can handle it properly. Don't sell your services if you are not 100 percent sure that you can satisfy your client's needs. Never perform a service when you feel that the client won't receive sufficient value for their money. Lastly, never give away business just to get your foot in the door: the long-term costs may lead you to resent the client later.

TRUST IS THE MIRACLE INGREDIENT

The importance of trust cannot be overstated. Remember these words from the last chapter; keep them in mind when facing difficult decisions.

> Trust is the fabric that binds us together, creating an orderly, civilized society from chaos and anarchy. If we can't trust our husband or our wife, if we can't trust our children, if we can't trust our boss or our colleagues, if we can't trust our preacher or our senator, then we have nothing on which to build a stable way of life. Trust is not an abstract, theoretical, idealistic goal forever beyond our reach. Trust—or a lack of it—is inherent in every action that we take and affects everything that we do. Trust is the cement that binds relationships, keeping spouses together, business deals intact, and political systems stable. Without trust, marriages fail, voters become apathetic, and organizations flounder. Without trust, no company can ever hope for excellence.

Trust is like love in a marriage: it bonds people together and makes them strong and effective. Trust in a relationship increases security, reduces inhibitions and defensiveness, and frees people to share feelings and dreams. Trust makes you free to put your deepest fears in the palms of your colleagues' hands, knowing that they will be treated with care. Trust allows you to be yourself and maintain your own values without worrying about acceptance. Trust makes colleagues willing to spend time together and make sacrifices for one another. Trust is an expression of faith that makes it easy for colleagues to have confidence in one another's ability to perform well and to know that they will be there if needed. Trust means that promises made will be kept, and it also means that when a promise is not kept, it was probably for good cause. And finally, trust means that a relationship will last not because it is good business, but because the relationship itself is valued.

THERE IS A DIRECT CORRELATION BETWEEN INTEGRITY AND BOTTOM-LINE PERFORMANCE

All too many people lose sleep because of an unfocused anxiety. They are worried about the future. They don't know if this is the last round of layoffs, whether their suppliers will make good on their promises, or if their clients will continue doing work with them. We no longer trust people to tell us the truth, to do what is right rather than what is politically expedient, to live up to their commitments, or to care about living up to a code of honor.

In a labor-intensive society, hard work resulted in tired bones and muscles. In the Information Age, our bodies tell us that enough is enough by reacting with stress-related ailments ranging from headaches to backaches to anxiety attacks. In fact, according to a *Wall Street Journal* article, "What makes an ethical executive tick? Nobody knows for sure, but London House [a consulting firm] thinks they may be happier, less tense and more responsible than people who are more willing to tolerate unethical behavior. . . . The most striking finding: The more emotionally healthy the executives, as measured on a battery of tests, the more likely they were to score high on the ethics test. High-ethics executives were also less likely to feel hostility, anxiety and fear."[27] The costs to society of everyone acting like random molecules bouncing off one another is just too great. We have no time to think about what is important. We judge someone's worth by what we see on the outside rather than their inner worth. We envy someone who has achieved success without thinking about what they did to earn it. In business, the new bottom line means you don't jump down peoples' throats when they make mistakes; you make it clear that you know they are trying their best—and they will respond in kind. It also means you don't hire bodies—you seek valued employees to join your business family. You invest in your people. You are not out to sell to your customers but to service them now and in the future. Your responsibilities go beyond the next quarter's financials to build a legacy for those who follow.

Being true to ourselves does not mean harming or even ignoring others; honesty has to be more than obeying the letter of the law because it is too easy to pervert the legal system to avoid acting the way we know we should. Being loyal to others means assuming that they will keep their word and letting them know that we will keep ours.

In the past, we assumed that people had integrity. Their actions rested on a foundation of values that made it very unlikely that they would act dishonorably. We need not try to re-create the past, but we ought to work toward a better future, keeping in mind that everyone can make a difference and that we can't wait for the next person to make the first move. In our complex society, contracts are needed to formalize arrangements, but they should not substitute for honorable relationships. We lose something very tangible when we abandon such intangibles as loyalty, trust, and honor.

NOTES

CHAPTER 1

1. "Best Global Brands 2010," *Interbrand*,
   http://www.interbrand.com/en/best-global-brands/best-global-brands-2008
   /best-global-brands-2010.aspx.

2. Robert Fulghum, *All I Really Need to Know I Learned in Kindergarten* (New York: Ivy Books, 1991), p. 4.

CHAPTER 2

1. Ken Shelton, "Plantation Management," *Executive Excellence*, vol. 7, no. 2, February 1990, p. 11.

2. Stephen R. Covey, *Principle-Centered Leadership: Teaching People How to Fish* (Provo, UT: The Institute for Principle-Centered Leadership, 1990), p. 139.

3. Jack Gordon, "Who Killed Corporate Loyalty?" *Training*, March 1990, p. 29.

4. Sarah Anderson, Chuck Collins, Sam Pizzigati, Kevin Shih, *Executive Excess 2010: CEO Pay and the Great Recession*, Institute for Policy Studies, http://www.ips-dc.org/reports/executive_excess_2010.

5. The Conference Board, "US Job Satisfaction at Lowest Level in Two Decades," Press release, January 5, 2010.

6. Ibid.

7. Ken Matejka and Jay Leibowitz, "A Commitment to Ex-S," *Manage*, February 1989, p. 3.

8. Amy Saltzman, "The New Meaning of Success," *U.S. News & World Report*, September 17, 1990, p. 56.

9. Alan Deutschman, "What 25-Year-Olds Want," *Fortune*, August 27, 1990, p. 44.

10. The Conference Board, January 5, 2010.

11. Gianni Zappalà, "Corporate Citizenship and Human Resource Management," Australian Centre for Industrial Relations Research and Teaching, University of Sydney, Working Paper 89, February 2004, http://www.orfeusresearch.com.au/.

12. "Research Study: 'TNS/Conference Board Report on Employee Engagement and Commitment,'" *Winning Workplaces* (TNS/Conference Board, September 2005), http://www.winningworkplaces.org/library/research/rs_engagement_commitment.php.

13. Thomas F. O'Boyle, "Fear and Stress in the Office Take Toll," *The Wall Street Journal*, November 6, 1990, p. B1.

14. Laurence Kelly, "Understanding Absenteeism," *The Worklife Report*, December 1989, p. 8.

15. The Conference Board, January 5, 2010.

16. William L. Ginnoda, "How to Build Employee Commitment," *National Productivity Review*, Summer 1989, vol. 8, no. 3, p. 251.

17. Shari Caudron, "Rebuilding Employee Trust," *Workforce Management*, October 2002, http://www.workforce.com/section/09/feature/23/33/47/index.html.

18. Tracy Benson and Robert Haas, "Vision Scores 20/20," *Industry Week*, April 2, 1990, p. 23.

19. Robert Howard, "Values Make the Company: An Interview with Robert Haas," *Harvard Business Review*, September–October 1990, p. 139.

20. Charles O'Reilly, "Corporations, Culture, and Commitment: Motivation and Social Control in Organizations," *California Management Review*, Summer 1989, p. 12.

21. Robert Waterman, *The Renewal Factor* (New York: Bantam Books, 1987), p. 71.

22. Covey, p. 260.

23. Ibid., p. 261.

24. Ibid.

25. Sue Shellenbarger, "Thinking Happy Thoughts at Work," *The Wall Street Journal*, January 27, 2010, http://online.wsj.com/article/SB10001424052748704905604575027042440341392.html.

26. Covey, p. 261.

27. Ibid., p. 262.

28. Max De Pree, *Leadership Is an Art* (New York: Dell, 1989), p. 22.

29. Thomas A. Stewart, "New Ways to Exercise Power," *Fortune*, November 6, 1989, p. 52.

30. Ibid.

31. Ibid., p. 53.

32. Ron J. Markin and Charles M. Lillis, "Sales Managers Get What They Expect," *Business Horizons*, June 1975, p. 52.

33. Ibid., p. 53.

34. Stanley Modic, "Whatever It Is, It's Not Working," *Industry Week*, July 17, 1989, p. 27.

35. Jim Braham, "A Rewarding Place to Work," *Industry Week*, September 18, 1989, p. 16.

36. Holly Rawlinson, "Make Awards Count," *Personnel Journal*, October 1988, p. 140.

37. Morton Grossman and Margaret Magnus, "The 2.1 Billion Rash of Awards," *Personnel Journal*, May 1989, p. 72.

38. Fran Tarkenton, "The Big Boss Is Dead," *Fast Track*, March 12, 1990.

CHAPTER 3

1. Erick Schonfeld, "GE Sees the Light by Learning to Manage Innovation: Jeffrey Immelt Is Remaking America's Flagship Industrial Corporation into a Technology and Marketing Powerhouse," *Business 2.0*, July 1, 2004.

2. "Leading in Tougher Times, A Presentation by Warren Bennis," summary report in *Investment in America Forum: Leadership and Organizational Challenges in an Age of Discontinuity*, United States Military Academy at West Point, June 25–27, 2002 (The Conference Board, 2002), http://www.leadertoleader.org/ourwork/iaf_2002.pdf.

3. James P. Andrew, Joe Manget, David C. Michael, Andrew Taylor, Hadi Zablit, *Innovation 2010: A Return to Prominence—and the Emergence of a New World Order*, The Boston Consulting Group, April 2010.

4. Roger von Oech, *A Whack on the Side of the Head* (New York: Warner Books, 1983), p. 30. See also von Oech's *A Kick in the Seat of the Pants* (New York: Harper & Row, 1986) for valuable insights on creativity.

5. Roger von Oech, *A Kick in the Seat of the Pants* (New York: Harper & Row, 1986), p. 14.

6. "The 50 Most Innovative Companies," *Bloomberg Businessweek*, April 22, 2010, http://www.businessweek.com/interactive_reports/innovative_companies_2010.html.

7. Gary Hamel, "Deconstructing Apple—Part I," *Gary Hamel's Management 2.0* (blog), *The Wall Street Journal*, February 22, 2010, http://blogs.wsj.com/management/2010/02/22/deconstructing-apple-part-i/.

8. Thomas Osborn, "How 3M Manages for Innovation," *Marketing Communications*, November–December 1988, p. 19.

9. "IBM 2010 Global CEO Study: Creativity Selected as Most Crucial Factor for Future Success," *United Business Media PR Newswire*, May 18, 2010. (This article discusses the fourth edition of IBM's biennial Global CEO Study series, *Capitalizing on Complexity: Insights from the Global Chief Executive Officer Study, 2010*, and contains a link to the study.) http://www.prnewswire.com/news-releases/ibm-2010-global-ceo-study-creativity-selected-as-most-crucial-factor-for-future-success-94028284.html.

10. Eric Schmidt, "Erasing Our Innovation Deficit," *The Washington Post*, February 9, 2010, http://www.washingtonpost.com/wp-dyn/content/article/2010/02/09/AR2010020901191.html.

11. Larry Reibstein, "For Corporate Speech Writers, Life is Seldom a Simple Matter of ABCs," *The Wall Street Journal*, June 30, 1987, p. 33.

12. Erik Brynjolfsson and Michael Schrage, "The New, Faster Face of Innovation," *MIT Sloan Management Review*, August 17, 2009.

13. Jack Adamson, "The Art of Managing Creative People," *Executive Excellence*, September 1989, p. 9.

14. "Siemens CEO: Fast Innovation as Key for Co's Future Report." *Dow Jones International News*, June 25, 2005.

15. R. Donald Gamache and Robert L. Kuhn, *The Creativity Infusion* (New York: Harper & Row, 1989), p. 25.

16. Robert H. Waterman, Jr., *The Renewal Factor* (New York: Bantam Books, 1987), p. 91.

17. Deborah Dougherty, "The Trouble with Senior Managers on Product Innovation: A View from the Trenches," paper published by The Wharton School, August 1988, pp. 11–12.

18. David Placek, "Creativity Survey Shows Who's Doing What," *Marketing News*, November 6, 1989, p. 14.

19. Dougherty, p. 8.

20. Von Oech, *A Whack on the Side of the Head*, p. 49.

21. Russell Mitchell, "Masters of Innovation: How 3M Keeps Its New Products Coming," *Business Week*, April 10, 1989, p. 58.

22. Schmidt.

23. Reibstein, p. 33.

24. Gamache and Kuhn, p. 34.

25. Dougherty, pp. 14–15.

26. Mark Frohman and Perry Pascarella, "Achieving Purpose-Driven Innovation," *Industry Week*, March 19, 1990, p. 20.

27. Stratford Sherman, "Eight Big Masters of Innovation," *Fortune*, October 15, 1984, p. 84.

28. Mitchell, p. 58.

29. Alicia Johnson, "3M Organized to Innovate," *Management Review*, July 1986, pp.38–39.

30. Dougherty, p. 22.

31. Edward de Bono, *Lateral Thinking* (New York: Perennial Library, 1973), p. 108.

32. Dougherty, p. 7.

33. Ronald A. Mitsch, "Three Roads to Innovation," *The Journal of Business Strategy*, September–October 1990, p. 8.

34. Vic Sussman, "To Win, First You Must Lose," *U.S. News & World Report*, January 15, 1990, p. 64.

35. Gary Meyers, "How to Nurture Creativity," *Public Relations Journal*, November 1988, p. 45.

36. Robert D. Hof, "Building an Idea Factory," *Bloomberg Businessweek*, October 11, 2004, http://www.businessweek.com/magazine/content/04_41/b3903462.htm.

37. Osborn, p. 20.

38. Von Oech, *A Whack on the Side of the Head*, p. 105.

39. Placek, p. 14.

40. Roderick Wilkinson, "50 Booster Rockets for Your Imagination," *Supervision*, January 1989, p. 25.

41. Royal Bank of Canada, "The Creative Approach," *NRECA Management Quarterly*, Winter 1988–89, pp. 39–40.

42. Ibid., p. 39.

CHAPTER 4

1. *Capitalizing on Effective Communication: How Courage, Innovation, and Discipline Drive Business Results in Challenging Times*, Communication ROI Study Report, Towers Watson, 2010, p. 3. This study looked at data collected in April and May 2009, from 328 organizations that collectively represented five million employees in various regions around the world.

2. Richard Saul Wurman, *Information Anxiety* (New York: Bantam, 1990), p. 32.

3. Jeanette A. Davy, Angelo Kinicki, John Kilroy, and Christine Scheck, "After the Merger: Dealing with People's Uncertainty," *Training and Development Journal*, November 1988, p. 57.

4. Dunhill Personnel Systems Inc. and the Columbia Business School, "Workplace Issues Top On-the-Job-Stress Points for Managers," *Inc.*, September 1990, p. 131.

5. *Capitalizing on Effective Communication*, p. 8.

6. The Conference Board, "U.S. Job Satisfaction Keeps Falling, The Conference Board Reports Today," Press release, February 28, 2005.

7. Alvie L. Smith, *Innovative Employee Communication* (Englewood Cliffs, NJ: Prentice-Hall, 1991), p. 231.

8. *The State of Employment Engagement–2008: North American Overview*, Blessing-White, 2008.

9. *Mercer's 2002 People at Work Survey*, Mercer Human Resource Consulting, 2002.

10. *IABC Research Foundation and Buck Consultants Employee Engagement Survey*, June 2010.

11. Ibid.

12. "Listen for the Answers: A New IABC Research Foundation Study Reveals Opportunities to Enhance Employee Engagement," *The Free Library*, 2009, http://www.thefreelibrary.com/Listen+for+the+answers%3a+a+new+IABC+Research+Foundation+study+reveals+...-a0207226689.

13. Alison Stein Wellner, "Lost in Translation," *Inc.*, September 1, 2005, http://www.inc.com/magazine/20050901/managing.html.

14. Nicole Perlroth, "Corporate Bullies," *Forbes*, May 5, 2010, http://www.forbes.com/2010/05/05/bullying-bosses-executives-leadership-careers-gorilla_2.html.

15. "Towers Perrin Survey Finds Almost Half of American Workers Doubt the Credibility of Employer Communications," Press release, *CSRwire*, January 6, 2004. (This press release refers to the Towers Perrin survey *Enhancing Corporate Credibility: Is It Time to Take the Spin Out of Employee Communication?*, released January 2004.) http://www.csrwire.com/press/press_release/20728-Towers-Perrin-Survey-Finds-Almost-Half-of-American-Workers-Doubt-the-Credibility-of-Employer-Communications.

16. Bill Lane, "Liberating GE's Energy," *Monogram* (GE Publication), Fall 1989, p. 3.

17. Robert E. Kelley, "Gold Collar Worker Survey," News release, Carnegie Mellon University, November 9, 1989.

18. Peter M. Senge, *The Fifth Discipline* (New York: Doubleday, 1990), p. 150.

19. Ibid., p. 212.

20. John K. Borchardt, "Who Puts Bad Apples in the Barrel?" *Today's Chemist*, April 2001, http://pubs.acs.org/subscribe/archive/tcaw/10/i04/html/TCAW04work.html.

21. Terrence E. Dean and Allen A. Kennedy, *Corporate Cultures* (Reading, MA: Addison-Wesley, 1982), p. 135.

22. Max De Pree, *Leadership Is an Art* (New York: Dell, 1989), p. 92.

23. Joanne Martin, Martha S. Feldman, Mary Jo Hatch, and Sim B. Sitkin, "The Uniqueness Paradox in Organizational Stories," *Administrative Science Quarterly*, September 1983, p. 448.

24. Ibid., p. 439.

25. Ibid., p. 144.

26. James A. Autry, *Love and Profit: The Art of Caring Leadership* (New York: William Morrow, 1991), p. 81.

27. Wellner.

28. Autry, p. 181.

29. Frank K. Sonnenberg, *Marketing to Win* (New York: Harper & Row, 1990), p. 183.

30. Timothy Schellhardt, "Slick Annual Reports Gloss over Employees," *The Wall Street Journal*, April 29, 1991, p. B1.

31. "When Employees Talk," *Communication Management*, July 1988, no. 107 [newsletter], Towers Perrin.

32. Sonnenberg, pp. 176–179.

33. *HR Focus*, May 1990, p. 7.

34. E. Zoe McCathrin, "Beyond Employee Publications," *Public Relations Journal*, July 1989, p. 15.

35. "Towers Perrin Survey Finds Almost Half of American Workers Doubt the Credibility of Employer Communications."

36. Terry Van Tell, "Communications with Your Employees and Boss," *Supervisory Management*, October 1989, p. 5.

37. McCathrin, p. 15.

38. Jay L. Johnson, "Internal Communication: A Key to Wal-Mart's Success," *Direct Marketing*, November 1989, p. 72.

39. McCathrin, p. 20.

40. Ibid.

41. John Thorbeck, "The Turnaround Value of Values," *Harvard Business Review*, January–February 1991, p. 56.

42. Valerie McClelland and Richard E. Wilmot, "Improve Lateral Communication," *Personnel Journal*, August 1990, p. 32.

43. Senge, p. 283.

44. Donald E. Petersen, speech before the Foundation for American Communications, Naples, Florida, January 16, 1987.

45. Maryann Keller, *Rude Awakening: The Rise, Fall, and Struggle for Recovery of General Motors* (New York: William Morrow, 1989), pp. 124–125, 129.

46. Johnson, p. 68.

47. Dean and Kennedy, p. 86.

CHAPTER 5

1. Jena McGregor, "Consumer Vigilantes," *Bloomberg Businessweek*, February 21, 2008, http://www.businessweek.com/magazine/content/08_09/b4073038437662.htm?chan =magazine+channel_in+depth.

2. "Satisfaction Not Guaranteed," *Bloomberg Businessweek*, June 19, 2006, http://www.businessweek.com/magazine/content/06_25/b3989041.htm.

3. Leonard Berry, "The Costs of Poor Quality Service Are Higher Than You Think," *American Banker*, June 24, 1987, p. 4.

4. Ibid.

5. Jennifer Harshman, "Bad Customer Service Stories Travel Faster," Suite101.com, May 22, 2009, http://customerrelations.suite101.com/article.cfm/bad_customer _service_stories_travel_faster.

6. McGregor, 2008.

7. "Quantifying Bad Word of Mouth," Consumerist.com, March 20, 2006, http://consumerist.com/2006/03/quantifying-bad-word-of-mouth.html.

8. The Forum Corporation, "Customer Focus Research," *Executive Briefing*, April 1988, pp. 3–4.

9. The PIMS Data Base, *PIMS LETTER*, No. 33, p. 8.

10. Jena McGregor, "Customer Service Champs 2010," *Bloomberg Businessweek*, July 2010, http://www.businessweek.com/interactive_reports/customer_service_2010.html.

11. "12 Lessons from the Best Customer Service Companies," Focus.com, http://www.focus.com/fyi/customer-service/12-lessons-best-customer-service-companies/.

12. Valarie A. Zeithaml, A. Parasuraman, and Leonard L. Berry, *Delivering Quality Service* (New York: Free Press, 1990), p. 21.

13. Carl Sewell and Paul B. Brown, *Customers for Life* (New York: Doubleday, 1990), p. 121.

14. Rosabeth Moss Kanter, "Think Like the Customer: The Global Business Logic," *Harvard Business Review*, July–August 1992, p. 9.

15. Ibid.

16. Sewell and Brown, p. 17.

17. Russell R. Miller, "Modest Alternative to Killing All Lawyers," *Manager's Journal*.

18. James Donnelly, Jr., *Close to the Customer* (Illinois: Irwin, 1992), pp. 76–77.

19. Ibid.

20. Adam Braff and John C. DeVine, "Maintaining the Customer Experience," *McKinsey Quarterly*, December 2008.

21. "12 Lessons from the Best Customer Service Companies."

22. Paula Haynes, "Seven Principles of Waiting. Hating To Wait: Managing the Final Service Encounter," *The Journal of Services Marketing*, Fall 1990, vol. 4, no. 4, pp. 20–26.

23. Donnelly, p. 21.

24. "12 Lessons from the Best Customer Service Companies."

25. Tom Peters, *Thriving on Chaos* (New York: Knopf, 1987), p. 91.

26. U.S. Office of Consumers Affairs, in cooperation with Chevrolet Motor Division of General Motors, *Increasing Consumer Satisfaction*, p. 4.

27. "12 Lessons from the Best Customer Service Companies."

28. Frank K. Sonnenberg, *Marketing to Win* (New York: Harper and Row, 1990), p. 203.

29. Kristin Anderson and Ron Zemke, *Delivering Knock Your Socks Off Service* (New York: Amacom, 1991), p. 14.

CHAPTER 6

1. Robert J. Kriegel and Louis Patler, *If It Ain't Broke . . . Break It!* (New York: Warner Books, 1991), pp. 9, 26.

2. *The Enterprise of the Future: IBM Global CEO Study 2008*, IBM Corporation, May 2008.

3. Michelle Nichols, "The Upside of Change: Increased Sales," *Bloomberg Businessweek*, September 21, 2007, http://www.businessweek.com/smallbiz/content/sep2007/sb20070921_024440.htm.

4. Seth Godin, "Survival Is Not Enough," *Fast Company*, December 31, 2001, http://www.fastcompany.com/magazine/54/survival.html.

5. "The 10 Questions Every Change Agent Must Answer," *Bill Taylor* (blog), June 18, 2009, quote attributed to an "unknown Texas genius," http://blogs.hbr.org/taylor/2009/06/the_10_questions_every_change.html.

6. John P. Kotter and Leonard A. Schlesinger, "Choosing Strategies for Change," *Harvard Business Review*, March–April 1979, pp. 106–113.

7. Godin.

8. Alan M. Webber, "Learning for a Change," interview with Peter Senge, in *Fast Company*, April 30, 1999, http://www.fastcompany.com/magazine/24/senge.html.

9. Peter M. Senge, *The Fifth Discipline* (New York: Doubleday, 1990), p. 55.

10. Alfred J. Marrow, David G. Bowers, and Stanley E. Seashore, *Management by Participation* (New York: Harper & Row, 1967).

11. *The Enterprise of the Future: IBM Global CEO Study 2008*.

12. Patricia A. Galagan, "The Learning Organization Made Plain," interview with Peter M. Senge, in *Training & Development Journal*, October 1, 1991, p. 42.

13. Chris Argyis, "Teaching Smart People How to Learn," *Harvard Business Review*, May–June 1991, p. 99.

14. Kriegel and Patler, p. 128.

15. Ibid., p. 34.

16. Galagan interview with Senge, p. 38.

17. Brooks Carder, "Kicking the Habit," *Quality Progress*, March 1991, p. 88.

18. Webber interview with Senge.

19. Carder.

20. *Making Change Work: IBM Global Study*, IBM Corporation, October 2008.

21. Kriegel and Patler, p. 85.

22. Therese R. Welter, "They're Afraid of You," *Industry Week*, October 1, 1990, p. 11.

23. Judith M. Bardwick, *Danger in the Comfort Zone* (New York: Amacom, 1991), p. 36.

24. Kathleen D. Ryan and Daniel K. Oestreich, *Driving Fear Out of the Workplace* (San Francisco: Jossey-Bass, 1991), p. 133.

25. General Electric, *Annual Report*, 1991, p. 5.

26. Richard J. Schonberger, *Building a Chain of Customers* (New York: Free Press, 1990), p. 122.

27. Walter Kiechel III, "The Boss as Coach," *Fortune*, November 4, 1991, p. 204.

28. *Vis à Vis*, March 1990, p. 80.

29. Kriegel and Patler, p. 167.

30. Richard Saul Wurman, *Information Anxiety* (New York: Bantam, 1990), p. 192.

31. Tom Peters, *Thriving on Chaos* (New York: Knopf, 1987), p. 259.

32. Dr. Tineke Bahlmann, "The Learning Organization in a Turbulent Environment," *Human Systems Management*, 1990, p. 255.

33. Alan Mumford, "Learning Styles and Learning," *PR*, March 16, 1987, p. 158.

34. Lucia Solorzano, "Helping Kids Learn—Their Own Way," *U.S. News & World Report*, August 31, 1987, p. 62.

35. Wurman, p. 172.

36. Galagan interview with Senge, p. 43.

37. Ibid., p. 43.

38. Jeremy Campbell, *Grammatical Man: Information, Entropy, Language, and Life* (New York: Simon & Schuster, 1983), p. 141.

39. Ikujiro Nonaka, "The Knowledge-Creating Company," *Harvard Business Review*, November–December 1991, p. 102.

40. Ibid.

41. Christopher Knowlton, "Shell Gets Rich by Beating Risk," *Fortune*, August 29, 1991, p. 82.

42. Ibid., p. 84.

43. Nonaka, p. 96.

44. Ibid., p. 97.

45. Ibid., p. 99.

46. Thomas A. Stewart, "GE Keeps Those Ideas Coming," *Fortune*, August 12, 1991, pp. 41–49.

CHAPTER 7

1. Robert J. Kriegel and Louis Patler, *If It Ain't Broke . . . Break It!* (New York: Warner Books, 1991), p. 53.

2. Harry Emerson Fosdick, as quoted at Brainyquote.com. No source provided.

3. Faisal Hoque, "The Speed of Business Today," *Baseline*, June 24, 2007, http://www.baselinemag.com/c/a/Innovation/The-Speed-of-Business-Today-720022/.

4. "Business Innovation – Changing Companies for a Changing World," *Principal Voices*, http://www.principalvoices.com/business.html.

5. Katharine Mieszkowski, "How to Speed Up Your Startup," *Fast Company*, April 30, 2000, http://www.fastcompany.com/magazine/34/startup.html.

6. "Is Your Company Up to Speed?" *Fast Company*, May 31, 2003, http://www.fastcompany.com/magazine/71/uptospeed.html.

7. Chuck Salter, "Speed Rules," *Fast Company*, October 31, 1998, http://www.fastcompany.com/magazine/19/speedrules.html.

8. Philip Kotler and Paul J. Stonich, "Turbo-Marketing Through Time Compression," *The Journal of Business Strategy*, September–October 1991, p. 24.

9. Mieszkowski.

10. Philip Kotler, "Turbo-Marketing," *Marketing Executive*, April 1, 1991, vol. 1, no. 2, p. 24.

11. "First-Mover Advantage," Pearson, http://www.pearsoned.co.uk/Bookshop/article.asp?item=312.

12. Jocelyn R. Davis, Henry M. Frechette, Jr., and Edwin H. Boswell, *Strategic Speed: Mobilize People, Accelerate Execution* (Boston: Harvard Business Press, 2010), p. 178.

13. Kotler and Stonich, p. 24.

14. Mieszkowski.

15. Davis, Frechette, and Boswell, p. 179.

16. Rosabeth Moss Kanter, "Ourselves Versus Ourselves," *Harvard Business Review*, May–June 1992, p. 8.

17. James P. Andrew, Knut Haanaes, David C. Michael, Harold L. Sirkin, and Andrew Taylor, *Innovation 2008: Is the Tide Turning?*, The Boston Consulting Group, August 2008, p. 20.

18. General Electric, *Annual Report*, 1991, p. 2.

19. "Is Your Company Up to Speed?"

20. Michael F. Dealey, "Changing Organizational Structures," *Fortune*, July 13, 1992, p. 49.

21. Hoque.

22. General Electric, *Annual Report*, 1991, p. 3.

23. Kriegel and Patler, p. 117.

24. Edward de Bono, *Six Action Shoes* (New York: Harper Business, 1991), p. 32.

25. Paul B. Carroll, "Story of an IBM Unit That Split Off Shows Difficulties of Change," *The Wall Street Journal*, p. 1.

26. Jim Harrington, *Business Process Improvement* (New York: McGraw-Hill, 1990), p. 153.

27. Charles A. Sengstock, Jr., "Pursuing the Not-So-Elusive Goal of Perfection," *Public Relations Journal*, August 1991, p. 22.

28. Brent Bowers, "The Doozies: Seven Scary Tales of Wild Bureaucracy," *The Wall Street Journal*, June 19, 1992, p. B2.

29. Harrington, p. 153.

30. "Leading in Tougher Times, A Presentation by Warren Bennis," summary report in *Investment in America Forum: Leadership and Organizational Challenges in an Age of Discontinuity*, United States Military Academy at West Point, June 25–27, 2002 (The Conference Board, 2002), http://www.leadertoleader.org/ourwork/iaf_2002.pdf.

31. Lester R. Bittel, *Right on Time* (New York: McGraw-Hill, 1991), p. 5.

32. Karen Matthes, "Clean Up Your Life . . . Or at Least Your Desk," *Personnel*, October 1991, p. 23.

33. Allen C. Bluedorn and Robert D. Denhardt, "Time and Organizations," *The Journal of Management*, vol. 14, no. 2, 1988, p. 310.

34. Bill Symonds, "No, They Can't Stop Time, But They Can Help You Manage It," *Business Week*, May 22, 1989, p. 179.

35. Carroll.

36. Mieszkowski.

37. Walter Kiechel III, "Over Scheduled, and Not Loving It," *Fortune*, April 8, 1991, p. 105.

38. Robert H. Waterman, Jr., *The Renewal Factor* (New York: Bantam, 1987), p. 201.

39. Bluedorn and Denhardt, pp. 310–311.

40. Richard Saul Wurman, *Information Anxiety* (New York: Bantam, 1990), p. 161.

41. "Is All Time Wasted on the Job a Waste?" *Training and Development Journal*, November 1987, p. 17.

42. Joe A. Cox and Raymond L. Read, "Putting It Off 'til Later," *Baylor Business Review*, Fall 1989, p. 10.

43. As quoted in Bittel, p. 84.

44. Paul Hellman, "An Interview with Father Time," *Management Review*, January 1990, p. 63.

45. Walter Kiechel III, "Beat the Clock," *Fortune*, June 25, 1984, p. 147.

CHAPTER 8

1. Roger Lewin, "The Reality of Complexity," *Business Spirit Journal Online*, No date, http://bizspirit.com/bsj/archive/articles/lewin1.html.

2. Jenny Carless, "Unlocking the Value of Strategic Alliances," *The Network*, November 17, 2003, http://newsroom.cisco.com/dlls/hd_111703b.html.

3. Pervin Shaikh, "Cultivating a Win/Win Mindset," Suite101.com, October 16, 2009, http://personaldevelopment.suite101.com/article.cfm/cultivating_a_winwin_mindset.

4. Ibid.

5. Jacqueline Trovato, "Best Practices for Bargaining—Winning," Suite101.com, July 27, 2009, http://businessmanagement.suite101.com/article.cfm/best_practices_for _bargaining_part_two.

6. John Emshwiller, "Suppliers Struggle to Improve Quality as Big Firms Slash Their Vendor Rolls," *The Wall Street Journal*, August 18, 1991, p. B1.

7. Bill Breen, "The Need for Speed," *Fast Company*, November 1, 2004, http://www.fastcompany.com/magazine/88/dell-fasttake.html.

8. "Corporations Scale Back Use of Outside Counsel," *The Wall Street Journal*, October 15, 1991, p. B1.

9. General Electric, *Annual Report*, 1989.

10. Harry S. Dent, Jr., "Corporation of the Future," *Small Business Reports*, May 1990, p. 55.

11. Jay Coen Gilbert, "The Golden Rule of Business," *Fast Company*, September 28, 2009, http://www.fastcompany.com/blog/jay-coen-gilbert/change-we-seek/golden -rule-business.

12. "Getting Together: The Importance of Business Relationships," Advancingwomen.com, July 2010, http://www.advancingwomen.com/strategicplanning /getting_together_the_importance_of_business_relationships.php.

13. Tom Taulli, "Picking a Partner," *Forbes*, December 7, 2005, http://www.forbes.com /2005/12/07/startup-strategicalliance-entrepreneur-cx_tt _1207straightup.html.

14. Jordan Lewis, "Competitive Alliances Redefine Companies," *Management Review*, April 1991, p. 15.

15. Linda Tischler, "Seven Strategies for Successful Alliances," *Fast Company*, November 30, 2001, http://www.fastcompany.com/articles/2001/12/alliances.html.

16. Larraine Segil, "5 Keys to Creating Successful Strategic Alliances," *Forbes*, July 18, 2002, http://www.forbes.com/2002/07/18/0719alliance.html.

17. Roger Fisher and Scott Brown, *Getting Together* (New York: Penguin, 1988), p. 4.

18. Jennifer Pendleton, "Matches Made in Heaven," *Advertising Age*, March 14, 1988, p. 3.

19. Mattel, Inc., "Mattel, Inc. Globalizes and Consolidates Its Advertising Agency Assignments," Press release, August 14, 2002, http://www2.prnewswire.com/cgi-bin /stories.pl?ACCT=104&STORY=/www/story/08-14-2002 /0001783374&EDATE=.

20. Glenn M. Parker, *Team Players and Teamwork* (San Francisco: Jossey-Bass, 1991), p. 16.

21. Richard Saul Wurman, *Information Anxiety* (New York: Bantam, 1990), p. 130.

22. Fisher and Brown, p. 21.

23. Gilbert.

CHAPTER 9

1. Bob Burg, *Endless Referrals: Network Your Everyday Contacts Into Sales* (New York: McGraw-Hill, 1999), p. 231.

2. AT&T and Early Strategies Consulting, *The Business Impact of Social Networking*, (White paper), November 2008, p. 7.

3. Howard Aldrich, Ben Rosen, and William Woodward, "Social Behavior and Entrepreneurial Networks," in *Frontiers of Entrepreneurial Research* (Babson Park, MA: Babson College, 1986), pp. 239–240.

4. As quoted in Leif Smith and Patricia Wagner, *The Networking Game* (Denver: Network Resources, 1981), p. 2.

5. Anne Boe and Bettie Youngs, *Is Your Net Working?* (New York: John Wiley & Sons, 1989), p. 50.

6. Robert R. Mueller, *Corporate Networking* (New York: Free Press, 1986), p. 21.

7. Emil Protalinski, "Facebook Confirms It Now Has 800 Million Users," *Friending Facebook* (blog), September 22, 2011, http://www.zdnet.com/blog/facebook/facebook-confirms-it-now-has-800-million-users/3949.

8. Ben Parr, "LinkedIn Surpasses 100 Million Users," *Mashable Business*, March 22, 2011, http://mashable.com/2011/03/22/linkedin-surpasses-100-million-users-infographic/.

9. Mark Hachman, "Twitter Continues to Soar in Popularity, Site's Numbers Reveal," PCmag.com, http://www.pcmag.com/article2/0,2817,2392658,00.asp#fbid=lj15_T5yABK.

10. AT&T and Early Strategies Consulting, pp. 2, 7. According to this AT&T report: "Dunbar's number was first proposed by British anthropologist Robin Dunbar and is the supposed cognitive limit to the number of individuals with whom any one person can maintain stable social relationships."

11. Mueller.

12. Regis McKenna, *The Regis Touch* (New York: Addison-Wesley, 1985), p. 57.

13. Pat Wagner and Leif Smith, *Manual for Using the Office for Open Network* (Denver: Network Resources, 1984), p. 28.

CHAPTER 10

1. Gordon F. Shea, "Building Trust in the Workplace," AMA Management Briefing, 1984, p. 7.

2. "The Trust Deficit," World Economic Forum January 26, 2006, http://www.weforum.org/s?s=trust.

3. L. Gordon Crovitz, "The Business of Restoring Trust," *The Wall Street Journal*, January 30, 2011.

4. Shari Caudron, "Rebuilding Employee Trust," *Workforce Management*, October 2002, pp. 28–34.

5. William Ouchi, *Theory Z* (Reading, MA: Addison-Wesley, 1981), p. 5.

6. Dale E. Zand, "Trust and Managerial Problem Solving," *Administrative Science Quarterly*, p. 229. Research has shown that "the level of trust in a relationship affects the degree of defensiveness. Gibb (1961) found that members of small groups that developed a 'defensive climate,' had difficulty concentrating on messages, perceived the motives, values, and emotions of others less accurately, and increased the distortion of messages. Other studies suggest that some interpersonal trust is required for effective problem solving in a group. Parloff and Handlon (1966) found that intensive, persistent criticism increased defensiveness and mistrust among members of a group and decreased their ability to recognize and accept good ideas. Meadow et al. (1959) reported that defensiveness induced a lasting decrease in problem solving effectiveness. They found that groups penalized for poor ideas and admonished to produce only good ideas while working on early problems produced poorer solutions to later problems when these restrictions were removed than groups that were not penalized and admonished during their early problem assignments."

7. Shea, p. 7.

8. Dale E. Zand, *Information, Organization, and Power* (New York: McGraw-Hill, 1981), p. 38.

9. Friedrich Nietzsche, as quoted at Thinkexist.com. No source provided.

10. Gerald Zaltman and Christine Moorman, "The Importance of Personal Trust in the Use of Research," *Journal of Advertising Research*, October–November 1988, p. 19.

11. Stephen R. Covey, *Principle-Centered Leadership* (Provo, UT: The Institute for Principle-Centered Leadership, 1990), p. 151.

12. Tracy E. Benson, "In Trust We Manage," *Industry Week*, March 4, 1991, p. 28.

13. Peter Drucker, as quoted at Thinkexist.com. No source provided.

14. Roger Fisher and Scott Brown, *Getting Together* (New York: Penguin, 1988), p. 125.

15. Fernando Bartolome, "Nobody Trusts the Boss Completely—Now What?" *Harvard Business Review*, March–April 1989, vol. 67, no. 2, p. 135.

16. Shea, p. 55.

17. Zand, p. 38.

18. Ibid., p. 140.

19. Ibid.

20. Fisher and Brown, p. 123.

21. "Needed: Less Bureaucracy," *USA Today*, April 1989, p. 14.

22. Shea, p. 319.

CHAPTER 11

1. Fred Moody, "Mr. Software," *The New York Times Magazine*, August 25, 1991, p. 56.

2. Tom Brown, "On the Edge with Jim Collins," *Industry Week*, October 5, 1992, p. 12.

3. HR.com, October 5, 2000.

4. Rafael Brusilow, "Work-life Balance Trumps Pay: Study," *Metro*, September 22, 2009, http://www.metronews.ca/calgary/work/article/317561--work-life-balance-trumps -pay-study.

5. Ronald Henkoff, "How to Plan for 1995," *Fortune*, December 31, 1990, p. 70.

6. John Cox, "Nokia Looks to Make Windows Phone 7 Hottest Mobile OS on the Planet," *Network World*, March 24, 2011, http://www.networkworld.com/news/2011/032411-ctia-nokia-windows-phone7.html.

7. Tamara Schweitzer, "U.S. Workers Hate Their Jobs More Than Ever," Inc.com, March, 7, 2007, http://www.foxnews.com/story/0,2933,257345,00.html?sPage=fnc .business/smallbusiness.

8. Leigh Branham, "Overcoming Cynicism, Misconceptions, and Apathy about Employee Engagement," Trainingindustry.com, February 4, 2010, http://www.trainingindustry.com/training-outsourcing/articles/overcoming-cynicism.aspx.

9. "Small Businesses Face Employee Loyalty Challenges, According to Metlife Study," *Small Business Trends*, July 28, 2011, http://smallbiztrends.com/2011/07/employee-loyalty-challenges-metlife-study.html.

10. W. E. Odom, "Changes and Choices: The Wisdom to Choose Wisely," *Vital Speeches*, June 1, 1991.

11. Ron J. Markin and Charles M. Lillis, "Sales Managers Get What They Expect," *Business Horizons*, June 1975, p. 52.

12. Ibid., p53.

13. Branham.

14. Mark Frohman and Perry Pascarella, "Achieving Purpose-Driven Innovation," *Industry Week*, March 19, 1990, p. 20.

15. Rosabeth Moss Kanter, "Think Like the Customer: The Global Business Logic," *Harvard Business Review*, July–August 1992, p. 9.

16. Anne B. Sisher, "CEOs Think That Morale Is Dandy," *Fortune*, November 18, 1991, p. 83.

17. Seth Godin, "Survival Is Not Enough," *Fast Company*, December 31, 2001, http://www.fastcompany.com/magazine/54/survival.html.

18. James A. Autry, *Love and Profit: The Art of Caring Leadership* (New York: William Morrow, 1991), p. 81.

19. Alan Farnham, "The Trust Gap," *Fortune*, December 4, 1989, p. 5B.

20. Mark Skousen, "Roaches Outlive Elephants: An Interview with Peter Drucker," *Forbes*, August 19, 1991, p. 72.

21. Coca-Cola, *Annual Report*, 1989, p. 4.

22. Benedict Carey, "Fear in the Workplace: The Bullying Boss," *The New York Times*, June 22, 2004, http://www.nytimes.com/2004/06/22/health/fear-in-the-workplace -the-bullying-boss.html.

23. Therese R. Welter, "They're Afraid of You," *Industry Week*, October 1, 1990, p 11.

24. Brian S. Moskal, "Is Industry Ready for Adult Relationships?" *Industry Week*, January 21, 1991, p.19.

25. Henry L. Stimson, as quoted at Brainyquote.com. No source provided.

26. "Towers Perrin Survey Finds Almost Half of American Workers Doubt the Credibility of Employer Communications," Press release, CSRwire, January 6, 2004. (This press release refers to the Towers Perrin survey *Enhancing Corporate Credibility: Is It Time to Take the Spin Out of Employee Communication?*, released January 2004.) http://www.csrwire.com/press/press_release/20728-Towers-Perrin-Survey-Finds -Almost-Half-of-American-Workers-Doubt-the-Credibility-of-Employer-Communications.

27. Amanda Bennett, "Unethical Behavior, Stress Appear Linked," *The Wall Street Journal*, April 11, 1991, p. B1.

INDEX

ABC (Above the call of duty) program, 27
Absenteeism, 14–15, 20
Access
    as element of quality service, 87, 100–101
    See also Communication
Ace Hardware, 86
Active participation, *See* Participation
Adia Personnel Services survey, 154
Adrenaline addiction, 155
Advertising
    agencies, 171–172
    negative, 82–83
    power of, 88, 90, 198, 199
A. Foster Higgins & Company survey, 72
Agreement, as change management strategy, 109
Aguire, Bob, 145
Allen, Thomas, 69
Alliances, *See* Partnerships and business
    relationships
*All I Really Need to Know I Learned in
    Kindergarten* (Fulghum), 7
Amazon.com, 32, 49, 86
American Productivity Center survey, 26
Analogies, as learning tool, 125
Analysis paralysis, 146
Anger, 97, 119, 156, 209–210
Apathy, employee, 15–16, 17–18, 221
Apologies, to clients, 96–97
Apple, 32, 85
Assets
    clients as, 6
    employees as, 18–19
    trust as, 212
    See also Resources
Attitudes
    of employees, 13–16, 17–18, 58, 221
    toward clients, 81–82, 84–85, 230–231
Authority
    carrot and stick method, 20
    delegating to employees, 23, 34, 203–204
    dictatorships, 36–38
    exercise of power and, 21–22
    resistance to, 156
Automobile companies, 77, 86, 95–96, 122,
    141–142, 152
Availability, as element of quality service,
    100–101

Baby boomers, 10, 219
Baby-bust generation, 11, 219
Bardwick, Judith, 117
Barnes & Noble, 86
Barrington, Linda, 10
Bartolome, Fernando, 207
Behavior(s)
    caste systems, 50–52, 68–69, 223–224
    causes of relationship failure, 163–164
    dissatisfaction, expressions of, 13–16, 17–18,
        221
    fear-producing techniques, 117–119
    resistance to change, 115–116
    time management, 153–157
    toward employees, 20–26, 63–64, 73,
        119–120, 151–152, 208–209
    See also Change management approaches;
        Communication; Trust
Beliefs, *See* Values, corporate; Vision, corporate
Benchmarking, 113, 131
Benetton, 136
Bennis, Warren, 29–30, 147
Berkeley, George, 2
Best practices approach, 130–131
Bezos, Jeffrey, 49, 86
Big Words, 135
Bill of rights, employee, 23–26
Blackshaw, Pete, 83
Blame, 95, 113, 118, 150
Boredom, 156
Boss, synonyms for, 19
Boston Consulting Group survey, 32, 138
BP oil spill, 201, 202
Brainstorming, 126
Branding, versus price, 3
Brown, Paul B., 88, 89
Brown, Scott, 169, 174, 206, 210–211
Budgets/budgeting, 90, 91, 144, 166
Buffett, Warren, 162
Bureaucracy
    as barrier to creativity, 42–43
    as barrier to organizational effectiveness,
        138–140, 223, 224
    decision making and, 151–152
    spider analogy, 140
    strategies for reducing, 141–143, 145–147
    as time waster, 148
Burg, Bob, 179

Business relationships, *See* Partnerships and business relationships
BYD, 32

Campbell, Jeremy, 127
Cannon, 160
Carder, Brooks, 114
CareerBuilder.com, 219
Caring
  employee beliefs about, 24
  importance of, 27–28
Caste systems, corporate, 50–52, 68–69, 223–224
Centralization, 42, 165
CEOs (chief executive officers)
  change management, views of, 111–112, 116
  communication patterns, 72
  creativity, views of, 33, 138
  pay and perk discrepancies, 10, 68
  speed of innovation, views of, 138
  See also Management styles
Ceremonies, 27, 62
Champions, functions of in partnerships, 173
Change, resistance to
  as barrier to creativity, 50
  fears and, 116–120
  reasons for, 115–116
  strategies to overcome, 108, 225–226
  success factors, 116
  as time waster, 145
Change management approaches
  companies as machines, 110–111
  fallacies leading to failure, 111–114
  learning styles and, 123–127
  organizational learning, 120–123, 128–132
  types of, 108–111
Cisco, 160
Citizenship, *See* Corporate citizenship
Clients
  attitudes toward, 81–82, 84–85, 230–231
  communication with, 58, 88–89, 101–103, 173–174
  conflict with, 165
  customer service champs, 85–86
  customer surveys, use of, 132
  feedback from, 104, 208, 232
  gaining trust from, 199–200
  importance of quality service to, 84–87, 230–231
  listening to, 105, 230, 231–232
  long-term relationships with, 85–86, 231
  online complaints, 82–83
  resolving problems with, 94–95
  understanding needs of, 104–105

Close to the Customer (Donnelly), 90–91, 93–94
Clothing companies, 136
Coca-Cola, 5, 225
Coercion, as change management strategy, 109, 114
Cognitive dissonance, 114
Collins, James C., 214–215
Commitment
  building, 20–21
  to clients, 6, 208
  employee, 12, 13–16, 17, 114, 214–215, 216
  in partnership relationships, 163, 164–165, 171
Communication
  barriers to, 67–70
  as basis for trust, 208–209
  cardiovascular system analogy, 55–56
  as change management strategy, 109
  changing nature of, 57–58, 229
  with clients, 58, 88–89, 101–103, 173–174
  creativity, promoting, 34–36
  diagonal, 76–77
  downward, 72–73
  effective, 71, 79
  as element of quality, 87, 101–103
  external, 58, 88–89, 101–103, 173–174
  importance of, 56–57, 66–67, 77–78, 148, 233
  informal, 57, 65, 79, 102
  lack of as source of job dissatisfaction, 56
  lateral, 75–76
  leadership roles and, 58–66
  need for, 53–55, 228–230
  nonverbal, 67, 69
  with partner organizations, 163, 168, 174
  phases of, 78–79
  productivity and, 53, 54–55, 68, 148
  resistance to change and, 116, 123, 145
  upward, 73–74
  word of mouth, 184
  written, 40, 57, 67–68, 70, 88, 154, 157
  See also Language use; Networking
Compartmentalization
  of information, 72, 75, 143, 144, 229
  of services, 86
Competence
  as basis for trust, 205
  as element of quality service, 87, 95–96
Competition
  versus alliances and teamwork, 161, 172
  competitive advantage, 1, 5, 100, 129, 200
  impact on creativity, 39
  internal, 128, 144
  objective treatment of competitors, 209
  quality, importance of, 84–85
  speed, importance of, 40, 43, 53, 134–138, 223

Competition (*Cont.*):
  studying competitors, 113–114
  trends, 19, 29–30, 40, 52, 147, 212, 224–225
Complaints, consumer, 82–83, 165
Conference Board surveys
  employee motivation, 55
  job satisfaction, 10, 11, 13, 15, 219
Conference reports, 101
Confidence
  as basis for trust, 203–204
  of clients, 88
  in employees, 6, 24, 44
  of employees, 16, 24, 43, 58, 117, 141, 150
  eroding, 39, 58, 88
  in leadership, 58, 72, 116
Confidentiality
  as element of quality service, 98, 99–100
  networking and, 189
  in partnership relationships, 168
Consistency
  as basis for trust, 197, 198, 209–210
  in communication, 71
  in employee recognition, 27
  as role of formality and protocol, 41
  of words and actions, 69–70
Consumer complaints, 82–83, 165
Consumers, *See* Clients
Contingency planning, 128–129
Continuity in relationships, 168, 176
Continuous change, *See* Change management
    approaches
Continuous education, *See* Education and
    training; Learning
Contracts
  need for, 235
  in partnership relationships, 170, 218
Control
  contingency planning and, 129–130
  of information, 58–59, 156, 208
  loss of, 119, 153
  management styles and, 18, 19, 20, 21–22,
      36–38, 118
  need for, 13, 54, 92–93, 116, 150
  social, 19
  See also Bureaucracy
Conviction, strength of, 202–203
Cooperation, *See* Partnerships and business
    relationships
Co-optation, as change management strategy, 109
Coordination, communication and, 71, 77
Corporate citizenship, 12, 215–216
Corporate culture
  as barrier to creativity, 30, 47–52
  caste system, 50–52, 68–69, 223–224

Corporate culture (*Cont.*):
  heroes and legends, 61–62
  influence on partnership relationships, 163, 165
  learning environments, establishing, 120–121
  politics, 49–50, 70, 143–144, 224
  weak cultures, signs of, 61
Corporate Cultures (Dean and Kennedy), 61
Corporate Networking (Mueller), 183
Costs
  of absenteeism, 15
  of job dissatisfaction, 56
  of losing customers, 82
  of products or services, 3, 84, 89, 90
  See also Pricing
Courtesy, 87, 96–97
Covey, Stephen, 9–10, 20–21, 160, 203
Cox, Joe, 155
Creativity
  corporate culture barriers, 30, 47–52
  corporate examples, 32–33, 36, 46, 48–49
  fostering, 31–33, 46–47, 48–49, 221–222
  importance of, 29–30, 52
  as intangible quality, 5
  management style barriers, 30, 33–40
  operational style barriers, 30, 40–47
  phases of, 31
  right brain/left brain differences, 31–32
The Creativity Infusion, 37–38, 42
Credibility
  in communication, 71, 88–90
  as element of quality service, 87, 98–99
Criticism
  of employees, 23
  fear of, 117
  See also Feedback
*Crucial Conversations: Tools for Talking When
    Stakes Are High* (McMillan), 67
Culture, corporate, *See* Corporate culture
Curiosity, 124–125
Customers, *See* Clients
Customers for Life (Sewell and Brown), 88, 89
Customer surveys, use of, 132
Cynicism, 40, 117, 192

Dale Carnegie organization, 27
Deadlines
  adrenaline addiction, 155
  consequences of, 153
  procrastination and, 39–40
Dealey, Michael, 140
Dean, Terrence, 61
de Bono, Edward, 142
Decision making
  avoidance of, 43, 116, 119, 155

Decision making (*Cont.*):
  empowering, 151–152
  improving speed of, 141, 148–149, 151–152
  partnership relationships and, 165, 175
  trust and, 193
  unilateral, 175
Degrees of separation, 179–180
Delays, 105
  See also Time
Delegating, 151
Delivering Quality Service, 87
Dell, 161
De Pree, Max, 21, 62
Diagonal communication, 76–77
Dictatorial style of management, 36–38
Discretion, 168
Disgruntled employees, 16, 17
  See also Dissatisfaction
Disney, 5
Dissatisfaction, 13–16, 17–18, 56, 221
Distractions, avoiding, 157
Distrust, *See* Trust
Donnelly, James, 90–91, 93–94
Downsizing, 65, 107–108
Downward communication, 72–73, 78, 208–209
Dress, appropriate, 89
Driving Fear Out of the Workplace (Ryan and
    Oestreich), 117–119
Drucker, Peter, 154, 205, 224
Dual career ladders, 46
Dunbar, Robin, 182
Dyadic learning, 124

Edelman Trust Barometer survey, 192
Education and training
  as change management strategy, 109, 113
  employee trust levels and, 205
  importance of, 152, 205, 227, 233
  supporting employee development, 24–25
  See also Learning
Effectiveness, organizational, *See*
  Organizational effectiveness
Efficiency
  barriers to, 143–145
  bureaucracy and, 138–140
  employee motivation and, 55
  improving, 141–143, 147–153
  in phases of strategic action, 138
  of vendors and suppliers, 161
  See also Time
E-mail
  as communication tool, 57
  importance of proofreading, 88

E-mail (*Cont.*):
  as source of misunderstanding, 67–68
  as time saver, 154, 157
Employee Bill of Rights, 23–26
Employees
  commitment of, 114
  dissatisfaction, expressions of, 13–16, 17–18,
    221
  empowering, 20–21, 41, 94, 151–152, 222
  fears, 117, 150, 226–227
  feedback to, 25, 27, 35, 45
  incentives, 46–47
  information, need for, 25, 53–55
  job satisfaction, 10–11, 16–18, 219
  lateral communication, 75–76
  learning styles, 123–127
  loss of confidence in leadership, 58
  needs and desires of, 12, 23–26, 215, 220–221
  physical/health problems, 14–15, 235
  recognition programs, 26–27
  turnover, 13–14, 176, 204
  upward communication, 25, 73–74
  work-life balance, 215
  workplace stress, 14–15, 235
Employee surveys, use of, 131
Empowerment of employees, 20–21, 41, 94,
    151–152, 222
*Endless Referrals: Network Your Everyday
    Contacts Into Sales* (Burg), 179
Enhancing Corporate Credibility (survey), 72
Epictetus, 124
Ericsson (company), 160
Ertel, Danny, 166
Ethics
  corporate values, 12, 200–209
  employee beliefs about, 24
  in networking, 189
  relationship to emotional health, 235
  strength of conviction and, 202–203
  See also Trust
Evaluation process
  approaches to organizational evaluation,
    130–132
  as barrier to creativity, 45
  bureaucracy and, 151–152
  performance evaluation approaches, 130–132
Executive Excellence (Shelton), 9
Executives, *See* CEOs (chief executive officers)
Expectation levels
  for employees, 24, 152–153, 220
  in partnership relationships, 166–167
Expertise, *See* Competence; Knowledge
Expression, freedom of, 25

External communication, 58, 88–89, 101–103, 173–174
External relationships, *See* Partnerships and business relationships
External resources, 147, 218
Exxon, 201, 202
Eyelab, 136

Facebook, 182
Facilitation, as change management strategy, 109
Failure
    of change management approaches, 111–114
    fear of, 47–49, 117, 155
    learning from, 24, 48–49, 113, 222
    of partnerships, reasons for, 163–168
    See also Success
Fairness
    as basis for trust, 205–206
    toward employees, 20, 24
Faith
    establishing in customers, 211
    See also Trust
Fear(s)
    consequences of, 226–227
    employee, 117, 150, 226–227
    of failure, 47–49, 117, 155
    resistance to change and, 115, 116–120
    of success, 155
    techniques for instilling, 117–119
Federal Express, 137
Feedback
    from clients, 104, 208, 232
    constructive, 25, 122, 148, 174
    to employees, 25, 27, 35, 45
    importance of, 35–36
    trust and, 193
    upward communication from employees, 25, 73–74
    See also Communication
The Fifth Discipline (Senge), 60
Firing of employees, 64, 65, 66
First impressions, 88, 170, 198
First-line management, role in communication, 66–71, 73–74
Fisher, Roger, 169, 174, 206, 210–211
Flaherty, Richard, 149
Flexibility, of organizations, 217–218
Focus, importance of, 216–217
Ford Motor Company, 77
Formalities, *See* Policies and procedures; Rules
Fortino, Michael, 153
Forum Corporation survey, 84
Fosdick, Harry Emerson, 134

Four Seasons Hotels and Resorts, 85
Fox, Bill, 172
Friendships with clients, 89
Fulghum, Robert, 7
Fun, *See* Play, as learning tool

General Electric
    alliances, 161, 165
    Best Practices project, 130–131
    brand equity, 5
    bureaucracy of, 139, 141
    corporate culture, 34, 43
    creativity and innovation, 29, 32
    incentives, 46
General Motors, 141–142, 152
Getting Together (Fisher and Brown), 169, 206
Gibbons, John, 11
Gifts, for clients, 99
Goals
    compared to corporate vision, 114
    employee reward programs and, 27
    of employees, 23, 215
    excessive emphasis on, 130–131
    planning, importance of, 146, 156–157
    realistic expectations in partnerships, 166–167
Godin, Seth, 108, 110, 223
Golden Rule, 201
Google, 5, 32, 36, 134–135
Graham, Katharine, 162
Grapevine, communication via, 57, 65, 79, 102
    See also Networking

Haas, Robert, 18–19
Halpert, Jane, 22
Harshman, Jennifer, 82–83
Health problems, 14–15, 235
Hellman, Paul, 158
Heroes, organizational, 61–62
Heskett, James, 60–61
Hewlett-Packard, 5, 32, 76–77, 160
Hierarchy, corporate, *See* Organizational charts
High Hopes, Little Trust survey, 215
Hiner, Glen, 165
Hiring employees, 6, 14, 97, 205
Honda, Soichiro, 122
Honesty
    as basis for trust, 207–208, 233
    in communication, 71, 77
    as element of quality service, 98
    with employees, 24
Hoque, Faisal, 141
Horizontal communication, 75–76
Horizontal work flow, 143

Human relations/resource management paradigms, 20, 21
Huntsman Chemical, 165

Iacocca, Lee, 116
IBM
    alliances, 160
    brand equity, 5
    bureaucracy of, 142
    communication strategies, 74
    creativity and innovation, 32
    Making Change Work study, 116
    storytelling example, 63–64
    survey of CEOs, 33
Ideas, *See* Creativity
If It Ain't Broke . . . Break It! (Kriegel and Patler), 107, 133
Image, corporate, 14, 82–83, 88–89, 170
    See also Quality service
Immelt, Jeffrey, 29
Impressions, *See* First impressions; Image, corporate
Incentives
    creativity and, 46–47
    See also Recognition, employee
Incremental change, 38, 45, 74
Individual relationships, *See* Personal relationships
Industrial Age, compared to Information Age, 2–3, 213
Industry Week survey, 24, 117
Inefficiency, *See* Bureaucracy; Efficiency
Informal communication, 57, 65, 79, 102
Informal learning, 124
Information
    about partner organizations, 167
    compartmentalization of, 72, 75, 143, 144, 229
    confidentiality and, 98, 99–100, 168, 189
    flow of, 72–77
    managing/controlling, 34–35, 58–59, 148, 156, 208
    need for, 25, 53–55
    sharing, 35–36, 77–78, 101–102, 129–130
    storytelling, 62–66
    See also Communication; Knowledge
Information Age, compared to Industrial Age, 2–3, 213
Information Anxiety (Wurman), 54, 173
Information Organization (Zand), 195–196
Innovation, *See* Creativity
Innovative Employee Communication (Smith), 55–56
Instinct, 4, 116, 129–130
Intangible qualities, 2–5, 84, 213–214

Integrity
    as basis for trust, 201
    as element of quality service, 98
    valuing, 232, 234–235
Intel, 5, 46, 160
Interbrand, 5
Internal communication, *See* Communication
Internal politics, *See* Politics, corporate
Interpersonal behavior, *See* Behavior
Intranet, communication via, 57
Investments
    in ideas, 38
    in partnerships, 162–163, 170, 171–172
    return on, 6–7
    in technology, 145–146
    in training, 152
Involvement, *See* Participation
Isolation of management, 67–68

Jaguar, 95–96
Japan, 2, 114, 127, 129, 150, 161
Job satisfaction
    of baby boomers, 10
    continuum of, 16–18
    cost of dissatisfaction, 56
    employee expressions of dissatisfaction, 13–16, 17–18, 221
    trends, 10–12
    of younger workers, 219
Johnson & Johnson, 4, 201–202

Kanter, Rosabeth Moss, 89, 138
Kearns, David, 26
Keller, Maryann, 77
Kelley, Robert, 59
Kennedy, Allen, 61
Kennedy School survey, 58
Kiechel, Walter III, 120–121, 151, 158
Kleinfeld, Klaus, 37
Kliman, Stuart, 166
Knowledge
    collective, 129
    compartmentalization of, 72, 75, 143, 144, 229
    in partnership relationships, 167, 173–174
    product, 96
    tacit versus explicit, 129–130
    understanding customers, 104–105
    See also Communication; Information
Knowlton, Christopher, 128–129
Kotter, John, 21, 60–61
Kriegel, Robert J., 107, 113, 122, 133
Krogh, Lester, 46

Language use
    clarity of, 87, 101, 127–128
    e-mail communication, 67–68
    metaphors and analogies, 127–128
    need for common language, 75
    nonverbal, 67, 69
    simplicity versus complexity of, 145
    See also Communication
Lateral communication, 75–76
Lawyers, 89, 161
Layoffs, 15, 23, 65, 107–108
Leadership
    changing nature of, 18–19, 214–215
    crisis of, 58
    qualities of, 232–233
    See also Management styles
Leadership Is an Art (De Pree), 21, 62
Learning
    encouraging, 25, 96, 120–123, 226
    need for ongoing learning, 113, 120,
        123–124, 227
    organizational, 128–132
    styles of, 123–127
    See also Education and training
Legends, organizational, 62
Lerner, Larry, 15
Levi Strauss Company, 136
Levy, Jeff, 137–138
Lewin, Roger, 159
Lexus, 86
LG Electronics, 32
Lightning Strikes program, 27
The Limited, 136
LinkedIn, 182
Listening
    barriers to, 70
    to customers, 105, 230, 231–232
    to employees, 230
    See also Communication
L. L. Bean, 85
London House, 235
Loyalty
    as element of quality service, 97, 98–99
    employee, 16, 17
    See also Commitment

Mackey, John, 139
Madden, Dick, 38
Mail-in systems for employee feedback, 74
Making Change Work (IBM), 116
Management by Participation (Marrow et al.), 111
Management styles
    as barrier to creativity, 30, 33–40

Management styles (Cont.):
    communication and, 67–68, 208–209
    displaying confidence, 203–204
    increasing efficiency, 147–153
    influence on partnership relationships, 163, 166
    learning styles and, 123–127
    organizational learning, 128–132
    plantation management, 9–11, 219
    trust and, 208, 220
    types of, 214
Manipulation, as change management strategy, 109
Manipulative learning, 124
Marketing
    benchmarking, 131
    of intangibles, 103
    3M strategy, 48
    trends, 3, 6, 105
    by word of mouth, 184
Marketing News survey, 39
Marketing to Win (Sonnenberg), 69, 70
Matson, Jack, 48–49
Mattel, 171–172
McDonald's, 5, 210
McKenna, Regis, 184
McMillan, Ron, 67, 68
Meetings
    ambiance and behavior in, 69, 100
    preparation for, 90, 149
    skip-level meetings, 74
    as time waster, 149–150
Mentoring, 127
Metaphors, as learning tool, 125
MetLife's 9th Annual Study of Employee
    Benefits Trends, 219
Michener, James, 121
Micromanagement, 18, 24, 151
Microsoft, 5, 32, 160, 213, 218
Mieszkowski, Katharine, 136
Milgram, Stanley, 179–180
Military model, 78
Mission, corporate, 18, 59–61, 216
Mistakes
    admitting, 122–123
    learning from, 24, 48–49, 113, 222
Mistrust, See Trust
Mitsch, Ronald, 48
Moorman, Christine, 203
Morale, See Job satisfaction
Motion, versus movement, 147, 217
Motivation
    employee, 16, 17, 214–215
    resistance to change and, 115
    social motivation, 19

Motivational Systems survey, 26
Mueller, Robert, 183
Multidirectional communication, 58, 71, 78
Mumford, Alan, 123
Murdoch, Rupert, 135

Napster, 223
Narcissism, 117
Negotiation, 109, 166
Networking
    barriers to, 184–185
    benefits of, 180–181
    close versus casual relationships, 182–183
    as communication strategy, 79
    definitions and overview, 181–182
    modes of, 179, 180
    rules and protocol, 185–189
    six degrees of separation, 179–180
    social media and, 182
    steps for developing networks, 183–184
    See also Partnerships and business relationships
Newsletters, as communication tool, 57, 228
New York Times, amount of information in, 54
Nietzsche, Friedrich, 196
Nokia, 5, 32, 218
Nonaka, Ikujiro, 128, 129–130
Nonverbal communication, 67, 69
Nordstrom, 86

Obedience, 16, 17
Objectives, *See* Goals
Objectivity, 71, 105, 130, 183, 205–206
O'Brien, William J., 222
Obsolescence, 110, 227
    See also Change management approaches
Odom, W. E., 220
Oestreich, Daniel K., 117–119
Ogilvy & Mather, 171–172
Open-door policy, 25, 230
Openness
    as basis for trust, 207–208
    in communication, 71, 77–78
    See also Honesty
Operational style
    as barrier to creativity, 30, 40–47
    See also Bureaucracy; Management styles
Oral tradition, 62–66, 126
Organization, importance of, 156
Organizational charts
    adherence to as communication barrier, 67, 223
    as element of quality service, 90–91
    vertical organization, 67, 143
Organizational citizenship, *See* Corporate citizenship

Organizational culture, *See* Corporate culture
Organizational effectiveness
    strategies for improving, 141–147
    trends, 138–140
Organizational learning, 120–123, 128–132
Organizational structure
    caste systems, 50–52, 68–69, 223–224
    spiderlike qualities of, 140
    trends, 18, 159–162
    vertical organization, 67, 143
    See also Bureaucracy; Change management approaches
Osborn, Thomas, 51
Ownership, employee sense of, 17, 24, 27

Packaging
    of ideas, 40, 44
    of products, 51, 201–202
Paperwork, *See* Bureaucracy
Paranoia, 117
Participation
    as change management strategy, 109
    as learning tool, 123, 124, 125–126
Partnerships and business relationships
    building, 170–173
    commitment in, 163, 164–165
    communication issues, 163, 168, 174
    corporate culture and, 163, 165
    courting phase, 170
    importance of individuals in, 164, 168, 172–173
    ingredients for success, 160, 162, 169–170, 171–177, 218
    maintaining, 173–176
    management style and, 163, 166
    reasons for failure, 163–168
    resolving problems, 174–175
    trends, 159–162, 176–177
    See also Networking; Trust
Paterno, Joe, 122
Patler, Louis, 107, 113, 122, 133
Pattern Research, 187–188
Patterns, seeing, 125
Pay, *See* Salaries
PepsiCo, 160, 166–167
Perfectionism, 155
Performance
    evaluation approaches, 130–132
    expectation levels and, 24, 152–153, 220
    See also Feedback
Perot, Ross, 141–142, 152
Personal relationships
    finding time for, 158
    importance of, 176
    influence on partnerships, 164, 168, 172–173

Personal relationships (*Cont.*):
   work-life balance, 215
Personal safety, 100, 204
Peter Pan Syndrome, 155
Peters, Tom, 212
Peterson, Donald E., 77
PIMS database, *See* Profit Impact for Marketing
   Strategy (PIMS) database
Planning
   contingency planning, 128–129
   importance of, 146, 156–157
   involving employees in, 76, 145
   as time saver, 156–157
Plantation management, 9–11, 219
Play, as learning tool, 127
Policies and procedures
   as barrier to creativity, 40–41
   as barrier to quality service, 93–94
   reasons for, 142
   simplifying, 142–143, 145
   See also Bureaucracy; Rules
Politics, corporate
   as barrier to creativity, 49–50, 117
   bureaucracy and, 224
   as communication barrier, 70
   as source of inefficiency, 143–144
Porras, Jerry I., 214–215
Power
   bureaucracy and, 42–43, 138–139, 141
   dispersing, 222–223
   types of, 21–22
   withholding information and, 70, 168, 207
   See also Authority; Empowerment of
      employees
Pragmatists, 123
Predictability, as basis for trust, 210–211
Presentations
   of ideas, 42, 44, 151
   preparation for, 90, 149
Pressure, *See* Stress
PricewaterhouseCoopers survey, 215
Pricing
   branding versus, 3
   as element of quality service, 89
   to gain competitive advantage, 136, 161
   importance of, 84, 98
Pride, as element of quality service, 88
Principle-Centered Leadership (Covey), 203
Prioritizing, 71, 154–155
Problems
   avoiding, 40, 103, 112, 209
   being prepared for, 103, 174–175
   resolving customer problems, 94
   See also Mistakes

Problem solving
   holistic approach, 86–87
   learning and, 113, 122
   in partnership relationships, 174–175
   resolving customer problems, 94
   See also Creativity; Decision making
Procedures, *See* Bureaucracy; Policies and
   procedures
Procrastination
   avoiding, 155–156
   as barrier to creativity, 39–40
   resistance to change and, 115
Productivity
   increasing, 6, 54–55
   influence of communication on, 53, 54–55, 68
   problems with, 11, 15, 16, 193–194
   of start-up companies, 68
   stress and, 153
   technology and, 145–146, 157
   See also Time
Profit Impact for Marketing Strategy (PIMS)
   database, 84
Progressive (company), 135
Progress reports, 102
Promises
   to clients, 66, 90, 103, 206
   to employees, 44, 208
   in partnership relationships, 170
Promotions, 46, 139, 194
Proofreading, importance of, 88
Protocol, *See* Policies and procedures; Rules
Psychological Bulletin survey, 20
Publicity, negative, 82–83, 165
Publix Super Markets, 86
Pygmalion effect, 24, 220

Quality, product, 210
Quality service
   access and, 100–101
   communication with clients and, 101–103
   competence and, 95–96
   contributing factors, 87–105
   credibility and, 98–99
   customer impressions, 88–90
   customer service champs, 85–86
   importance of, 84–87, 230–231, 233
   as intangible, 84
   price and, 84, 89
   reliability and, 90–91
   responsiveness to clients and, 92–95
   security and, 99–100
   understanding customers, 104–105
Quantification, of intangibles, 2, 213–214

Questions
   from clients, 90, 96
   facilitating learning, 121
   Socratic method, 126
Quick Response Systems, 136
Quitting employment, 13–14

Read, Raymond, 155
Recognition, employee
   creativity and, 46–47
   importance of, 23
   programs, criteria for, 26–27
Record keeping, 90
Red tape, *See* Bureaucracy
Redundancy, as learning tool, 128
Referent power, 21, 22
Reflective learning, 123, 126–127
The Regis Touch (McKenna), 184
Reinforcement, *See* Feedback; Rewards
Relationships, *See* Partnerships and business
      relationships; Trust
Relevancy of information, 55, 71, 125, 208–209
Reliability, 87, 90–91, 206
The Renewal Factor (Waterman), 19, 152
Reputation
   importance of, 3, 7, 98, 193, 199–200
   negative, 14, 93, 200
   See also Respect
Research, purpose of, 146
Resentment, 110, 170, 175
Resources
   allocating, 1, 134, 147
   external, 147, 218
   time as, 92, 137–138, 153–154, 224–225
   See also Assets
Respect
   as element of quality service, 87, 96
   lack of, 66, 77, 92
   in networking, 180, 185, 187
   in partnerships, 171, 177
   strength of conviction and, 202–203
   toward employees, 6, 22, 23, 24
   See also Trust
Responsibility
   avoidance of, 118, 119, 155
   corporate citizenship, 12
   of employees, 23, 24, 52, 94
   managerial, 20–22, 33–34, 166
   in relationships, 174, 201–202
Responsiveness, 87, 92–95
Review process, *See* Evaluation process
Revlon, 64
Revson, Charles, 64

Rewards
   employee recognition programs, 26–27
   incentives, 26, 46–47
Rights, employee, 23–26
Risk taking
   change and, 121–123
   value of mistakes, 24, 48–49, 113, 222
Rituals, 62
Ritz-Carlton, 86
Role models, 61–62
Routines, *See* Policies and procedures
*Rude Awakening: The Rise, Fall, and Struggle
      for Recovery of General Motors* (Keller), 77
Rules
   as barrier to creativity, 40–41
   as barrier to quality service, 93–94
   networking, 185–189
   reasons for, 142
   as reflection of corporate culture, 63–64
   See also Bureaucracy
Ryan, Kathleen D., 117–119

Safety, 100, 204
Salaries
   discrepancies in, 10
   employee views of, 13, 26, 215
Sales
   automobile, 2, 95–96
   clothing companies, 136
   as immediate, isolated events, 82, 85, 199
   strategies for improving, 87, 136–138
   3M, 32–33, 51
   trust and reputation, effects of, 192, 200
   See also Pricing; Quality service
Satisfaction, *See* Job satisfaction
SBC, 160
Scheepbouwer, Ad J., 107
Schellhardt, Timothy, 69–70
Schmidt, Eric, 33, 41
Scientific management, 20, 21
Seaborn, Emmett, 192
Secretiveness, 207–208
Security
   as element of quality service, 99–100
   See also Confidentiality
Self-concept, 155
Senge, Peter, 60, 110–111, 112, 114, 115, 127
Service quality, *See* Quality service
Sewell, Carl, 88, 89
Shared vision, *See* Vision, corporate
Shaw, Mona, 81
Shea, Gordon, 191, 194, 207, 212
Shelton, Ken, 9

Sherman, Stratford, 46
Shewmaker, Jack, 73–74, 78
Simplification of procedures, 142–143, 145, 173
Sirota, David, 224
Six Action Shoes (de Bono), 142
Six degrees of separation, 179–180
Skip-level meetings, 74
Smith, Alvie, 55–56
Smith, Fred, 137
Social media
    as communication tool, 57
    consumer complaints on, 82–83
    networking and, 182
    number of users, 182
    See also Networking
Social motivation, 19
Social uncertainty, 208–209
Socratic method, 126
"Soft" issues, 1–2, 213
Solorzano, Lucia, 124
Sony, 32, 160
Specialization, 51
Speed
    value placed on, 133–138, 223
    See also Time
Staff, *See* Employees
Starbucks, 160, 166–167
Start-up companies, 34, 68, 165, 223
Status, *See* Caste systems, corporate
Stayer, Ralph, 22
Stengel, Casey, 182
Stimson, Henry, 229
Storytelling
    negative stories, 64, 66
    role in corporate culture, 62–66
Strategic alliances, *See* Partnerships and business relationships
Strategic planning, *See* Planning
Strategic Planning Institute, Profit Impact for Marketing Strategy (PIMS) database, 84
Strategic Speed, 137, 138
Stress
    as consequence of low trust, 193–194
    health-related consequences, 14–15, 235
    lack of information and, 54
    managing, 153
    productivity and, 153
Strohecker, Ben, 203–204
Success
    critical factors, 5–6
    fear of, 155
    personnel changes and, 114
    relationship to failure, 48, 113, 122
    "soft" issue determinants of, 1–2, 213

Success (*Cont.*):
    See also Failure
Suppliers/vendors
    building relationships with, 6, 147
    credibility and integrity of, 98–99
    cutting number of, 160–161
    See also Partnerships and business relationships
Support, as change management strategy, 109
Surveys, use of
    customer, 132
    employee, 131

Tacit knowledge, 129–130
Tangibles, as elements of quality service, 87, 88–90
Tarkenton, Fran, 27–28
Team Players and Teamwork, 172
Teamwork, 172–173
Technology
    productivity and, 145–146
    as time saver, 154, 157
Telephone calls, 74, 100, 189
Territorialism, 117, 144
Theorists, 123
Thinking styles, 31–32
3M Company
    brand equity, 5
    corporate culture, 41
    creativity and innovation, 32–33, 48, 51
    incentives, 46
Time
    as barrier to creativity, 38–39
    deadlines, 39, 40, 153, 155
    management of, 153–158
    as resource, 137–138, 153–154, 224–225
    strategies for improving speed, 141–143, 145–147
    timeliness as element of quality service, 92–93
    value placed on, 133–138, 154
    wasting, 143–145, 148–150, 154, 156, 224–225
    See also Bureaucracy
Top-down communication, *See* Downward communication
Towers Perrin reports
    corporate communication, 58, 229–230
    employee engagement, 192
Towers Watson survey, 55
Toyota Motor, 32
Trainees, 96, 127
Training, *See* Education and training; Learning
Transitions
    employee turnover, 13–14, 176
    impact on partnership relationships, 168, 176

Trust
    as asset, 212
    benefits associated with, 194–195, 234
    consequences of mistrust, 192–194, 196
    importance of, 191–192, 193, 212, 233–234
    levels and degrees of, 195–196
    mistrust, environment of, 151, 229–230
    public trust levels, 192
    resistance to change and, 116
    stages of, 197, 198–211
Turnover, employee, 13–14, 176, 204
Twitter, 182
Tylenol, 4, 201–202

Uncertainty
    fear of, 115
    managing, 102
    social, 208–209
Understanding clients, 87, 104–105
Uniformity, 203
Unilateral decision making, 175
Universum student survey, 215
Upward communication, 73–74
USAA, 85, 94
Utilicorp United, 69–70

Values, corporate
    as basis for trust, 200–209
    importance of, 59–61, 215–216
    promoting, 61–66
Vendors, See Suppliers/vendors
Verbal abuse, 119, 210–211
Vertical communication, 72–74
Vertical organization, 67, 143
Vision, corporate
    compared to goals, 114
    hologram metaphor, 60
    importance of, 59–61, 216–217
Visual learning, 124
von Oech, Roger, 31, 41, 51

Wal-Mart, 73–74, 78
Walton, Sam, 73

Waste
    avoiding, 147
    of time, 143–145, 148–150, 154, 156, 224–225
Waterman, Robert Jr., 19, 152
Watson, Thomas J., 49, 63–64
Watson Wyatt surveys
    employee confidence in leadership, 16
    Employee Engagement Index, 221
    Work USA 2002 survey, 192
Weintraut, J. Neil, 135
Welch, Jack Jr., 34, 46, 119–120, 147, 161
Wellner, Alison Stein, 67–68
Wharton School survey, 39
Whole Foods Market, 139
Whole person management paradigm, 21
Word of mouth communication, 184
Work environment
    Employee Bill of Rights, 23–26
    facilitating growth, 171–173
    learning, enhancing, 120–121
    workplace stress, 14–15, 153, 235
    See also Corporate culture
Work force, See Employees
World Economic Forum survey, 192
Written communication
    e-mail, 57, 67–68, 154, 157
    of ideas, 40
    proofreading, 88
    simplicity versus complexity of, 145
    time devoted to, 70
Wurman, Richard, 54, 125, 173
Wyatt Company survey, 73

Xerox Corporation, 199

Yaffe, Bruce, 14–15
Yahoo!, 160
Yates, JoAnne, 57
Young, John, 76–77

Zaltman, Gerald, 203
Zand, Dale E., 195–196, 208–209

ABOUT THE AUTHOR

Frank K. Sonnenberg, a marketing strategist and partner at Sonnenberg & Partners, has written four books, published over 300 articles, and appeared on CNN as "a nationally recognized expert in the field of marketing." Frank served as the National Director of Marketing for Ernst & Young's Management Consulting Group for over a decade. He and his marketing firm have consulted to some of the largest and most respected companies in the world.

IndustryWeek named the first edition of *Managing with a Conscience* one of the Top Ten Business Books of the Year. Salon.com named Frank's blog among the top 100 in 2009, and Trust Across America called Frank one of the Top 100 Thought Leaders of 2010. In 2011, *Social Media Marketing Magazine* (SMM) selected Frank as one of the top marketing authors in the world on Twitter. He has served as an expert panelist for *Bottom Line Business*, as the marketing columnist for *The Journal of Business Strategy*, and on the editorial board of *The Journal of Training and Development*. He is active within his community and has served on several boards.

Visit Frank's blog: www.franksonnenbergonline.com. "Our mission is to spur conversation about the urgent need to reawaken personal values and personal responsibility."

Frank is also on Twitter: @FSonnenberg.

Made in the USA
Lexington, KY
04 January 2012